seven faces

Charles A. Perrone

seven faces

Brazilian Poetry

Since

Modernism

DUKE UNIVERSITY PRESS   DURHAM AND LONDON 1996

© 1996 Duke University Press
All rights reserved
Printed in the United States of America on
acid-free paper ∞
Typeset in Galliard by Keystone Typesetting, Inc.
Library of Congress Cataloging-in-Publication Data
appear on the last printed page of this book.

contents

acknowledgments

Primary research for this book was conducted in 1991 with a Fulbright Regional Research Fellowship and in 1987 with an award from the Division of Sponsored Research of the University of Florida. Preliminary findings were made during a previous stay in Brazil with a PRA grant from the Organization of American States. Since work on this project began, I have had useful, inspiring, and friendly contact with so many poets, professors, critics, scholars, publishers, and independent writers in Brazil that listing them presents a problem, for all the reasons known to those who gather information over a period of years and encounter countless generous people. This result would hardly have been possible without all their help. Those who have assisted me in the present endeavor know who they are and have my gratitude. Almost all of these individuals appear in chapter endnotes. At the risk of omitting anyone here, or of giving any wrong impressions of order, I prefer to give a collective and energetic thank you very much — *muito obrigado* — to all in Brazil who lent a hand, an ear, or an eye, from the *eixo* Rio de Janeiro–São Paulo to Curitiba, Belo Horizonte, Brasília, Salvador, Fortaleza, Belém do Pará, and points in between.

During the writing stages here, I was fortunate to have the editorial advice and professional encouragement of colleagues around the country whom I would like to recognize: Roland Greene, Randal Johnson, Vicky Unruh, Jon Vincent, Amelia Simpson, and Irwin Stern. Claus Clüver was very helpful with materials. Since one chapter and parts of others have their origins in my dissertation, I would also like to recognize the doctoral committee again for long-term, as well as more recent, contributions to the research for and ultimate realization of the present

project: Fred P. Ellison, Merlin Forster, K. David Jackson, Naomi Lind-
strom, Lily Litvak, and Gerard Béhague.

I am grateful to all those artists of the word who have granted permis-
sion to reprint and/or translate their work or titles to which they hold
rights. Good faith effort has been made to contact all authors and/or
copyright holders. All unattributed translations are my own. Portions of
this book have appeared previously in journals, to which I extend re-
newed thanks. Parts of chapter 2 and chapter 5 are derived from "The
Imperative of Invention: Brazilian Concrete Poetry and 'Intersemiotic
Creation,'" *Harvard Library Bulletin*, New Series, 3, no. 2 (1992): 44–
53. Chapter 3 is a somewhat revised version of "The Social Imperative:
The Politics of Poetry in the 1960s," *Brasil Brazil* 11 (1994): 25–51. A
section of chapter 4 is based on "Lyrics (Song Text) as Lyric (Poetry):
The Case of Brazil," *Ars Lyrica* 4 (1989): 37–45. A shorter version of
chapter 5 appeared as "Margins and Marginals: New Brazilian Poetry of
the 1970s," *Luso-Brazilian Review* 31, no. 1 (Summer 1994): 17–37, re-
printed with permission.

We gratefully acknowledge permission for use of the following poems
and lyrics: "Poema de sete faces" and "No meio do caminho," © 1996 by
the estate of Carlos Drummond de Andrade. "Seven-Sided Poem" from
The Complete Poems 1927–1979 by Elizabeth Bishop © 1979, 1983 by Alice
Helen Methfessel. Reprinted by permission of Farrar Strauss & Giroux
Inc. Oswald de Andrade, "National Library," trans. Jean Longland; João
Cabral de Melo Neto, "Education by Stone," trans. James Wright, from
An Anthology of Twentieth-Century Brazilian Poetry © 1972 by Wesleyan
University Press, reprinted by permission of University Press of New
England. Ferreira Gullar, "The Pears" trans. William Jay Smith; Mario
Faustino, "Life Nothing but Language," trans. Richard Zenith, from
Brazilian Poetry 1950–1980 © 1983 by Wesleyan University Press, re-
printed by permission of University Press of New England. Adélia
Prado, "With Poetic License," trans. Ellen Watson, from *Alphabet in the
Park* © 1990 by Wesleyan University Press, reprinted by permission of
University Press of New England. Mário de Andrade, "Ode to a Bour-
geois Gentleman," trans. Jack Tomlins, from *Hallucinated City* © 1969 by
Vanderbilt University Press. João Cabral de Melo Neto, "O engenheiro,"
"Educação pela pedra." Editora Nova Fronteira, Rio de Janeiro, Brazil.
Lyrics of "Cobra criada" (João Bosco-Paulo Emílio) © 1979 Editora
Musical BMG Arabella Ltda., Rio de Janeiro, Brazil. All rights reserved.
Lyrics of "Clara" (Caetano Veloso) © 1967 by Musiclave Editora Musi-
cal, São Paulo, Brazil. All rights reserved. Lyrics of "O estrangeiro"
(Caetano Veloso) © 1989 and "Terceira margem do rio" (Milton Nasci-

A note on bibliographical documentation: each section of endnotes is self-contained. Sources utilized in more than one chapter are cited in full in each segment in which they are used. Regarding the translation of titles in Portuguese: all such items are enclosed in parentheses, following the original. When a published translation of a poem title exists, the title of the English version is given in quotation marks. When no translation exists, a literal rendering of the title follows with no quotation marks. Published books of translations are given in italic; if no translation has been published, an English equivalent in roman type is given.

Facets, Phases, Titles, Trends:

Brazilian Lyric 1950–1990

In the second half of the twentieth century, the domain of lyric — in the general sense of genre — has expanded in curious and instigative ways far outside the bounds of conventional verse. Poetic endeavor in Brazil has been remarkably creative and diverse, at times with notable international projection. Makers of poetry have drawn from graphic arts, music, interdisciplinary theory, and other nontraditional elements in addition to literary heritage. Such exercises in lyric difference had begun in Brazil with its modernist movement in the 1920s. More so than in any other nation in the Americas, the avant-garde of Brazilian modernism had a tremendous impact on cultural discourses. The prime impetus of the modernist enterprise was poetry, which was a centerpiece of early-century intellectual life beyond the field of literature. Lyric remained a key frame of reference for aesthetics into midcentury and later, and ideas that were argued vis-à-vis poetry in the twenties have continued to stimulate discussion. Especially with the emergence of loquacious neovanguards in the late 1950s and 1960s, poetry has been at the forefront of dispute and dialogue about numerous matters: the nature of nationalism, the social duties of artists, the practice of experimentalism, limits and variant uses of the arts, Brazil's place in the international arena.

This book is about practices of Brazilian poetry in the contemporary period, from the 1950s to the final decade of the century. Since informed discussion of this span depends on reference to the legacies of modernism in Brazil, an introductory chapter reviews that early-century movement to set the stage for what follows. The ensuing chapters study movements, currents, tendencies, and environments, phenomena that overlap in time and purpose. Consideration of groups, generational manifestations, and novelty here takes deliberate precedence over attention to individual authors and the late modernist verse of what has been termed "the tradition of the image." It should remain clear that the many voices of a more "standard" lyrical expression are an implicit presence throughout. After the introduction, chapters 2 through 6 concern, respectively, concrete poetry and other vanguard groups, politically committed verse in the sixties, the lyricism of popular music, strains of youth poetry in the seventies, and rethinkings of lyric in the final decades of the century. While this coverage is wide, it does not claim to be comprehensive. This book seeks to characterize the programs, problems, and interrelations of poetry in varied forms, relating aesthetic factors to sociocultural milieu and addressing a number of related questions: how avant-garde, socially engaged, and alternative writers grapple with the marginalized status of poetry; how they approach parameters of identity and implications of underdevelopment; how they respond to modernization and authoritarianism; and others. These discussions of the spheres of poetry explore how varieties of lyric may invoke an assumed national spirit, interrogate the status of culture during the rise of a consumer society, and react to the growing influence of electronic media. The aim of these chapters is to elucidate social and aesthetic tensions in contemporary Brazilian poetry, contrasting and evaluating the pursuit of consciousness, and, to use Jonathan Culler's title, the pursuit of signs.

The main purpose of chapter 1, again, is to provide essential background about *modernismo,* or Brazilian modernism, to establish fundamental points of reference for the presentation of subsequent artistic endeavors. Those figures whose voices have been most influential in the second half of the century are emphasized. To frame the necessarily condensed portrait of the modernist movement, this first chapter synthesizes both the old-school mindset against which the youthful nationalists rebelled in the 1920s and the reception of the poets of the Generation of 1945, who reacted against the dominant modernist aesthetic. Significant individual names in the verbal arts of the decade of transition of the 1950s are also highlighted. The present title *Seven Faces* is drawn from a symptomatically oppositional poem by Carlos Drummond de Andrade, "Poema de sete faces" (1930), which is interpreted in chapter 1. This "heptagonal poem" stands as a monument in Brazilian lyric and, with its diverse yet interconnected parts and polygonal levels of suggestiveness, is an appropriate point of departure for a study such as this one that explores risk, difference, and dissonance. While the poem's spirit of multiplicity motivates the title of the book, there is no sole topical count herein nor is there any intention of a discrete correlation between the seven strophes of Drummond's landmark modernist text and the trends taken up in the chapters.

The most substantial segment of *Seven Faces* is chapter 2, which examines in detail the ascendance and stages of the midcentury neo-avant-garde of concrete poetry, and further weighs other experimental experiences. During the "developmentalism" of the late fifties in Brazil, the concrete poets solidified a sophisticated "verbivocovisual" poetics of invention. They would achieve, as national conditions changed in the sixties, unprecedented projection abroad. Taking the lead in a cosmopolitan movement, these artists of a peripheral country reversed the normal flow of European cultural influence. Since 1960, no other aspect of Brazilian poetry has received as much critical attention overseas. The outright distinctiveness of concrete poetry — as a theorized verbal art — continues to make it of special interest to an international audience. The present study extends analysis of texts, of reception, and of retrospection into the 1990s, well beyond the limits of the bulk of extant English-language criticism. Original concretism's experimental writing and conceptual apparatus generated tremendous controversy in Brazil. The academic establishment attacked concrete poetry on literary grounds, which merit another look in the light of historical perspective. Fueled by conflict and successes alike, the creative output and critical production of the movement became inescapable points of reference for lyric in Brazil. The concrete poets forcefully aired some issues that became constants in contemporary discussions: programmatic exposition of poetry's foundations, the interplay of theory and practice, the relationship of national and international literatures, the impact of translation on original composition, interrelations of the arts and technology. From the outset, antiexperimental and committed writers charged concretism with apoliticism and lack of humanism. Yet social aspects of the movement have been downplayed and also deserve a more careful sounding.

Concern with historical consciousness and political relevance marked all the arts in Brazil's nationalist and populist period of the early 1960s. These years produced a body of literature and criticism that focused sharply on ethics, conjuncture, and change, giving rise to ongoing debate about the social functions of art and making consideration of the dialectic of societal and existential factors imperative. Chapter 3 examines instances of committed poetry in Brazil, beginning with an account of antecedents to antiestablishment poetic discourse of the sixties. Since the Russian Revolution, *engagé* writing and authorial responsibility have inspired zeal at different times in different nations around the world.

With both transnational and local factors in mind, this segment comprises a Brazilian case study with a declared literary bias. It investigates the objectives and outcomes of an early-sixties project that emerged from the setting of student activism. In experimental and more conventional forms alike, participation in public discourse has proven, well after the trials of the sixties, to be an unyielding, if often sublimated, preoccupation in Brazilian lyric.

Sociopolitical metaphors were but one aspect of specialized contemporary songwriting that established a strong link between music and poetry. At home and around the world, Brazilian popular music became a truly prominent cultural practice in the 1960s. Among the achievements of this field was the frequent attainment of a lyrical level of "literary quality." Significant portions of the repertories of numerous poet-composers and lyricists prompted the establishment of a topic rightly called the "poetry of song." That is the subject of chapter 4, which opens with general deliberations about the treatment of song texts, as poetic as they might be, as "literary items," and with a look at Luso-Brazilian precedents to the erudite-popular musical lyricism of the sixties. Given the early experience of noted singer-songwriter Bob Dylan, it is interesting to note, in comparatist perspective, how the phenomenon of the poetry of song in Brazil was, relative to the Anglo-American realm, so much more diversified and contextually important. The star of poetry-in-music was especially bright from the late sixties to the late seventies in Brazil, but it has continued in individual instances past the eighties. An unusual, more recent manifestation of the muse further links the field of rock music to youth poetry of the seventies, as well as to the historical presence of concrete poetry and technological updates decades later.

After the experimentalism of the vanguards, the political emphases of the sixties, and the initial impact of song, new poetry in the seventies was searching and various. Chapter 5 explores two broad interrelated phenomena: the eruption of so-called "marginal poetry" in a small-press boom in the 1970s, and the "constructive" approach of verbal arts and poetry associated with what has been termed "intersemiotic creation." These young and inquiring faces of contemporary poetry appeared largely under the sign of dictatorship. New production is viewed in terms of the potential for "democratization" of text-making through the proliferation of publishing facilities; behavioral response to circumstances; and the aesthetic consequences of spontaneity, permissiveness, and experimental posturing. Concurrent with the informalism of "marginal" practice, other activities illustrate the interpenetration of theory and practice following the local development of information theory, structuralism, and semiotics, which began with concretism. One multifaceted figure synthesizes and "textualizes" the shared and competing interests of this time.

The 1980s would become a decade of open-ended reflection and new contextualizations. One of the prisms through which to view the late century, in Brazil as elsewhere, is the postmodern. Following up on chapter 2's revelations of cosmopolitan and utopian elements in the Brazilian vanguard, chapter 6 probes a pair of stirring incidents that involve the principals of concrete poetry and concern the question of postmodernism as manifested in lyric. The involvement of the concrete poets in these expressive moments of eighties lyric is no surprise. Positing places in a "post-" ambience is of lesser importance to younger poets, who may have debated engagement vs. alienation, the status of song in lyric, or marginality vs. constructivism. Concern with postmodernist hypotheses is naturally more intense for the concrete poets, who made a special transition from *modernismo* to a new phase with their movement of experiment. Postmodern issues are compelling to the former leaders of the most significant neo-avant-garde in Latin America, or perhaps the West, because the continuity of liberally conceived modernist ways, the avant-garde as inventive practice, and the contemporary definition of lyric are all in play and at stake. Chapter 6 features Brazilian responses to international versions of postmodernism, offers explications of a polemical (late concrete?) poetic text of the eighties, and queries a critique of that poem by a prominent Brazilian critic who, having staked a claim to a certain position of recognition in Anglo-American criticism of Brazilian literature, should have a reply in that same terrain. Uncovering and examining the circumstances and details of these Brazilian cases will, I hope, contribute to an understanding of issues of lyric and its contexts that transcends the national level.

Within the extension of the chosen focal points of the present study, there are constants of adjustment, contrast, confrontation, and evolution. Dimensions of private emotivity are de-emphasized in favor of more public sensibilities, and that which is distinctive, setting Brazilian cases apart from those of other nations, is favored. A comprehensive account without constraints of scope or selectivity could accommodate many more additional themes and countless individuals. In each of the experiences that are explored here, the factor of difference — be it through theoretical speculation, mode of communication, or other channels — makes a difference. The varying proposals and kinds of poetry that come under consideration deliver a range of artistic results; all attract attention, interest, and critiques for their own reasons. With these multiple features and expressions, the faces of contemporary poetry in Brazil — in a wide-angle view encompassing textuality, functions, inno-vations, and situations — give shape to a dynamic and vibrant subject, appreciation of which surely benefits from an open-ended imagination.

chapter one

Leaders and Legacies: From *Modernismo*

to Reactions and the Contemporary

Eu ouço o canto enorme do Brasil!
[I hear the enormous song of Brazil!]
— Ronald de Carvalho (1926)

Even as the end of the twentieth century approaches, the most funda-
mental point of reference for all artistic endeavors in Brazil is *modernismo*,
the national incarnation of European modernism in the fine arts and
literature.[1] *Modernismo* was a broad-based movement of renovation,
transformation, and self-realization in the dynamic decade of the 1920s
and after. All kinds of assumptions about creating art, writing literature,
understanding the structure of thought, and instituting values hark back
to that decade of growth and cultural assertion. In general terms, *mod-
ernismo* can be regarded as a reaction to the exhaustion of established
artistic principles, as an endeavor in making new forms, and as an ex-
ercise of intent to modify the cultural order, especially in literature. As in
Europe, where the well-known succession of -isms (futurism, cubism,
etc.) and diverse individual contributions configure modernism, Brazil's
coming of age did not comprise any unified program but rather several
different projects with shared interests in aesthetic liberty and in the
notion of being "modern." What most distinguishes the Brazilian case
is its nationalistic dimension, the search for New World modes of ex-
pression and definitions of national psyche. This aspect of *modernismo*,
while naturally reminiscent of the concern with *Volkgeist*, a prime facet of
nineteenth-century romanticism, is bound essentially to the particular
developments of the early twentieth century.

Winds of change had begun to blow in Brazil's artistic circles in the
1910s as received practices suffered from old age, inconformity with

reigning *passadismo* (past-ism) grew, and avant-garde information filtered into the country. Inaugural activities in 1922 (the centenary of independence from Portugal) would represent the culmination, agglutination, and organization of transformational energies. The official starting point of *modernismo* was the Modern Art Week, a three-day series of public events and performances in São Paulo in February 1922. Those happenings constituted a monument, a historical marking unique to Brazil, as no other major nation has so enshrined the time and place of its artistic maturation. The outcry of *modernismo* was founded on general rejection of conservative immobility in the arts, and of staid linguistic convention and empty pomposity in letters. Brazilian modernists held utopian beliefs in progress, in the possibilities of reform, and in the wonders of technology. They endeavored — often being deliberately provocative and scandalous — to overcome taboos and prejudices and to consecrate new languages. Leaders of the movement would appeal to colleagues in the arts to ensure their own originality through consideration of *all* (i.e., multiracial, multicultural, multiregional) aspects of Brazilian life. While this awakening of national consciousness largely characterized the thematic side of the Modern Art Week, stylistic issues played out as attacks on bad (antiquated) taste and literary senility, as efforts to demystify an ingrained rhetoric that had for years restricted expression. The Modern Art Week launched campaigns for change and agendas of experimentation, making a fundamental contribution to an aesthetic and psychological climate in which a generalized critique of the thought and creative options of preceding generations could take place. At the outset, the Modern Art Week was a point of convergence for new artistic currents that had been appearing in São Paulo and Rio de Janeiro since World War I; at its conclusion, it was a springboard for further adventures and a platform for consolidation of publications and groups. The most important of these merit treatment from the perspective of vanguardism.[2]

In literature, *modernismo* is commonly considered in two phases or divisions. The Modern Art Week marks the beginning of the vanguardist "heroic" phase of rebellion and rupture, which extends to the turn of the next decade. During these initial years, poetry was the driving force of the movement. The lyric genre enjoyed high prestige and, with its accumulated cultural capital, was a focal point of intellectual life in the 1920s. As David William Foster writes with reference to Brazil, "it is important to underscore how the fundamental instrument of modernism . . . was poetry . . . wherein resides the foremost testing ground of the modernist project."[3] Geographically, the cosmopolitan and future industrial center of São Paulo was the main stage of the heroic phase. As *modernismo* also solidified in the political and cultural capital of Rio de Janeiro, and spread with enthusiasm to other states, national spirit abounded and different manifestations evolved. A second commonly recognized phase runs from about 1930 to the middle of the decade of the forties, when some landmark retrospective essays appear. During this less militant second phase, often portrayed as having a more positive outlook and constructive approach, regional studies emerged (most notably the work of Gilberto Freyre), the novel gained increasing recognition, and lyric diversified in groups and individual endeavors. For some, *modernismo* may mean everything in the modern period, i.e., all literature since 1922, or serve as a historical designation whose extension remains open to debate. In the present study, the term *modernismo* will be employed in the more standard manner to refer to developments until about 1945, when, as seen below, an organized reaction to the liberties of modern verse took place. This usage is also understood to encompass the later work of the major voices who began in the twenties and thirties.

The young proponents of *modernismo* made significant inroads against entrenched models of declamatory eloquence in Brazilian letters in general, and antiquated Parnassian conventions in poetry in particular. Concurrently, the movement emphasized Brazilian content, including language itself, and drew heavily on European avant-gardes for technical support. It is possible to make a fundamental bipolar simplification of *modernismo* in poetry as the advent of free verse and the affirmation of nationalism. The study of *modernismo* has encompassed diachronic and synchronic efforts to trace the organization and realization of the Modern Art Week, to understand individual and collective projects involved in the Week, and to follow the subsequent unfolding of the movement.[4] To capture its guiding spirit of rupture, one must first look back at the mind-set and the poetry to which the Brazilian *modernistas* were so opposed.

Parnassianism and the Cult of Belles-Lettres

Parnassianism, which was relatively prominent in late nineteenth-century lyric of the mother country Portugal, still dominated Brazilian poetry at the outset of the third decade of the twentieth century. The practices of this French school were grounded in reverence for form — versification, meter, rhyme scheme, strophe — and in denial of romantic excess, strong emotion, and hyperbole. In the Brazilian parallel of this European aestheticism and *écriture artiste,* noble diction (read, classical

Continental Portuguese), mastery of technique, and exquisite taste (in language and content) were appreciated for their own sake. Parnassianism gained the status of a normative regime in literature and of an institution in high Brazilian society. For Benedito Nunes, the particular literary way of being shaped a certain social alienation:

> verbal decorum and refinement determined the "literary" behavior of the Brazilian intelligentsia. . . . Affectation of style in writing gave luster to such behavior and was part of a life style that masked, with the ritual of the vernacular purity of the language and of the self-sufficiency of the Beautiful, the frustrated and evasive social role of writers and artists who saw themselves in European molds, through which they idealized a superior station to attribute to themselves in a society from which they were effectively separated.[5]

The codified and restrictive Parnassian positions, so wrapped up in senses of propriety and prestige, created unavoidable distance from real-life circumstances, notably linguistic practice. While typically cultivating things exotic (Oriental or classical Greco-Roman) and reifying writerly rules, Brazilian Parnassianism did aim at inculcating civic pride in a conservative vein and managed to pay some attention to local culture. Olavo Bilac (1865–1918) was, before *modernismo*, recognized as a master of versification and a model of elegant erudition, and as the "Prince of Poets." His sonnet "Língua portuguesa" ("Portuguese Language," 1919) communicates the traditionalist attitude toward the instrument of expression:

> Última flor do Lácio, inculta e bela,
> És, a um tempo, esplendor e sepultura:
> Ouro nativo, que na ganga impura
> A bruta mina entre os cascalhos vela . . .
>
> Amo-te assim, desconhecida e obscura,
> Tuba de alto clangor, lira singela,
> Que tens o som e o silvo da procela,
> E o arrolo da saudade e da ternura!
>
> Amo o teu viço agreste e o teu aroma
> De virgens selvas e de oceano largo!
> Amo-te, ó rude e doloroso idioma,
>
> Em que da voz materna ouvi: "Meu filho!",
> E em que Camões chorou, no exílio amargo,
> O gênio sem ventura e o amor sem brilho!

Last flower of Latium, wild, uncultured beauty,
You are at once both splendor and the grave:
You're gold which, in the gang's impurity,
Doth veil a giant mine in graveled lave.

I love you thus, unknown, obscure and hidden,
A blaring trumpet, lyre of singleness,
Your fury's like the sea that's tempest ridden,
Your lullaby's of love and tenderness!

I love your lush green woods and perfumes, wrung
From virgin jungles and expansive sea!
I love you, rude and sorrowful native tongue,

In which my mother called: "Dear son of mine!"
In which Camões bemoaned, grieved exile he,
His luckless genius and love's tarnished shine![6]

In the early twentieth century, the Parnassian style in poetry, and its corollaries in official public discourse, remained the style of the ruling class, of cultured and semicultured bureaucrats. Liberal professionals were accustomed to conceiving of poetry as "ornate language" according to consecrated models that could guarantee "good taste" through imitation. In schools and society salons, which respected the Academy of Letters, the vogue was the descriptive sonnet. It was against this fallow provincial culture that the literary protests of *modernismo* would rise.[7] Though still firmly in place, Parnassianism was certainly ready to fall by the 1920s. While its principal poets had already died, other known poets were weak artists and disinterested cultivators. What remained of the movement was empty, formulaic rhetoric. The unusual pervasiveness of Parnassianism was yet to be challenged in its foundations and, finally, overcome.

Literary Modernism Brazilian Style

The dual impetus of *modernismo*—formal liberty and the search for Brazilian identity—had inherent potential for contradiction, surging from both cosmopolitan and local sources. The former meant contact with, and adaptation of, the novel ideas and formal proposals of the European avant-gardes, while the latter led to a nationalism of resistance to the foreign and to emphasis on Brazilian originality, even on the autonomy of local intellectual life. There was no avoiding oscillation between, and sometimes mixture of, these two aesthetic and ideological positions.

Wherever new projects might lead, an iconoclastic impulse was foremost in the first phase of *modernismo*. As Nunes underscores: "the rebelliousness of the generation of '22 against the immobility and academic self-sufficiency of the national intelligentsia that aestheticism had strengthened and safeguarded was manifested in an outward expression of rejection as an act of rupture" ("Pensamento estetico," 111). Breaking with the established institutions of literature would be achieved through, and allow for, both further patriotic opportunities and exploration of modern forms.

The principal European influences on *modernismo* were futurism and cubism. The futurist manifesto (1909) of the Italian F. T. Marinetti encouraged audacity, revolt, and artistic blows against the status quo. It affirmed the beauty of velocity and technology in the urban age of the machine and offered "words in liberty" as the cry of rebellion in poetry. Poets in Brazil absorbed the ideas of Guillaume de Apollinaire, whose antitraditionalist *manifesto de syntese* (1913) clamored for "words in liberty" too and sought for poetry the multidimensionality of pictorial cubism. The later *esprit nouveau* (1920), constructive in character in comparison to the destructive vanguards of the 1910s, also inspired Brazilian intellectuals. Other influences were German expressionism in painting, with its exaltation of the elemental, and the manifestos of dadaism (1916–1919), with their derisive and clowning attitudes toward everything, including the autonomy of art, and their attractive appeals to primal laughter, ingenuity, and primitivism that challenged all literature and its encompassing society. The surrealism of André Breton (manifesto, 1924) also called for permanent revolt and a kind of "literary terrorism," while valuing, above all, the subconscious. This line, centering on liberation and projection of unconscious material, could lead to a kind of experimentation of primitivist character, of natural interest in tropical and largely undeveloped Brazil.

In the 1910s and 1920s, a few Brazilian writers were exposed to and responded to avant-garde agitation to varying degrees. In terms of attitude and technical applications, the manner in which authors understood and used European avant-garde vices and devices were as heterogeneous as *modernismo* itself. In a larger sense, the big difference between Europe and Brazil, with respect to the significance of the artistic vanguards, is that the European avant-gardes were produced as the result of a fundamental crisis of thought. There is a pervasive agonistic character in the early decades of the twentieth century, and the proponents of various -isms come out against art and the entire social structure that supports it. During the "heroic phase" of Brazilian modernism in the

1920s, what was sought was not so much an activist lyric, or a reformulation of civilizational values per se, nor a general break with the social structure, but rather a kind of artistic making up for backwardness and lost time, a modernizing "resetting of the clock."[8] The rupture of *modernismo* was with the past and was carried out with an eye to literary revitalization, and to affirmation of the right to pursue a fresh creative consciousness.

In the pursuit of new expressive means and goals, the poets and prophets of *modernismo* fell into a series of different groups. One Brazilian observer established five convenient divisions with distinctive traits: (1) the *dinamistas* (dynamists) of Rio de Janeiro, including venerable essayist J. P. da Graça Aranha (1868–1931) and poet Ronald de Carvalho (1893–1935), who stressed material progress, technical greatness, and the cosmic destiny of Brazil; (2) the *desvairistas* (loonies) of São Paulo, especially in the person of the multifaceted national cultural leader Mário de Andrade (1893–1945), who theorized poetic making, underscored freedom in artistic research, and proposed a national language; (3) the *primitivistas* (primitivists) led by the central figure of Oswald de Andrade (1890–1954), author of two key manifestos of *modernismo*, with their suggestions of return to origins and flight from illustrious old culture; (4) the *nacionalistas* (nationalists), patriotic writers who spoke against prejudice and advocated a kind of paternalistic reform; and (5) the *espiritualista* (spiritualist) group called Festa, who, in the 1930s, reexplored symbolism, tradition, and mystery.[9] Beyond this scheme, one must highlight the places of two widely respected and influential independents: Manuel Bandeira (1886–1968), some of whose pre-1922 verse effectively marks the transition to *modernismo*, and much of whose subsequent poetic work so vividly embodies the modern spirit, and Carlos Drummond de Andrade (1902–1987), who headed the modernist platform in the state of Minas Gerais and would become the leading lyric voice in Brazil in the twentieth century. Many other poets represent collective and individual directions of *modernismo*.[10]

A Complete Story: Mário de Andrade

In the estimation of many, the most dynamic and characteristic figure of *modernismo* was Mário de Andrade. Internationally, he is perhaps best known for his experimental prose "rhapsody" *Macunaíma* (1928).[11] In conjunction with his innovations in fiction, and beyond, Mário was a folklorist, musicologist, teacher, administrator, literary critic, and poet. In this last capacity, he authored two statements of principle that remain

absolutely essential to the consideration of *modernismo:* "Prefácio inter-
essantíssimo" ("Extremely Interesting Preface," 1922) and "A escrava
que não é Isaura" ("The Slave Who Is not Isaura," 1924). In these
manifestos, lyric poetry is understood as a necessity of expression that
becomes art when filtered by a creative intelligence. In modern poetry,
surpassing antiquated rules supposedly based on beauty, the "imagina-
tion is set free . . . and finds, in the epoch of the twenties, in synthetic,
quick and cinematic expression, the culmination of a process of libera-
tion of lyric impulses" (Nunes, "Pensamento estético," 115). Mário thus
combines the intuitive, the laborious synthesis of futurist poetics, and
the shock-images of expressionism. The "Preface" opens the collection
Paulicéia desvairada (Hallucinated City). Actually written some two
years before the Modern Art Week, it is the first showcase of *modernista*
verse in Brazil, with its avant-garde intellectual disquiet, passionate ur-
ban approach to the city of São Paulo, and multiple voices.[12] The dis-
putatious side of this collection is best felt in the local illustration of
épater les bourgeois of "Ode ao burguês" ("Ode to the Bourgeois Gentle-
man"), which the poet recited at the central event of the Modern Art
Week. It opens:

> Eu insulto o burguês! O burguês-níquel,
> o burguês-burguês!
> A digestão bem feita de São Paulo!
> O homem-curva! o homem-nádegas!
> O homem que sendo francês, brasileiro, italiano,
> é sempre um cauteloso pouco-a-pouco!
>
> . . . .
>
> I insult the bourgeois! The money-grubbing bourgeois,
> the bourgeois-bourgeois!
> The well-made digestion of São Paulo!
> The man-belly! The man-buttocks!
> The man who being French, Brazilian, Italian,
> is always a cautious little take-your-time!
> (*Hallucinated City,* 36–37)

Among Mário's objectives was the elimination of middle- and upper-
class prejudice against truly national cultural manifestations, including
folk art and popular speech. A sustained concern with the lexicon and
syntax of everyday language, and with common people's art, made
Mário a model for politically motivated poets decades later.[13] Beyond
the "folk" element per se (celebration of aspects of the indigenous pres-

ence, African-Brazilianness, the Northeastern region, the Amazon, etc.), Mário was a staunch advocate of linguistic realism and native expression against the defenders of Lusitanian grammar and exclusionary classical culture.

As far as literary history is concerned, Mário's main contribution was the retrospective address "O Movimento Modernista" (1942), in which he states what he believes to be the three main points of the enduring legacy of *modernismo:* the permanent right of aesthetic research, the updating of national artistic intelligence, and the stabilization of a national creative consciousness. These were not really innovations in the 1920s; elements of each are to be found all through Brazilian artistic history. What really distinguished the endeavors of *modernismo* was the articulation of these conquests into an organic whole with collective results. These points are certainly applicable to Mário's own work, and they continue to provide an honest, and oft-cited, synthesis of the movement he led.

Appropriation and Confrontation: Oswald de Andrade

A very different departure from romantic-symbolist idealization, Parnassian rigidity, and realist representation is to be found in the work of Oswald de Andrade, the foremost polemicist, iconoclast, and manifesto-maker of *modernismo.* This key avant-garde instigator explored the boundaries of prose in autobiographical cubist experiments and forged poetry in a similar vein.[14] His *Poesia Pau-Brasil* (Brazil-wood poetry, 1925), while inspired in European primitivism, sought a "native originality" whose cultivation could lead to a modern poetry of export (Brazil-wood having been the first product sent abroad in the sixteenth century).[15] In his new antiverse, Oswald achieved a radical reduction of poetry into brief, synthetic, telegraphic instances. In this *poesia-minuto,* he isolated working materials — phrases from historical documents, circumstantial language, descriptions of local phenomena — into lyrical fragments which, in a sui generis montage with frequently parodic intentions, were linked together in chronological, geographical, or thematic subheadings. A good example of Oswald's mischievous text-making comes in "Biblioteca Nacional" ("National Library"), evidently a selection of suggestive titles from the bookshelves:

A Criança Abandonada
O doutor Coppelius
Vamos com Ele

Senhorita Primavera
Código Civil Brasileiro
A arte de ganhar no bicho
O Orador Popular
O Pólo em Chamas

The Abandoned Child
Doctor Coppelius
Let Us Go with Him
Miss Spring
Brazilian Code of Civil Law
How to Win the Lottery
Public Speaking for Everyone
The Pole in Flames[16]

This example illustrates the poet's characteristic point-blank utilization of the "readymade" in a satirical setting involving history, literary heritage, and public discourse. It is a clear renunciation of ornamental language and of what supposedly constituted good taste and elegant diction in poetic language. The peculiar selection of titles juxtaposes different social elements and has humorous intent as well. In this sense, it can be associated with one of the main practices of the combative phase of *modernismo,* the so-called *poema piada,* or joke poem.[17] This mode was used as an arm in the campaign against the predominance of the values of the literary academy.

Such short poems of Oswald's as "National Library" achieve given effects but may easily fall flat when extracted or isolated from the group in which they were composed. It is essential, then, to take into account the encompassing frames of Oswald's verse, whether the historical Portuguese chronicles of discovery or accounts of exploratory voyages through the Brazilian provinces, to appreciate the individual instances of the inaugural collection of Brazil-wood poetry, which is best understood as a self-contained sequence. On the formal plane, the very use of new procedures — fracture, fragmentation, capsulization — means, in many instances, that image-making may take precedence over the communication of any particular idea.[18] This constructive approach would interest, in a fundamental way, Brazil's principal midcentury neovanguard, the concrete poets.

Poesia Pau-Brasil had been preceded by the publication of a manifesto announcing the operative approaches of this new type of lyric and proclaiming, in creative tones, its strengths.[19] The governing principles of this playful document included, in the compositional vein, synthesis, geometrical balance, and technical finishing. In the avant-garde mode, invention and surprise were highlighted, and in a celebratory primitivist spirit, simplicity, innocence, and purity were advocated. These were, however, to be filtered by "cultured practice" to meet an aesthetic standard. Appropriate literary progress was to be made through fusion and contrast of native phenomena with modern elements, especially technological advances, as suggested in the phrases "Nostalgia for the medicine man and military air fields . . . The forest and the school." Oswald's liberating outlook here is encapsulated in the italicized phrase *Ver com olhos livres / See with open eyes*, which calls for freedom of technique and for apprehension of surrounding (i.e., Brazilian) realities. It bears stressing, finally, that the poetry was conceived of as an export product, as something to combat the historical imitation of European models, and thus as a source of pride. This is a key de-centering gesture of a New World vanguard.

Oswald's aesthetic project evolves with a second, more celebrated, declaration of principles, "O manifesto antropófago" ("The Cannibalist Manifesto," 1928), which has intrigued and challenged Brazilian and foreign critical readers alike.[20] Oswald's rebellious, antiestablishment, and culturally proactive sentiment is developed in this none too diaphanous follow-up document through the metaphors of deglutition, devourment, and anthropophagy. Critical perspective on Brazilian cultural history, beginning with the contact of Portuguese and Amerindian populations, is gained through an encounter with the primitive forces of the unconscious. The pivotal symbol of cannibalism is an attempt to comprehend a native totemic sense of eating one's enemies to absorb their forces via magical disposition. This, in literature, would be understood as a critical assimilation of foreign (or even nonliterary) information and experiences for reelaboration in local terms. The polemical juxtaposition of foreign and Brazilian material in the manifesto is best felt in the phrase "Tupy, or not Tupy, that is the question," a cosmopolitan pun involving the family of South American indigenous peoples, Hamlet's existential dilemma, and the choices facing sentient New World artists. In conjunction with the assertions of *Pau-Brasil*, Oswald's anthropophagy comprised a vanguard relativization of the nation's peripheral status, which would also be taken up by the theoreticians of concrete poetry in their own efforts to situate their innovative art in a conjuncture of purpose.

In the insurgent mode of *modernismo*, Oswald's cannibalist group, with its standard-bearing publication and associate members, started out, as one participant has written, as "an independent movement of negativist fun-making. It marked an epoch. It impiously knocked over figures who were mere literary shells, with no heart. It shook up inconsistent hierarchies."[21] At this point, the target was not just Parnassians but less-adventurous rival modernists as well. With Anthropophagy, Oswald was going after the proponents of another submovement, *Verdeamarelismo* (Green-yellowism, 1926), later *Anta* (Tapir, 1927), which may have been formulated as ultranationalistic responses to Oswald's earlier project.[22] This other faction included Menotti del Picchia (1892–1988), one of the original organizers of the Modern Art Week, Plínio Salgado (1895–1975), who would later head Brazilian *integralismo* (a fascistic political organization), and Cassiano Ricardo (1895–1974), truly one of the most enduring figures of Brazilian poetry in the twentieth century. These writers elaborated an idealistic neo-Indianism and proved to be xenophobic. While essential for a socioliterary study of the 1920s–1930s, their cultural symbols and guiding metaphors would not have much lasting effect. Their adversary, to the contrary, would enjoy a vibrant revival and reevaluation in the sixties and beyond. As one of Brazil's most respected critics affirmed half a century after the Modern Art Week: "without a doubt the most important figure of *modernismo,* and the most influential on the newest generation, is Oswald de Andrade."[23]

The Length of a Century: Manuel Bandeira

One of the central personalities of Brazilian poetry of the twentieth century — before, during, and after *modernismo* — was Manuel Bandeira. Better than any other single figure, this key poet embodied and expressed the evolving and exploratory spirit of modern lyric in his country. In the late 1910s, Bandeira's work still showed the lasting influences of Parnassianism, as well as crepuscular interests in symbolism, but he was already positioning himself against phony noble diction and literary regulations. His collection *Carnaval* (1919) included "Os sapos" ("The Toads"), which poked fun at Parnassian rigidity and was performed at the Modern Art Week.[24] In view of his opposition to staid tradition and his encouragement of innovation, Bandeira earned the nickname "The St. John the Baptist" of *modernismo*. With *O ritmo dissoluto* (Dissolute rhythm, 1924), the poet moved definitively toward free verse, forcefully questioned the hierarchy of subjects in poetry, blurred the boundaries between the "poetic" and the "prosaic," and brought numerous thematic and lexical novelties in a nationalist vein. He transferred the symbolist preoccupation with mellifluous verse into a more accommodating musicality, incorporating the rhythms of speech and the particular sonorities of Brazilian Portuguese (cf. the example of "Berimbau" in chapter 4).

The multifarious poems of *Libertinagem* (Libertiny, 1930) best represent the poet's combative spirit, dark humor, characteristic irony, controlled colloquialism, and occasional desire to shock well-behaved society. "Poema tirado de uma notícia de jornal" (Poem taken from an item in a newspaper, "Found Poem") illustrates the poet's ability to transform quotidian events with an interpretive intonation of defamiliarization. The relatively long "Evocação do Recife" ("Evocation of Recife") blended individual and collective perspectives in a nonlinear and associative "folk" implementation of modern diction.[25] Bandeira stated his position at the end of the belligerent stage of *modernismo* in "Poética: "Estou farto do lirismo comedido . . . bem comportado . . . funcionário público . . . namorador / Político / Raquítico / Sifilítico . . . Não quero mais saber do lirismo que não é libertação" ("I'm fed up with restrained lyricism . . . of well-behaved . . . Of public servant . . . courting love lyricism / Politic / Ricketic / Syphilitic . . . I want nothing more to do with lyricism that isn't freedom," Williams, 37). From the 1930s on, this "dean" of Brazilian poetry continued to build on tradition and rebellion, inner sentiment and external observation, and a peculiar subtle diction, to diversify his poetic world. His desires and gains represent key points of reference for the lyric of *modernismo* and of the contemporary period alike.

In the Middle of the Road: Carlos Drummond de Andrade

For many, the axial figure of modern poetry in Brazil is Carlos Drummond de Andrade. Iconoclastic at the outset, existentially acute and socially perspicacious for a lifetime, Drummond's widely studied and translated poetry is consistently intellectual, hinges on awareness of language as an instrument, and keeps a metaliterary level in sight.[26] He made an audacious debut with "No meio do caminho" ("In the Middle of the Road"), a singularly repetitious text and a roadmarker of *modernismo:*

No meio do caminho tinha uma pedra
tinha uma pedra no meio do caminho
tinha uma pedra
no meio do caminho tinha uma pedra.

Nunca me esquecerei desse acontecimento
na vida de minhas retinas tão fatigadas.

Nunca me esquecerei que no meio do caminho
tinha uma pedra
tinha uma pedra no meio do caminho
no meio do caminho tinha uma pedra.

In the middle of the road there was a stone
there was a stone in the middle of the road
there was a stone
in the middle of the road there was a stone.

I'll never forget that having happened
in the life of my oh so tired retinas.
I'll never forget that in the middle of the road
there was a stone
there was a stone in the middle of the road
in the middle of the road there was a stone.

Since its appearance in Oswald's *Revista de antropofagia* (1928), critical responses to this bold poem — ranging from outrage and derision to celebration of its antinormative implications and careful examination of its structural strategies — have merited an entire volume.[27] Among the abiding legacies of this joco-serious lyrical stab is its inspiring textualization of the confrontation of impediments, be they societal, existential, or literary.

It is another landmark poem of Drummond's first book that inspires, through its multidimensionality, the title of the present study. The variously translated "Poema de sete faces" is significant as a characteristic text of the second, less nationalistic degree of *modernismo* in poetry and, in a wider-angle view, as a representation of the opening up to a variety of possibilities for the decades to follow. This heptagonal composition, the "Seven-Sided Poem," is like an unfolding fan that is suggestive — in its fabric, patterns, and contextualizations — of a series of factors relevant to the march of twentieth-century Brazilian lyric:

Quando nasci, um anjo torto
desses que vivem na sombra
disse: Vai, Carlos, ser *gauche* na vida.

As casas espiam os homens
que correm atrás das mulheres.
A tarde fosse azul
não houvesse tantos desejos.

O bonde passa cheio de pernas:
pernas brancas pretas amarelas.

Para que tanta perna, meu Deus, pergunta meu coração.
Porém meus olhos
não perguntam nada.

O homem atrás do bigode
é sério, simples e forte.
Quase não conversa.
Tem poucos, raros amigos
o homem atrás dos óculos e do bigode.

Meu Deus, porque me abandonaste
se sabias que eu não era Deus
se sabias que eu era fraco.

Mundo mundo vasto mundo
se eu me chamasse Raimundo,
seria uma rima, não seria uma solução.
Mundo mundo vasto mundo,
Mais vasto é meu coração.

Eu não devia te dizer,
mas essa lua
mas esse conhaque
Botam a gente comovido como o diabo.

When I was born, one of the crooked
angels who live in the shadow, said:
Carlos, go on! Be *gauche* in life.

The houses watch the men,
men who run after women.
If the afternoon had been blue,
there might have been less desire.

The trolley goes by full of legs:
white legs, black legs, yellow legs.
My God, why all the legs?
my heart asks. But my eyes
ask nothing at all.

The man behind the moustache
is serious, simple, and strong.
He hardly ever speaks.
He has a few, choice friends,
the man behind the spectacles and the moustache.

My God, why hast Thou forsaken me
if Thou knew'st I was not God,
if Thou knew'st that I was weak.

Universe, vast universe,
if I had been named Eugene
that would not be what I mean
but it would go into verse
faster.
Universe, vast universe,
my heart is vaster.

I oughtn't to tell you,
but this moon
and this brandy
play the devil with one's emotions.[28]

The opening lines here reveal a wealth of attitudinal factors and pro-
cedural directions. Adjectivization, for instance, breaks the natural rela-
tion of words, suggests "ideas through unsuitable concepts," and proves
to be a principal vehicle of humor and a "powerful instrument of en-
chantment."[29] This first strophe ironically sets up the rest of the poem as
the fractured words of a contrary self and can even key an interpretation
of Drummond's lyrical world. *Gauche* means maladjusted, marginalized,
and, for the displaced person, "left out," a notion that crystallizes the
"aesthetic personality of the poet."[30] Each of the stanzas particularizes a
state of mind and a mode of perception or expression; visual focus, for
instance, governs the second and third stanzas, while containment and
reserve can be gleaned from the fourth. There is, nevertheless, surface
disjuncture, a lack of clear connection between the seven parts. This
compositional difference among the parts reflects a complex conscious-
ness. Self-awareness involves lacks of harmony. After the introductory
stanza, the next six "reflect tensions at different levels and in different
ways. Not only does each stanza suggest a conflict but the very an-
gularity, the disjointedness with which the poem moves from stanza to
stanza, is symptomatic of conflict as well."[31] The variety of the stanzas is
like a cubist effort at representation of simultaneity of perception and
consciousness. In a rhetorical sense, the poetic fragmentation is a move
away from linearity and dominant discursiveness. Thus the internal con-
flicts of the poem are not defeating, but rather constitutive of a searching
self and of an artistic newness. The very propriety of the lyrical event, at
the poem's conclusion, is questioned as it is enunciated.

With all this, the oddly formed "Poema de sete faces" incarnates the general break from strictures of the past in *modernismo,* technical modernizations, individualization of rhythm, the role of ironic apprehension, manipulated colloquialism, opposition to conventional coherence, acceptance of dissonance, appeals to shape and visuality, an intense portrait of the fractured modern self and text, and an overall enabling of poetic diversity to come.

A Fest of a Different Stripe: The *Festa* Group

In contrast with the transformational, ethnically focused, and ludic currents of *modernismo,* a number of poets of the late 1920s and 1930s availed themselves of the liberating effects of the movement to pursue different courses of modernity. Grouped around the journal *Festa,* a number of new voices opted for a more solemn poetry. Their versemaking was marked by serene gravity, prophetic tones, and spiritual (largely Catholic) concerns. These poets included poet-essayist Tasso da Silveira (1895–1968); publisher Augusto Frederico Schmidt (1906–1965); Murilo Mendes (1901–1975), who rejected an early *Pau-Brasil*–like approach and would become a late surrealist stylist; the neosymbolist Cecília Meireles (1901–1964), Brazil's most important female poet; Jorge de Lima (1895–1953), who also participated in Northeastern regionalism; and Vinícius de Morais (1913–1980), who would move toward a more worldly verse and become a key figure in the emergence of the poetry of song in the 1960s, but started out immersed in youthful mysticism. When one tries to fit the collective Festa stance into the confines of Brazilian modernism *strictu sensu* (i.e., avant-garde), one is "assaulted by perplexity," as one honest historian puts it.[32] Still, this group does participate, in a broad sense, in the move away from canonical Lusitanian domination, the intellectual decentralization, the national introspection, and the resolve to participate in national life that characterized *modernismo.* The distinguishing traits of this group further suggest the possibility of the conservative countertendency of the mid-forties.

Rereaction and Reenactment: The Generation of 1945

About a quarter-century after the Modern Art Week, there occurred in poetry an organized reaction to the "permissiveness" that the movement had ushered in. Despite massive social change and wholesale shifts in literature, the lyric genre had not lost its place as a key cultural practice, as Nunes points out: "With the ebb of *modernismo* in the 1940s, literature, and particularly poetry, linked to the tradition of modern lyric since 1922, was still the catalytic means of aesthetic reflection" ("Pensamento Estético," 120). Counting on the prestige of poetry but reflecting differently, poets known collectively as the Generation of '45 rejected free verse and colloquialism in favor of a return to lofty themes, refined language, precious metaphors, and classical vehicles (ode, sonnet). Among their objections to modern lyric in its local manifestations — which were voiced in more accommodating terms by many modernists themselves — were the loss of rhythm (i.e., metrification), the sterility of the machine (as celebrated in futurism), the natural limits of the joke-poem, and the excessive concern with folklore.[33] While without a manifesto per se, these oppositional values were made clear in creative and expository texts, as were the influences held to be "aristocratic" (T. S. Eliot, Paul Valéry, Rainer Maria Rilke). Thematically, this anti-populist group, convinced of its own serious mission, focused on psychic states, philosophical doubt, problems of being, hermetic symbols, and temporality.

This in effect neo-Parnassianism was widely perceived as retrograde and lacking in necessary social concern. Since the late forties, Brazilian critics of several different persuasions have objected to what the Generation of '45 proposed. It will be instructive to see a series of responses to them to reveal both their poetic values and the scope of critical positions of midcentury, as these critiques are indicative of lines of thought that would emerge more forcefully in the fifties and beyond. Sérgio Buarque de Hollanda, in the role of literary critic, was taken aback by the '45 poets' fetishization of learned rules and techniques. As a leading historian, he recalled that "nostalgia for rigid regulations and inflation of form never represented an emblem of those epochs truly rich in poetry."[34] The individual and collective dangers of retrocession are well expressed by a later analyst: "The crisis of 1945 was a crisis of the 'poem.' Losing all sense of the modernist revolution, the poets fell into an involution — a fact verified in the work of many writers of the period — that threatened Brazilian poetry with a return to premodernist processes."[35]

Natural comparisons to the products of *modernismo* via the logic of the poem are as much a question of content as of mechanics. In this regard, the mythification of '45 can be related to what some of them saw as a "deficiency" of mainstream '22, to wit, "the absence of philosophical-psychological content, of doubt and inner disquiet." To whatever degree this may be true, or relativized in a wider-angle view of the twenties and thirties, the extremism and negativity of '45 remain clear in the eyes of a veteran observer:

the generation that denied *modernismo* went to the other extreme, worrying to excess about the things of the Eternal. They live with their heads buried in Mystery. . . . sometimes the most trivial of things are treated with an air of transcendental nebulosity, of hermetic grandeur, of complicated and esoteric eloquence. . . . an obsessive passion with a new Mythology was born. (Peregrino Júnior, 6, 8)

In the wake of the Second World War, and in the midst of a local emphasis on national growth, extraliterary aspects increasingly concerned many Brazilian critics in the 1950s. Thus poet-essayist Affonso Ávila— cofounder of the progressive Minas Gerais journal *Tendência,* organ of what was termed *nacionalismo crítico*—worried whether '45 poet Domingo Carvalho da Silva was excessively formalist, remote, and difficult, and asserted that another, José Paulo Moreira da Fonseca, ought to restructure his poetry to "uncover other horizons in the conquest of the major issue of poetry of our century, that is man in his relationship with the world and his fellow men."[36] Evident here is a social preoccupation that peaks, as seen in chapter 3, in the 1960s, but which provides needed perspective on the poetic enterprise that proposed to surpass *modernismo.*

In an organic assessment of the group, finally, a young José Guilherme Merquior noted how the meters of '45 verse betray the psychological flexibility of '22, lamented the newer poetic language as a dictionary vocabulary, and found fault with the "rarefied anemia and abstraction" of its typical images. He saw, rightly, the insistence of this "degeneration" on a return to order as misguided, since, following the destructive heroic phase of *modernismo,* the forties were already "a decade of serene construction," as Mário de Andrade himself had proposed.[37]

Given these kinds of reactions, it is no surprise that the Generation of '45, though active in their own circles and publicly recognized, never really took. Such poets as Péricles E. da Silva Ramos, who worked on the party's journal, the *Revista brasileira de poesia* (1945–1949, reborn in 1976 as *Revista de poesia e crítica*), feel underrepresented and unappreciated in the sphere of contemporary poetry. And, objectively, they are. Beyond the type of negative reaction seen here and their own self-study, there is a clear lack of critical studies of this group.[38] But given the impression of their project as "the biggest bluff of our contemporary literature," what is to be expected?[39] *Modernismo* was a mammoth enterprise and marked a major shift in literature and cultural thought, so the Generation of '45 was taking on no less than artistic nationalism and the institution of modernity in lyric. The type of rigor they offered depended on rules and regulations instead of individualized care, creativity within formal restraints, and pondered nonspontaneity, three traits rightfully attributed to one widely celebrated contemporary poet.

A Case Apart: The Engineer-Bard João Cabral de Melo Neto

The most important poet of the second half of the twentieth century in Brazil, João Cabral de Melo Neto (b. 1920), coincides chronologically with the Generation of '45, but his outlooks and practices set him clearly apart. While he may share a concern with formal discipline in the most general sense, he opposes their cult of the sonnet, focus on psychic states, and bias toward elevated poetic lexicon.[40] Cabral grounds his verse in the tangible reality of objects and things and favors rational compositional procedures over any kind of romantic inspiration or personal expression. Through calculated (yet flexible) metrification and semantic manipulations, Cabral aims at a geometric rigor and the functional approach of architecture. His operative self-image is that of the title poem of *O engenheiro* (The engineer, 1945).

> A luz, o sol, o ar livre
> envolvem o sonho do engenheiro.
> O engenheiro sonha coisas claras:
> superfícies, tênis, um copo de água.
>
> O lápis, o esquadro, o papel;
> o desenho, o projeto, o número:
> o engenheiro pensa o mundo justo,
> mundo que nenhum véu encobre.
>
> . . . .
>
> Light, sun and the open air
> surround the dream of the engineer.
> The engineer dreams clear things:
> surfaces, tennis-courts, a glass of water.
>
> A pencil, a T-square, paper;
> designs, projects, numbers.
> The engineer imagines the world correct,
> a world which no veil covers.[41]

As suggested in the last line here, the precision and objectivity of language in Cabral's poetry are links to real settings (the backlands of the Brazilian Northeast, the city of Recife, Andalusia) and social facts. The poet's severe verse avoids sentimental cadences, yet his very nominal lines sharpen perceptions of human situations and landscapes. Perhaps his most revealing title is *Duas águas* (Dual waters, 1956), as two central currents of his work, metapoetic reflection and "realistic" dramatic verse, are represented in the two parts: the long poem "Uma faca só lâmina" ("A Knife all Blade"), a meditation on writing in which the knife symbolizes poetic language, and "Morte e vida severina" ("The Death and Life of a Severino," originally 1955), a Christmas play and Cabral's best-known work.[42] In *A educação pela pedra* (Education by stone, 1966), it is mineral symbolism that figures prominently in the questioning of (literary) self, as in the title poem:

> Uma educação pela pedra: por lições;
> para aprender da pedra, freqüentá-la;
> captar sua voz inenfática, impessoal
> (pela de dicção ela começa as aulas).
> A lição de moral, sua resistência fria
> ao que flui e a fluir, a ser maleada;
> a de poética, sua carnadura concreta;
> a de economia, seu adensar-se compacta:
> lições de pedra (de fora para dentro,
> cartilha muda), para quem soletrá-la.
>
> Outra educação pela pedra: no Sertão
> (de dentro para fora, e pré-didática).
> No Sertão a pedra não sabe lecionar,
> e se lecionasse, não ensinaria nada;
> lá não se aprende a pedra: lá a pedra,
> uma pedra de nascença, entranha a alma.
>
> An education by stone: through lessons,
> to learn from the stone: to go to it often,
> to catch its level, impersonal voice
> (by its choice of words it begins its classes).
> The lesson in morals, the stone's cold resistance
> to flow, to flowing, to being hammered:
> the lesson in poetics, its concrete flesh:
> in economics, how to grow dense compactly:
> lessons from the stone, (from without to within,
> dumb primer), for the routine speller of spells.
>
> Another education by stone: in the backlands
> (from within to without and pre-didactic place).

In the backlands stone does not know how to lecture,
and, even if it did would teach nothing:
you don't learn the stone, there: there, the stone,
born stone, penetrates the soul.[43]

Again, human presence in an actual physical landscape coordinates a text intensely focused on its own factitious nature. It is this capacity for simultaneous appeal to a linguistically sublime domain and the terrain of being in the world that makes Cabral a singular case in Brazilian literature. The influence of his "antilyrical" aesthetic of self-containment, as illustrated in chapters that follow, is felt in concrete poetry, poets of song, regional poets, and all those who value rigor over emotivity.

Other Indelible Voices

Cabral, Drummond, Bandeira, Oswald, Mário, *modernismo,* a movement inspired in a wealth of national phenomena and in appropriate appeals to a worldwide arsenal of artistic means and forms of organization, including avant-gardism—these are the principal established frames of reference for the development of lyric and its discussion after 1950. Three other names should be mentioned for their contributions to poetic literature and criticism, and as points of reference in the examination of contemporary ideas and reprises. The first of these is the most important figure in Brazilian prose fiction of the twentieth century, João Guimarães Rosa (1908–1967), whose masterpiece was published in 1956.[44] While he did not publish a book of poetry in his lifetime, the master linguist Rosa influenced all artists of the word in Brazil with his inventive stylings. Largely working out of archaic rural settings, Rosa was universal and cosmopolitan, having elaborated wholly modern texts with transcendental dimensions. Poets appreciate his workings with verbal materiality, sound strata, portmanteau words, neologisms, creations on the basis of foreign languages, and other features. The impact of this Joycean figure on writers' consciousness in Brazil is at times subtle yet always true.

Where the lyric genre per se is concerned, a most salient name in the second half of the twentieth century is Ferreira Gullar (b. 1930), who has made marks in experimentalism, social poetry, and polemics. His book *A luta corporal* (Bodily struggle, 1954) is a benchmark in modern Brazilian lyric, a point of departure for the contemporary. This markedly diverse collection moves from metrified verse and more conventional lyric to brief epiphanies, dense prose poems, automatic writing, and other audacious linguistic trials. The existential anguish and artistic disquiet that move the poet are suggested in "As peras" ("The Pears"), which may symbolize a discourse ripe for change:

> . . . .
> Oh as peras cansaram-se
> de suas formas e de
> sua doçura! As peras
> concluídas, gastam-se no
> fulgor de estarem prontas
> para nada.
> . . . . .
>
> Oh the pears have tired
> of their shape and
> sweetness! The pears
> have spent themselves
> in the final glow of preparation
> for oblivion.[45]

In the final sections of this conflictual book, Gullar challenges rationality and confronts the limits of his instrument and of literary experience, dismantling syntax and pulverizing language, as in the closing strokes of "negror n'origens" (blackness 'norigins), with its seemingly random combinations and nonword particles:

> . . . .
> URR VERÕENS
> ÔR
> TÚFUNS
> LERR DESVÉSLEZ VÁRZENS[46]

Such explorations in the suppression of discourse exercised the *modernista* right to "research" in poetry and further opened space, on an individual level, for radical nonconformism. Gullar, a nervous artistic personality, went on to pursue, energetically, different interests; his evolving work will figure variously in subsequent chapters.

Any discussion of Brazilian poetry after *modernismo* must include poet-critic Mário Faustino (1930–1962). Unlike any other figure of the 1950s, Faustino sought an up-to-date reconciliation of classical models and innovations in verse. His at once existentially and linguistically intense involvement with poetry is reflected in this anthological piece:

Vida toda linguagem,
frase perfeita sempre, talvez verso,
geralmente sem qualquer adjetivo,
coluna sem ornamento, geralmente partida.

. . . .
. . . imortal sintaxe
à vida que é perfeita
    língua
      eterna.

Life nothing but language,
an always perfect phrase, perhaps verse,
generally without any adjectives,
an unornamented column, generally split.

. . . .
. . . immortal syntax
for the life that is perfect
    eternal
      language.[47]

Faustino follows the modern line of poetry conceived of as verse-making and as cultivation of the image. Such practice continues throughout the sixties, seventies, eighties, and nineties in Brazil, even as other proposals emerge with strength to gain attention. There are many accomplished poets in the late modern vein in Brazil. Though they are not the chosen focus of the present study, an all-inclusive study of the domain of lyric would consider them.[48] For his part, the young critic-translator Faustino showed an Ezra Pound–like curiosity as director of a Rio de Janeiro literary supplement. There he pondered aspects of compositionally focused poets from Edgar Allan Poe to Jorge de Lima, and welcomed the stimulation and literary challenges that came with the explosion of concrete poetry.

chapter two

The Imperative of Invention: Concrete Poetry

and the Poetic Vanguards

Every authentic poem is an adventure — a planned adventure.
The poet is a designer of language.
— Décio Pignatari (1950, 1964)

After the fallout of the Modern Art Week and the iconoclasm of high *modernismo,* the most provocative and distinctive development in Brazilian lyric is concrete poetry. The creative output of this trend may be limited compared to the extensive corpora of modernist lyric, with its many authors, but the overall phenomena of concretism — encompassing theory, debates, criticism, translations, and interdisciplinary forays — are considerable and have had their own significant effects on artistic practice. The experiments and innovations of the concrete poets, from their inception to current irresolutions, have been influential and quite controversial in Brazil. Outside the country, concrete poetry has lived another life. The international movement was, in diverse versions, an active and notable latter-day avant-garde. It grew, in many respects, out of Brazilian initiatives, despite the natural restrictions of operating from a nonhegemonic nation.[1] It is noteworthy in itself that in the peripheral, Portuguese-speaking nation of Brazil, the theory and practice of concrete poetry developed more intensively than anywhere else. Concrete poetry garnered more attention abroad for Brazilian poetry, if not for literature in general, than any other contemporary manifestation. One might venture to say that concretism has been to Brazil, in terms of international recognition, what the writings of Octavio Paz are to Mexico, or the poetry of Pablo Neruda to Spanish America. Whatever the status of its citation index, variations in the perception of Brazilian concrete poetry merit extended consideration.

The history of the movement of concrete poetry in Brazil has been well documented, and many have examined its theories and products in Brazil and abroad.[2] The aim of the present chapter will be to identify and evaluate important foundational and transitional moments of Brazilian concrete poetry, balancing elements of history and reception with textual inquiry. While some misunderstandings of the goals and processes of concrete poetry are taken up here in an effort to appreciate them as unprecedented and evolving aesthetic proposals in their Brazilian contexts, it is not the purpose of this account to offer any new theoretical angle on concrete poetry. In the presentation of the creative and critical literature of the movement, the international presence is kept in sight, but the prime focus remains on national aspects, from diachronic and synchronic perspectives. With attention fixed on the trajectory of the Brazilian movement and its impact in cultural spheres, there is no extended specific treatment here of the conceptualization of this manifestation as a "vanguard." It is still worth emphasizing that concrete poetry was postulated, and emulated, as a midcentury avant-garde. The theoretical issues of vanguardism act here not in a separate venue, but as part of an overall picture.[3]

Stages, Terms, and Guidelines

Concrete poetry in Brazil developed in three stages. The first (1952–1956) involved the organization of the self-named Noigandres group by the São Paulo poets Décio Pignatari, Augusto de Campos, and Haroldo de Campos. In this "organic" or "phenomenological" phase, creative texts were still verselike but visual factors and verbal dispersion began to play leading roles. In the second stage, a spatially syntaxed poetic minimalism developed. In this so-called "heroic phase" (1956–1960) — the echoes of *modernismo* are intentional — manifestos were issued and the theory of concrete poetry evolved significantly. This period saw the making of "classical," "high," or "orthodox" concrete poetry, texts composed according to rational, "mathematical" principles. More flexible notions of creativity and "invention" prevailed in the third stage, beginning about 1961. The last phase witnessed both definition of social concerns and extreme challenges to the conventions of poetry, as well as intense discord and the emergence of other vanguard groups.

In discussions of Brazil's paramount poetic avant-garde, it is useful to distinguish between the coined term *poesia concreta* and *concretismo,* which referred to abstract, nonrepresentational practices in music (cf. *musique concrète*) and the plastic arts (painting and sculpture), in Europe and Brazil.[4] *Poesia concreta,* strictly speaking, denotes the experimental creative texts of the Noigandres group and affiliated poets, published from the mid-1950s to the early 1970s; by intimate association use of the term also normally implies the accompanying manifestos and theoretical writings that speak directly of the vanguard project in poetry. The Noigandres poets, hoping to set themselves apart and to avoid being labeled another -ism in the succession of (ephemeral) literary movements, voiced preference for the term *poesia concreta* (and, in conjunction, *poetas concretos*) in lieu of *concretismo* (or *concretistas*). Practice outweighed express preference, however, and those terms came to be used interchangeably. In their application to contemporary Brazilian literature, *concretismo* and the corresponding adjectival form *concretista* can have wider meanings, which will be respected in the course of the present chapter. The terms have come to designate the work and advocacy of the Noigandres group in general, which, beyond the specific products of *poesia concreta* in the decades of the fifties and sixties, included translations of inventive poetry from the age of troubadours to the present day, concomitant critical appreciations of select foreign authors, reappraisals of unusual national figures (e.g., Oswald de Andrade, the anomalous romantic poet Sousândrade, and the unique symbolist Pedro Kilkerry), essays on general, largely formalist, literary theory, and interdisciplinary studies.[5]

Further distinctions should be drawn between the original concepts of concrete poetry and the term's accumulated meanings and international usages. Concrete poetry (from Portuguese *poesia concreta* and French *poesie concrète*) was launched in the mid-fifties by the São Paulo poets in conjunction with the Swiss-Bolivian poet Eugen Gomringer. From this purposefully international literary gesture, a calculated poetic practice emerged. Since about 1960, however, "concrete" often also refers to numerous different experiments on the printed page — typographical designs (often nonsemantic), pattern poems, neoletterism, "chaotic" text, scribbles, and some nonverbal practices of page art — which are not comparable to Gomringer's foundational texts nor to what the Brazilians called the "verbivocovisual ideogram."[6] Because of the many possible associations the term *concrete poetry* may now conjure up, it is important to underline from the outset here how profoundly poetic and conceptual the Brazilian project was, and how different its "classical" material was from other less verbally grounded experiments. Concrete poetry was not conceived as figured word-designs but rather as a spatiotemporal juxtaposition of verbal material. If some later visually oriented practices of page art — including Brazilian — can be said to be "against" language, it should be stressed that concrete poetry was founded *on* literary language and is often *about* words. The Brazilian concrete poets, even while taken with Ezra Pound's notion that poetry is more like painting and music than literature, aspired to his characterization of great literature as "language charged with meaning to the utmost possible degree."[7] The term *concrete poetry* will be used here, for the most part, as a translation of the more narrow sense of *poesia concreta* rather than as an umbrella term encompassing the wide transnational spectrum of textual experiments.

Origins and Formation of Brazilian Concretism

The first phase of concrete poetry in Brazil, from 1952 to late 1956, involved the formation of the Noigandres group, their investigations and thinking about poetics, and the organization that would lead to the actual movement. In the atmosphere of the antimodernist Generation of '45, Pignatari, Haroldo, and Augusto demonstrated daring metaphorical imaginations and distinctive lexical, syntactical, and rhythmic traits. Their early output already suggests aversion to the aesthete approach of the neo-Parnassians of '45, with their metrical preoccupations and theme-driven focus on intimacy and the psyche.[8] While examining *The Cantos* of Ezra Pound, the young poets discovered an enticing reference to the enigmatic *noigandres,* a word in a song of the Provençal troubadour Arnaut Daniel that had baffled romance philologists.[9] The São Paulo poets adopted the word as an emblem of free artistic experimentation, and with the allusion to Daniel, whom Pound considered *il miglior fabbro,* and to Pound himself, the young Brazilians staked a claim to his paradigm of poet-inventor. *Noigandres* was the name of the poetry series they published (1952–1962), and the title would be used to refer to the poets as a group with common interests. In the early fifties, they met to brainstorm about modern poetry, with the aim of discovering and charting new directions. Dissatisfied with current national and international thinking in poetry, they wanted to get beyond both the stiff retrograde formalism of the '45 poets and the "automatic factory of metaphors" of surrealism, the only surviving historical avant-garde and a dominant force in French and Spanish American lyric.[10] The leap that was made to concrete poetry was so radical that it cannot be attributed simply to reaction against prevailing values. The ingenious "planned adventure" of the Noigandres poets could not have occurred without their unusual literary preparation and dedication to research in poetics.

    The group's efforts led them to four principal sources: Pound, the adventurous French symbolist Stéphane Mallarmé (1842–1898), the high modernist James Joyce (1882–1941), and the singular North American poet e. e. cummings (1894–1962). Of greatest influence in Pound were his musical interests and his relational ideogrammic method of composition (in *The Cantos*), which, inspired by Fenollosa's studies of Chinese characters, counterposed and juxtaposed related elements drawn from different sources with visible effects. A "crisis of verse" was already evident in Mallarmé's *Un coup de dés* (1897), whose "prismatic subdivision of ideas" — through meaningful variations of type size, distribution of blank spaces and words all over the page, and physical dispersion of lines — implied a new structural syntax for poetry. In Joyce's experimental word craft, the Noigandres poets admired portmanteau words, lexical montages, what he called the "verbivocovisual" word-ideogram, and the interpenetration of time and space. e. e. cummings' poems offered expressive typography, instigating verbal dismantlings, and calculated placement of fragments on the page. These various non-conventional concepts of text-making, synthesized in the Noigandres poets' own particular ways, would be cornerstones of continual theorizations about new forms of poetry.[11] Other points of reference were the shaped text of Guillaume Apollinaire's *calligrammes* (the vision more than the actual mimetic practice) and his phrase "il faut que notre intelligence s'habitue à comprendre synthético-ideographiquement au lieu de analytico-discursivement," as well as the material emphasis (sound, print, page, color) of the historical avant-gardes of cubism, futurism, and dadaism. The Noigandres poets would adapt to their purposes specific elements of the experimental works of these key modern authors in the formulation of concrete poetry.

Brazil's emerging experiment in lyric had key interdisciplinary links. Augusto proclaimed in 1955: "In synch with terminology adopted by the visual arts, and to a degree, by avant-garde music (concretism, concrete music), I would say there is a *concrete poetry.*" He described the basis for such new poems as an "irreversible and functional idea-generating sound-optical structuring [that] creates an entirely dynamic 'verbivoco-visual' entity . . . of ductile words capable of being molded and amalgamated into the shape of the poem" (*Teoria* 34). The most fundamental principle here was the integration of appeals to sight, semantics, and sound. As for the role of music, the emergence of concrete poetry was clearly fortified by the poets' regard for experimental composers. It is consistent that the first identified *poesia concreta* should have been Augusto's *poetamenos* (composed 1953, published 1955), a set of texts marked by de-sentimentalization of lyrical impulses, fragmentation, spatial arrangement, and polychromatic design. The multivoice sequence was modeled

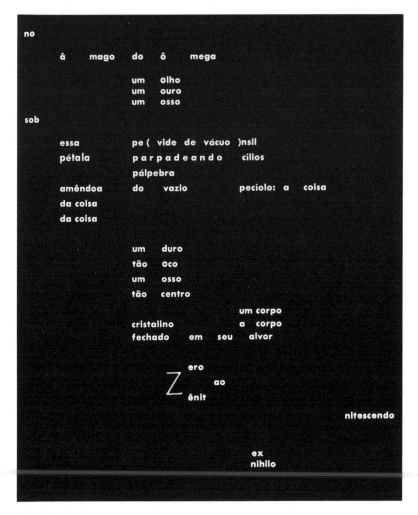

Example 1*

*[in the /es sence of the O mega / an eye / gold / a bone / under / that pen (vine of vacuum) sile / petal blinking lashes / eye lid / almond of emptiness petiole: the thing / of the thing / of the thing / of the thing / a hardness / so empty / a bone / so center / a body / crystalline / to body / closed in its whiteness / Z -ero / to the / -enith / splendoring / ex nihilo]

on Anton Webern's *klangfarbenmelodie* (tone-color-melody), whose application has been aptly analysed by Claus Clüver.[12]

This colorful series and other early concrete poems were characterized by the authors as "organic" or "phenomenological," modifiers which respectively suggest the planting of seeds for later forms and working emphasis on the surface qualities of language. Concrete poetry would be transgressive vis-à-vis inherited lyric, especially the spontaneity of free verse, through tight control and precise manipulation of elements. Production was still verselike at this juncture, though keyed by spatialization of lines and dispersion of words. It was already a type of writing that acted in space and welcomed visible form, valuing alphabetic and phonetic patterns. Haroldo sought integrated verbal and visual effects in the series "o âmago do omega ou fenomenologia da composição" ("The Heart of the Omega or Phenomenology of Composition") with the use of white lettering on black pages and a kind of "de-versification" through distribution of words over the area of the page, as in the title piece of the series shown in example 1.

Such poetry is beginning to move toward the substitution of the linear syntax of verse by nominal structures juxtaposed on horizontal and vertical axes, which would characterize later concrete. Other examples of this early stage and the emphasis on textual physiognomy are the serial rounded texts of "ovo novelo" and the criss-crossed crucigrams of "terremoto" by Augusto, as well as Decio's wavering "um movimento" (example 2).[13]

High Concrete: Models, Practice, Theory

Articulation of the movement of concrete poetry in Brazil and abroad began in 1955–56, even as goals and poetic concepts evolved. On the international level, a noted starting point was Pignatari's encounter with Gomringer, author of reductive poems he called "constellations." As an outcome of that meeting (in 1955), he and the Noigandres group agreed to identify their respective projects as "concrete poetry" and to organize an international anthology. While the original publication plan never materialized, Gomringer began to promote concrete poetry in Europe, especially Germany, laying groundwork for subsequent visits by the Brazilians.[14] On the home front, groups of experimental painters and sculptors in Brazil had also helped to create favorable conditions for the emergence of concrete poetry. The inaugural 1956 exhibition of cooperative *arte concreta,* at the Museum of Modern Art of São Paulo, featured poster texts alongside artwork and marked the official launching of con-

```
                    u m

                           m o v i

                    m e n t o

              c o m p o n d o

        a l e m

                                    d a

      n u v e m

              u m

              c a m p o

                           d e

              c o m b a t e

                    m i r a

        g e m

                    i r a

                           d e

        u m

                    h o r i z o n t e

    p u r o

        n u m

              m o

              m e n t o

    v i v o
```

Example 2*

*[a move-ment composing beyond the clouds a field of combat mir-age ire of a pure horizon in a live mo-ment]

crete poetry.[15] Artists and poets alike aimed at nonrepresentational impersonality, eschewing self-communication in favor of an objectification that would foreground shape and the physical properties of working materials, as seen in a pair of key examples below.

Exhibited poetry included some of the "organic" pieces of the Noigandres poets, as well as experimental works by new adherents to the creed: Ronaldo Azeredo (b. 1937), and two poets who would later lead dissenting factions, Ferreira Gullar, with parts of *o formigueiro,* and Wlademir Dias-Pino (b. 1927), with a noted decompositional piece called "sólida."[16] The two items in the inaugural exhibition that would be representative of the central repertory of concrete poetry in its "classical" form were two stark nonverse texts in bold futura font: Pignatari's celebrated "terra," a word field based on multiple fractures of that single word, and Augusto's "tensão."[17]

In an early manifesto (1956), Augusto had concluded with one of the best capsule definitions of concrete poetry: "tension of word-things in time-space" (*Teoria* 45). The poem "tensão" (example 3) was the creative embodiment of that crystallizing phrase and remains an ideal example to gain an initial understanding of the officially articulated concrete genre.

This prototype illustrates such orthodox concrete approaches as the appeal to simultaneity, the reliance on geometric plotting, the visual layout of phonolexical connections, and the manipulation of relations of proximity and likeness. It was presented at the time as an example of a "fully realized concrete poem" with an internal movement "produced by and producing graphophonetic functions-relations" which become the equivalent of rhythm.[18] Revolving around the express nerve-center of "tension," the poem is a meticulously constructed web of sound and semantic linkages. The text invites a close examination in order to make explicit its systematized effects and to appreciate the nonmetaphorical intricacy of the poem.

The basic design of "tensão" comprises three sets of pairs that can be seen as three horizontal rows, diagonals, or vertical columns, with 2-3-2 items. While elements may be connected mentally to form a series of triangles, the most evident implications of the pairings are two squares (upper left, lower right) linked at the center. In terms of words and numerical organization, and reading top left to bottom right, the first and last pairs are made up of two three-letter words, while all the pairs in between are six-letter words divided in half. This morphological division makes for visual symmetry, additional phonetic links, and some semantic variants: the second-person plural imperative or present subjunctive,

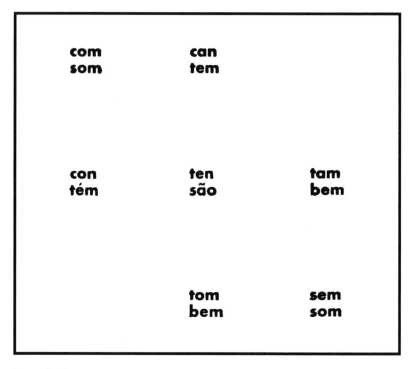

Example 3*

cantem, when split leaves an isolated nonmeaningful syllable (*can*) and the present indicative singular of "to have" (*tem*); when the center word is split it generates an echo-effect vocable (*ten*) and a plural copulative verb form (*são*). Although multidirectional readings are possible here, there is a more conventional or normative left-to-right reading with three basic syntagms: presence of sound, transition toward loss, absence of sound. This "content" plus the interplay of graphed sounds and blank spaces make for the on-off tension of sound and silence that founds the poem. The sound field is constructed both to ensure a melodic dimension to that reading and to set up multiple internal relations that, when visually depicted, substantially diversify the phonovisual map. A phonetic transcription will facilitate hearing and visualizing the web of sound made of exact reiterations, rhymes, and alliterative similarities (example 4). The consonantal dimension is comprised of interplay of

*[with-sound / si-ng! (it has)
(it) con-tains / ten-sion (they are) / as-well
(tone) tum-ble! (well) / without-sound]

the frequent silibant /s/ and the locally dominant occlusives (stops): /k, t, b/. The vocalic side, in turn, is purely nasal; the simple nasal /õ/ is complemented by the results of fractures (/ã/, /ẽ/, and additional /õ/), while two nasal dipthongs form other patterns. Like elements when connected imply a series of lines, angles, triangles, and diamond shapes that, centered by the semantically consistent "tension," overlay the basic plan of the text. Thus /b/-to-/b/ and /ãw/-to-/ãw/ yield short diagonal strokes, while linked /s/ and /õ/ descend across the text field, the first and last instances providing an open-close rhyme and alliteration. The velar stops /k/ form a prominent triangle at upper left, while both /t/ and /ẽy/ form central flat-diamond shapes. With the /t/ of the axial "tension," the cardinal points cross at the center. Unlike the basic visual design, all of these links are not symmetrical, so the implied sound map enriches the simplicity of the most obvious primary surface. If plotted and graphed the phono-visual web might take on a countenance such as given in example 5.

The combination of various factors makes a thick textual fabric in "tensão," which is a historically apt instance of the application of new poetic concepts. Indeed, one critical reader identified it as a "neuralgic" text that incorporates "all the 'productive operationality' of the movement."[19] This example and "terra" both mark the transition to the "geometric-isomorphic" phase of concrete poetry.

In terms of theory, the shift in perspective was articulated in Haroldo's declaration "Da fenomenologia da composição à matemática da composição" (*Teoria* 93–94, originally 6-23-57). The new compositional process was to replace the "one-word-leads-to-another" approach, in

kõ   kã
sõ   tẽy

kõ   tẽ   tãw
tẽy   sãw   bẽy

      tõ   sẽy
      bẽy   sõ

Example 4

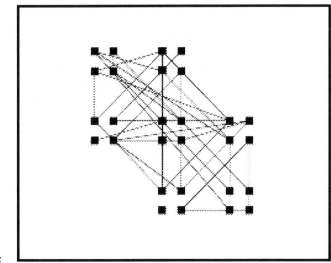

Example 5

which structure results from the interaction of words or fragments produced in a spatial field, where each new word implies a kind of structural option [allowing] a more accentuated intervention on the part of chance and the availability of intuition." Now, the desired yield will be preplanned poems in which creativity is rigorously controlled to make the poem lean toward a "constructive rationality." Emphasis will fall on condensation, directness, and brevity: "Simple words in live circulation — highly economical and reduced." In concert, the aim will be the "elimination of descriptive poems: the content of poems will always be their structure." With this, the progressive radicalization of ideas about synthesis and reduction has come to the point of definition of a model practice. It is here that Gullar, citing over-objectification of language as well as a desire to leave room for expressive subjectivity and temporality within contemporary experiments, breaks with the movement. His neoconcretism, though hardly active, was the first splinter group to emerge from the concrete project.

Reaction-Reception-Response

Before his defection, Gullar had participated in the second staging of the exhibition of concrete art, in Rio de Janeiro in early 1957, when criticism and response began to increase considerably. The curve of reception of concrete poetry rose sharply at this point because in addition to specialized publications, there was mainstream press coverage of events.

Reactions, not unexpectedly, included shock and dismay about the fate of the literary arts. Loud and sarcastic phrases like "nobody understood!" and "the rock 'n' roll of poetry" echoed throughout the artistic community. Journalistic reaction and incomprehension turned hysterical and virulent. While modernist poet Olegário Mariano declared that concrete poetry was "something fit for mental retards," novelist José Lins do Rego called the young poets "heretics" and wrote: "What are the concretists' intentions? Only to undo God's doing! . . . it's a shower of stupidity! The concrete poets are planning things more terrible than the atomic bomb!"[20] Manuel Bandeira did sympathetically receive the concrete poets in the first wave, even composing a few textual experiments himself, but their best ally proved to be Mário Faustino, who backed their notions of poetic invention in the literary supplement he directed for the major Rio daily, *Jornal do Brasil*.[21]

On the side of serious criticism, one of the first analytical and theoretically informed articulations of skepticism about concrete poetry was Antônio Houaiss's response to a lecture by Pignatari. It is worthwhile to consider that essay as a critical signpost, as a fair third-party summary of concrete thought at that time, and, in conjunction, as a set of remarks to respond to in order to comprehend better the new poetic practice.[22] Houaiss set down objections, which continue to this day, to the nonlinear syntax of concrete poetry and to the resultant emotive and expressive constraints. This type of comment gave rise to the frequently employed topical metaphor for concrete poetry as a "dead end" or "blind alley." Houaiss begins with a respectful recapitulation of six main points around which Pignatari's "militant" presentation revolved: that with the general failure to utilize the blank space of the page, the historical cycle of poetry as verse was over; that early concrete poetry had already been "ideogrammatical" and suggested a new kind of syntax; that literature should abandon the lyrical for the direct synthesis of concrete poetry; that it was a self-contained expression of autonomous structure; that there were precursors to concrete poetry but, with its nonlinear approach, it was most apt for the media age; and that concrete poetry could fruitfully exploit typographical resources.

Houaiss explains these areas of concern well but cannot accept any of the lecture's premises or conclusions. From his vantage point, only frustration and limitations are ultimately visible. After an extended discussion of linguistic evolution and literary change, he asserts that "the attempt to create a new syntax — a new, systematic and functional structuring of linguistic signs, deprived of the syntax in which they necessarily fit, and on which they in essence depend — is a *voluntary castration*" (emphasis added). Poetry, he states, can only work within the natural linguistic system, since "linguistic signs when abstracted from their system are no longer signs" (242). The posited concrete variety, as a result, must be a nonlinguistic and nonliterary art. Houaiss does note that concrete poetry is against cliché, the commonplace, and the reproduction of stale language; but since this is no novelty — all new (and good) poetry aspires to that stance — no special credit should be granted. Instead, Houaiss insists that concrete poetry lacks an essential affective experience by depriving words of their necessary insertion into richer environments, and such abandonment of "the contextual concept" is, again, "a voluntary castration" (249). The concrete poets, he believes, ought to follow the "natural" path of expressing and penetrating nature. Their project is "fated to failure" by the elimination of two-thirds of language's humanity. With the replacement of natural syntax and the supposed decimation of semantic charges, Houaiss thinks only isolated articulations of the sound dimension would remain in concrete poetry. These mere "insignifications" (254) do not suffice to achieve the desire for "a beehive of signification" (the phrase is Pignatari's).

These arguments — as the Noigandres poets would be quick to point out — typify a common difficulty: how to judge a new, ideogrammic concept of poetry by traditional parameters. When Houaiss asserts, for instance, that concrete poems as explained would ultimately yield nothing but sound data, he seems to bypass the whole notion of "verbivoco-visual" as dynamic integration. In the critic's terms, this new material cannot aspire to the status of lyric poetry as constituted in romantic, expressionistic forms. Indeed, it was precisely against this concept that the Noigandres group was struggling. As emphasized in a treatment of concrete poetry as a classical (i.e., nonromantic) formalism, "in the concrete poem there is simply no speaker."[23] As a linguist, however, Houaiss grounds his arguments in a sort of speech-act theory of Western languages. His approach proves to be limiting both in a general sense, as there are not appropriate distinctions between pragmatic and creative levels of language, and in a specific sense, as he apparently discounts the possibility of artistic inspiration in Oriental writing (i.e., ideograms). When at one point he affirms that "it is not conceivable that systematic sedimentation, . . . that system which is created in human linguistic syntax, thanks to a long and slow collective task of thousands of years, should be able to be modified all of a sudden . . . by a theory or pseudo-theory" (242), the critic seems to think that the concrete poets are trying to change the actual language rather than to institute a specific artistic application of it. Houaiss's objections would be quite valid if what was at issue were standard oral communication, expository writing, or even discursive verse, rather than an experimental poetry in search of a new mode of aesthetic communication. Houaiss is so concerned with the role of syntax in, to use Jakobsonian terms, the referential function of language — which is indeed essentially altered in concrete poetry — that he underestimates the poetic function, not to mention the self-oriented phatic function. Even with respect to the "signifying" functions of language, Houaiss seems to forget readers' powers of association and imagination when he affirms that the words of concrete poetry would effectively lose their semantic charges in their asyntactical environments.

In another part of his exposition, Houaiss himself notes that the experimental poets' use of bare words is not really objective or concrete but open to individual interpretation and therefore to some symbolic or mythical content and mystery. Here, he rightly states that the concrete poets' goal of nonmystery cannot be fully achieved, but he also weakens his own case against concrete's semantic limitations. Contrary to the implication that concrete poets cannot really express and penetrate nature, and despite their stated ideal of textual self-constitution, there is inevitable "penetration" of nature in some concrete poetry, as will be suggested below. Finally, with respect to the allegations of linguistic impoverishment, Haroldo articulated an extensive response and counterdemonstration in "The Informational Temperature of the Text."[24]

Further to the question of semantics and natural syntax in concrete poetry, it is useful to cite an explanation of German poet Max Bense:

> it is a poetry that does not confer aesthetic or semantic meaning to its elements — words, for example — through the habitual construction of contexts ordered in linear and grammatical ways, but rather that supports itself in visual connections. The basic principle of construction of this poetry is, then, not the sequence of words in the flow of consciousness but their co-existence in the act of perception. Words are not primarily used as intentional supports of signification but, beyond that function, they also have at least that of being a concrete element of composition, in such a way that meaning and graphic composition mutually express and condition each other: simultaneity of the semantic and aesthetic functions of language.[25]

Precisely because concrete poetry was thought to comprise not so much a variation of lyric but a new structure, as much in Germany as in Brazil, it was imperative to underscore not just the nonlinearity of the poetic approach but the intentional relativization of semantic charges as well, especially in relation to the normally ignored, or underplayed, dimension of primary sensorial (visual) apprehension. This said, it will be helpful to keep in mind that simultaneity will not be an absolute function. The creative possibilities of concrete poetry will include some examples of kinetic character and of linear readings within texts.

Set in Concrete: The Classical Repertory

Such explanations of syntax would apply most coherently to the principal production of the high, geometric phase of Brazilian concrete poetry, which was brought together in *Noigandres,* no. 4 (1958), an exhibition-ready portfolio composed of the "pilot plan," twelve poster-poems, and Pignatari's oft-cited six-frame sequence "LIFE." The avant-garde ideal of collective work was sought in the joint presentation of poems by four authors (the original trio plus Ronaldo Azeredo). Ten of these classical examples have appeared in North American reprints and studies, most notably Pignatari's transformational anti-advertisement "beba coca cola."[26]

While adhering to basic principles of construction, each concrete poem should also, ideally, embody a distinctive singularity. Still, the portfolio items and other late-fifties' orthodox poems display certain shared creative tacks and "thematic" qualities. Thus, like "LIFE," Azeredo's "velocidade" is a one-word kinetic poem. Related movement-oriented items include his "ruasol" and "vai-e-vem" by Noigandres's new associate, José Lino Grünewald.[27] Given the interest in paronomasia, several concrete texts are centered around lexical coincidences, such as Pignatari's "love poem" in Spanish, "hombre," and Augusto's unfolding "colocar a máscara."[28] The impulse toward renewal of language is evident in a series of texts that might be regarded as "anti-cliché." These include the above-cited "beba coca cola," as well as Haroldo's "anamorfose" (built around the phrase "sem sombra de dúvida" [without a shadow of a doubt]), "mais menos" (more less), and "ver navios."[29] Such phrase-deconstructing texts are particularly curious from the perspective of Michel Rifaterre's theory of the matrix, whereby poems may be defined as the "unsaying" of literary antecedents or linguistic formulas.[30]

While formalist considerations may seem to dominate the concrete agenda, numerous texts of the period have direct social intentions or significant social overtones. These include Pignatari's "terra" (with the issue of land reform) and Augusto's "sem um número" (numberless), as well as Grünewald's "petróleo" (petroleum, 1957), "fome" (hunger, 1959), and "forma" (form-s, 1959), which carries notions both of change and of linguistic relations (example 6).

```
        f o r m a
      r e f o r m a
    d i s f o r m a
t r a n s f o r m a
  c o n f o r m a
    i n f o r m a
        f o r m a
```

Example 6

This text can also clearly be viewed within a (meta-) paradigm of formal aspect. In this way, it is related to concrete texts of abstraction, with little evident reference to the world outside of the text, such as Augusto's "eixo" and titles by Haroldo closer to the ideal of self-containment, including "mais menos," "fome de forma," "fala prata," and "branco."[31]

One of the most distinguished items in the corpus of "high" concrete is Haroldo's "nascemorre" (birthdeath), which merits reproduction and further explication here.[32] This is at once one of the more "lyrical" concrete poems and an exemplary instance of planned construction (example 7).

Knowing only that *nasce* means "is born" and that *morre* means "dies," one can imagine the subsequent combinatory verb forms and therefore the basic syntagms here: birth, death, rebirth, re-death, dis-birth, dis-death. For a true reading, the polysemantic role of the first-last word is significant: *se* both means "if" and designates the impersonal subject "one" (cf. French *on*, Spanish *se*). This makes for simultaneous doubt/uncertainty and affirmation/declaration. The ambivalence, coupled with the necessity for the auxiliary verb with English "born," precludes good translation in the same verbal mode. As far as other conjugations are concerned, while Portuguese *renasce* is as normal as the English phrase "is reborn," (cf. renascence), *remorre* (re-dies) is equally neologistic. This integrated lexico-conceptual strategy continues with *desnasce* (is un-born) and *desmorre* (un-dies). The strangeness of the verb forms is

```
            se
           nasce
         morre nasce
         morre nasce morre
                    renasce remorre renasce
                            remorre renasce
                                    remorre
             re                           re
           desnasce
        desmorre desnasce
   desmorre desnasce desmorre
                    nascemorrenasce
                    morrenasce
                    morre
                    se
```

Example 7

amplified if one assumes a third function for the word *se,* that of third-person reflexive pronoun. The verbs *nascer* and *morrer* do not take reflexive pronouns in standard speech (as the second may in Spanish, for instance). If a reflexive *se* is understood to govern all the verb forms here, what results are strange phrases something like "one borns oneself," or, with the articulation of an implied subject, "he/she dies him/herself," "you re-birth yourself," or "you dis-die yourself." Such less obvious undertones work with the neologisms, repetitions, and combinations in a process of radical defamiliarization and create an atmosphere, "mood" if you will, of disquiet. Through these verbal unfoldings, the birth-death cycle is constituted, not as a progression with starting and ending points, but rather as a process of continuity and circularity with occurrences, emphases (re-), and reversals (des-). The binomial semantic (life/death), then, does not comprise a simple split, dichotomy, or opposition.

These relationships are reinforced in visual structures and phono-orthographic patterns. The first thing that strikes the reader-viewer of "nascemorre" is the text's shape: the four parts are mirrored pairs of triangles. Yet some of the symmetries in this picture are exact, while others are near-exact or equivalents. The pivotal points are identical in their graphic representation (*se, re*), as are the syllabic counts of counter-poised horizontal lines (1-2-4-6 / 9-6-3-1 above and vice versa below). Actual physical space is one degree greater in the third triangle, since the prefix *des-* has three letters instead of the two of *re-,* and lesser in the last triangle, since the verbal components are run together, consistent with the conjunctive spirit of the poem. The textual idea is derived from two axial syllables, *re-* and *se-*, in which spelling and normal pronunciation are at variance.[33] The full phonetic grid has only six syllables: /si/, /na/, /mó/, /Ri/, /Re/, /des/. The initial *se* (/si/) reverberates incessantly in the perfect rhyme of the second syllable of *nasce* (/nasi/) and so on and in the vocalic rhyme of *morre* (/móRi/) and so on. While phonetically *se* is derived from the second syllable of *nasce*, the particle *re* appears to be detached from *morre*. The word *morre*, connected to the counterpart *nasce* via the vowel /i/, links with the prefix *re-* via the consonant /R/. The last two letters of the other element *des-*, finally, are like a flipflop of *se*. Through these sets of interrelations, the poem's objectified linguistic material opens up the "subjective," existential dimension. The internal dialectic of sounding, spelling, doing, re-doing, and undoing makes strange the real-life progression toward death, and will not allow such linearity to penetrate the poem.

Deals, Ideals, and Concretizations

Such poems as "nascemorre," with its wide resonances, invite contemplation of certain aims of the Noigandres agenda. A central ideal to which concrete poetry aspired is encapsulated in the formula "form = content / content = form" (Solt 13). The first level of projection of a poem—like concrete sculpture or painting—should be its own structure; a poem should communicate, in theory, its own idiosyncratic formal self, not interpret extratextual reality. Consistent with such principles, the concrete poets in Brazil declared themselves to be against the traditional mythical, symbolic, and mysterious elements of lyric and for superseding them with the fabrication of self-contained objects. Clearly, such ideals are met to varying degrees. There is, in general, a gap between programmatic ideas and practical results. In terms of self-containment, one might posit a variant, if you will, of the intentional fallacy. Just as structures of the concrete poem can eclipse assumed bounds, lexical components can "unexpectedly" fortify texts. What sets the poetry apart from the plastic arts, of course, are the inescapable "contents" of language. The nonreferentiality that might have been imagined for independent concrete poems was simply not fully achievable. Even outside normal syntactical contexts, words carry a deeply entrenched semantic substance. As suggested in the commentary on the Houaiss essay above, readers are prone to associations when presented with actual words-in-situation, even if these are extremely vague or organized in highly unconventional modes. Most observers of concrete poetry have noted, in one way or another, how the referential or communicative functions of language can be recognized in concrete poems, and to some extent be functional, yet still be consistent with the concern for structural innovation. In a historical account of change in Brazilian literary language, for example, it is affirmed that concrete poems "continue to be communication on the social level, without losing their self-representational character." While an absolute theoretical value may be given to words as signs (rather than as signifiers), such radical positions do not stand up in creative applications, "because language with nothing but the presence of isolated signs does not exist. The simple fact of putting word-signs in space projects a word-space relationship."[34]

The achievement of concrete poetry — somewhat like that of any good poetry — can be thought to be best when there is a productive level of interplay between self-sustainment and invocations, however obtuse these may be, of extratextual realms. Creative tension results when what might be termed "discursive residues" interact with objectified language. The interrelations of quasi-nonreferential words may be the primary stuff of a given poem, and that in itself may create an enigmatic quality. There is a particular kind of success when the conventional sense of lyric is stripped bare and exposed in its parts, but not reduced to zero. Rather than undermining the prioritizing of self-manifestation, overtones of words enrich texts, making them more accessible to "transitional" readers. While critics in Brazil attacked the lack of content in concrete poetry, the poets themselves regarded their nonrepresentational efforts as modern and cosmopolitan. But in practice, again, they either stopped short of total isolation or were limited by the natural echoes of language-in-situation. What emerges from such a confrontation of ideal and practice is a need to recognize different levels of abstraction and semantic range in concrete poetry and to affirm the *relative* favoring of autonomous structuring over nonstructural content.

Theory, Plans, and Such

The position on self-sufficiency and other main points of the theory of concrete poetry had already been articulated when the two-page "pilot plan for concrete poetry" appeared. It was issued in both Portuguese and English with the international movement in mind.[35] The manifesto presented no real new ideas; it was, rather, a compilation, a careful synthesis of particularized literary and interdisciplinary frames of reference, key phrases, and theoretical statements from previously published critical articles and manifestos by Pignatari, Augusto, and Haroldo. Having drawn from varied sources, the concrete poets clearly wanted, somewhat optimistically, to be many things at the same time. By 1958, the spectrum of interests spanned the original literary beacons (Pound, Mallarmé, et al.) and several other areas. Universal and national currents flowed together in the plan. The prime inspirations from Brazilian literature were Oswald de Andrade — with his cubist *poesia-minuto* and "Cannibalist Manifesto" (which contains the phrase "we are concretists") — and the exemplary verse of the contemporary João Cabral de Melo Neto. Musical sources, so essential to Augusto's early work, had expanded, as had references in the plastic arts, including both noted individuals and concrete art in general. Film pioneer Sergei Eisenstein's approach to visual composition — ideogram and montage — was also cited. Advances in information theory (cybernetics) and linguistic science (e.g., Sapir), as well as Gestalt, were incorporated into a broad concept of perception. With these and other diverse components, it is difficult to establish an authoritative hierarchy of values in the pilot plan. One can, of course, infer something about the relative importance of elements from their order of presentation. The initial two points were certainly audacious, as they presented concrete poetry in a historical dimension as a "product of a critical evolution of forms," taking for granted the "end of the historical cycle of verse." In terms of textual construction, the authors of the manifesto foregrounded the supraverbality of graphic space and analogical spatiotemporal structuring. The idea that agglutinated terms of text-making was that of isomorphism, conceived as "form-and-content in search of identification."

In addition to the spheres of "high art," there was an important addition to the theoretical mechanism by 1957: links with communication technology and mass media. Concrete poetry was held by its creators to be consistent with "a kind of contemporary 'forma mentis' imposed by posters, slogans, headlines . . . [that] makes urgent the rapid communication of cultural objects."[36] The isomorphic optical fields of concrete texts would, in theory, allow for a reception in keeping with the mindset of the age of billboards, more sophisticated visual programming, and electronic media. Concrete was presented as a poetic solution in the era of mass communication, from newspapers to radio and television, as an artistic language adapted to the technologically modern present. The makers desired that their poetry be regarded as a configuration of forms designed, again, not to provide an outlet for subjective expression but to set in motion readers' internal dynamics, which were determined both by reading and environment. Beyond the relatively small readership with a literary education, the concrete poets could also imagine approaching a mass audience of workers by incorporating elements from the sign fields of everyday industrial life. The poetic vanguard could thus envision a shrinking of the barriers between "high" and "low" spheres as well as closer relations between the utilitarian, the artistic, and the political.

The effort to incorporate the implications of print and electronic media for lyric into the overall framework that justified and explained concrete poetry comprised a pivotal moment in the development of its theory and posed one of the toughest questions the Noigandres poets had to face: how to reconcile and, as an attentive student put it, "to present the new poetry as a synthesis of two basically distinct forms of symbolic production: cultural industry, or mass media, and erudite culture, to which the authors of the concretist paideuma belong."[37] In the pilot plan, nonliterary inputs and factors—page design, advertising technique, radio, cinema, television, the general rapidity of modern information exchange—were implicit in the appeal to "nonverbal communication" and in the concluding assertion of a "general art of the word" and of a "poem-product, useful object." Such aspects—ever to be more provocative than conducive to solutions of cultural dilemmas—resurface in discussions of the ideological reverberations of concrete poetry and in its semiotic manifestations of the 1960s.

"By putting emphasis on the materiality of language in its visual and sonorous dimension," Augusto later said, "concrete poetry responded to the provocation of the new communication media."[38] In this declaration, one may wonder: what provocation and what new media? Specific reference is made to newspapers, film, and billboards. Assuming an additional implication of concrete as the poetry of the television age, the frame of reference would have to be international. Brazilian television was hardly off the ground when the pilot plan was issued and did not become a major factor in the shaping of national consciousness until the 1970s. In this sense, concrete poetry was well ahead of its time in Brazil; it was an anticipation of, rather than a response to, the power of new communication media. The fact that concrete poetry was ahead of its time may partially explain the outcry against its program, for literary circles were not necessarily attuned to the progressive mind set of the late fifties, as presented below.

With the issuance of the pilot plan, the major corpus of writings that would make up *Teoria da poesia concreta* is in place, and one has access to sufficient material to justify discussion of the theoretical side as a whole.[39] If the collected essays are considered as an overall argument with supporting parts, there is ample ammunition for anyone in search of changes in position, imperfections, and incongruencies. This should come as no surprise, since the ideas of the Noigandres group naturally matured in the course of the decade, and each had individual preferences and emphases (Augusto on intermedia, Pignatari on information theory and industrial design, Haroldo on world literature). Specific titles and the collected essays become balancing acts that, Augusto himself admits, "even feed on divergence."[40] One could follow up on any given line in the pilot plan—the poem as "useful object," for instance—trace it through the creative repertory and find numerous confirmations or non-compliances. Indeed, as suggested in the discussion of the ideal of self-projection above, the poems may often simply not match up to the theory—which may be greater or lesser than creative results. "Not that this invalidates concrete poetry," Rosemarie Waldrop calmly observes. "All it does is show that the manifestos are overstated (which is hardly surprising)" (148). In the long run, it is generally not profitable to hold concrete poems—or any programmatic art form—to strict application of specific manifesto points. These are best considered not as inflexible measures for the poems but as purposefully polemical statements, elements in an overall attack on poetic convention and in an aggressive proposal of a new way of text-making.

Even granting that the pilot plan, like all manifestos, has statements overblown for rhetorical effect, a few of these call for considered response. The plan's opening salvos are probably the two sorest points, since they do not regard the poetry per se but are put in larger historical terms. These points are the assertion of concrete poetry as the "product of an organic evolution of literary forms" and the assumption of the death of verse. The first point implies a questionable sort of literary Darwinism that even friends of concretism view as a historical illusion.[41] Concrete poetry was not the product of natural evolution but rather a *planned adventure* of contrived invention. The conscious elaborations of the Noigandres poets were a synchronic intervention that does not, in and of itself, justify their diachronic claims. In the declaration about the end of the historical cycle of verse, in turn, the use of "we" is nodal in strategic and pragmatic evaluations. Iumna Maria Simon observes that the Noigandres poets, as a group in a specific cultural conjuncture, had first taken on the Generation of '45 as a natural adversary. The narrow literary specialization of '45, however, offered insufficient opposition to the technomodernization and social broadening of scope that concrete poetry envisioned. Thus verse itself came to be viewed as an anachronism to target ("Esteticismo," 125–126). Now, verse might have lost its usefulness for the makers of the statement about its end themselves and for their followers who were set irrevocably against convention, but even at the height of its influence, concrete poetry totally stood out in the mainstream continuation of verse-making as the standard for poetry in Brazil. The many and undeniable effects of concretism on poetry in general are wholly another question.

Concrete Poetry and Sociohistorical Context

The Noigandres group, operating in times of democratic growth and cultural assertion, sought to reconcile formalism, technology, and social relevance. In the mid-1950s, much Brazilian cultural discourse was tinged by historical awareness, notably of the hegemonic relationship of industrialized and Third World nations. Intellectuals were particularly sensitive to the implications of underdevelopment. During the presidency of Juscelino Kubitschek (1956–1960), master plans for industrialization and economic advancement—with the slogan "fifty years in five"—fostered a climate of optimism. *Poesia concreta* was conceived, drawing on diverse artistic and other sources, in the years immediately preceding the Kubitschek administration. The actual movement unfolded in, and somehow reflected, the characteristic forward-looking euphoria of what was called "developmentalism." In this conjuncture, it was in the interest of concretism as a declared vanguard to make "a poetry on the level of a modern society." Within and beyond the literary sphere, "the signs of modernity and technique . . . were appraised as the bearers of a transforming consciousness, able to overcome archaic structures." The wish for modernity could lead to "abstract affirmations of a vocation for the future, as if the perspective of overcoming underdevelopment were imminent," and the concrete poets "celebrated the signs of modern times."[42] The most vivid enactment of the growth of the new Brazil was the "pilot plan" for the construction of the new capital, Brasília, which Haroldo retrospectively called "an epistemological metaphor for the capacity for innovation of the Brazilian artist."[43] The concrete poets echoed the innovative capital-city project by calling their manifesto a "pilot plan" and would recognize architecture as the representative art of the period. However, this identification was general and spiritual, not specific, political, or partisan, as concrete poetry was not actually linked to any government agency or cultural plan. In retrospect, different responses have been given to the question of what role developmentalism might have in the picture of concrete poetry. Asked if Pignatari's aim of "making poems on the level of industrial objects rationally planned and produced" coupled the concrete endeavor to the institutional thought of the late 1950s, Haroldo elected to emphasize epochal ambience and disavowed links with official "developmentalist ideology." This position came in response to latter-day critiques of the Kubitschek regime and its failures, and, by association, of concrete poetry. Augusto has confirmed the points of contention:

> The connection with developmentalism that characterized his [Kubitschek's] administration were used by criticism of a sociological orientation as an allegory, in an attempt to identify artificially the cosmopolitanism of CP [concrete poetry] with such facts as the implantation of an automotive industry in Brazil by multinational companies: it was a demagogic comparison that aimed at representing the protagonists of CP antipathetically, as reactionaries or *entreguistas* (in the sense that development is the delivery [*entrega*] of the wealth of the nation for the exploration of foreign capital), at a moment in which the demands of the nationalists were in ascendence again. The military dictatorship that was installed in Brazil for twenty years from 1964, creating a cultural stew that exacerbated the so-called "ideological patrols" carried out by the left, sanctioned this negative vision of Kubitschek, in spite of his having been exiled, and in connection with this view maintained a preconception against the poetry of his era. Today, after the collapse of the Marxist utopia, the same Kubitschek administration is viewed with other, more positive eyes.[44]

Reservations about the identification of concrete poetry with developmentalism do not preclude, logically, the recognition of "interesting coincidences." Rather than any conscious attachment to any program of (extra-artistic) action, what proves to provide best perspective here is the intellectual mood of the fifties. Utopian designs did provide a "contextual backing" for concrete poetry, Haroldo also affirmed, but it was always essentially a "literary rupture against discursive poetry" in an "excentric" country where such thinking was possible.[45] It was the *Zeitgeist* of the period that favored the concrete vanguard as a collective which, with the possibility of imagining a more just society on the horizon, could produce new poetic forms. The utopian element of the period and that inherent in its poetic vanguard carry over and evolve in the next phase of national life, and, as the reactions of the Noigandres poets to the issue of developmentalism suggest, will resurface as an aspect of evaluation three decades later.

Invenção: The Phase of Semiotics and Politics

The political and cultural climate of the early 1960s was increasingly radical, as detailed in chapter 3, and the concrete poets reacted to changes in environment. A brief postscriptum was added to the pilot plan in 1961: "without revolutionary form there is no revolutionary art." This phrase of the celebrated poet of the Russian Revolution, Vladimir Mayakovsky (1893–1930), was adopted to express the Noigandres group's insistence on aesthetic innovation in socially aware art. These outward-looking notes are an important aspect of the loosening of the "orthodox" concepts of concrete poetry that marked the third phase of the movement. The common threads here are the attack on convention and the challenging of facile stances, whether political or artistic. At the turn of the decade, the Noigandres poets formed a new collective that they dubbed *Invenção,* the rubric for a creative section in a São Paulo newspaper as well as the title of an interdisciplinary journal (1962–1967). New associates included former symbolist poet Edgard Braga (1898–1985), haikai specialist Pedro Xisto (1901–1989), as well as the enduring modernist poet Cassiano Ricardo, and poet-essayist Mário Chamie (b. 1938), who would defect to form, as seen below, an alternative vanguard with idiosyncratic social pretensions.

In the early 1960s, objections to concrete poetry's assaults on natural syntax and conventional lyricism gave way, in keeping with the times, to critiques based on sociopolitical attitude and relevance. In a public address about contemporary poetry, Pignatari announced an imminent shift toward more evident social responsibility with the words "concrete poetry is going to make the participatory-semantic-content leap."[46] Left without much elaboration, the key phrase was open to interpretation and sparked numerous responses. One symptomatic statement manifested the persistence of values by which concretism had been judged: "We feared their becoming bourgeois and we condemned their isolationism, self-sufficiency, and the alienation of their artistic process . . . They failed to conceive poetry as a universe of ideologically organized units."[47] Representative comments also came from the established critic Adolfo Casais Monteiro, who reiterated a characterization of concrete poetry as overly technical and nonmusical, and wondered whether the announced "leap" would not signify internal contradictions.[48] On this score, it is worthwhile to recall, even granting the Noigandres group's general preference for formal exploration, that such early poems as "terra" and "beba coca cola" had demonstrated that there was no *inherent* contradiction between orthodox concrete poetry and potential social roles. The vocation of the concrete poets was always more poetic than ideological, but formal emphases invalidate neither what social content did exist nor pertinent overtones of seemingly removed poems. As the distinguished historian of Brazilian literature Alfredo Bosi writes: "The fact of denying *theme* does not signify in any way that [the poetry] is lacking in psychological or ideological content, as its detractors, gratuitously, sometimes suggest. . . . And, truthfully, it is not difficult to recognize in concrete poems the referential universe that their structure proposes to communicate: aspects of contemporary society, based on the capitalist regime and bureaucracy, and saturated with marketable objects, advertising images, commercial eroticism and sentimentalism, odd commonplaces that hinder language and weaken its critical and creative tonicity."[49] These comments are applicable both to fifties material and inventions of the early sixties. Yet there were indeed modifications in textual strategies when more consciously social material was produced in the third phase.

The opening up of the concretist approach did lead to fruitful dialogue with another active literary collective, the Tendência group of Minas Gerais, which, since 1957, had proposed a "critical nationalism." While the poets of this group — Affonso Ávila (b. 1928), Affonso Romano de Sant'Anna (b. 1937), and others — also vigorously rejected the regressive lyricism of the Generation of '45, they maintained faith in (some form of) verse and focused attention on historical themes and current social conditions. Discussions between the two groups were mutually beneficial: Tendência reconsidered recalcitrant positions on formal research, and the Noigandres group was encouraged in their turn toward social themes. The search for common ground further led to exchanges of creative and critical material for their respective journals. The key poetic voice of Tendência, the ever-inventive Ávila, contributed to *Invenção* (nos. 2, 4, 5). In 1963, the two groups participated, together with independent poets and critics, in a week-long national seminar on avant-garde poetry (Semana Nacional de Poesia de Vanguarda, University of Minas Gerais). The collective post-conference communiqué asserted the viability of a participatory vanguard and stressed a dual responsibility toward language and society.[50]

Many were still challenging the appropriateness and the very notion of concrete poetry as an experimental avant-garde in a severely imbalanced, underdeveloped country. It was precisely in *Tendência* that Haroldo addressed the central question of whether a "literature for export" can be produced in peripheral conditions such as those in which Brazilian literature operated. The primal attempt to de-alienate Brazilian literature had

been Oswald de Andrade's cannibalistic "deglutition," critical assimila-
tion of foreign information and reelaboration in national terms. Con-
temporary support for the concrete project was found in the concept of
"sociological reduction": in given circumstances, a people can develop a
"critical consciousness" and, no longer satisfied to import finished prod-
ucts, endeavor to "produce other objects in the forms of, and with their
functions adjusted to, new historical demands."[51] This "reduction" can
apply not just to things but, Haroldo argued, to ideas as well. Passage is
made from importation to production of new things/ideas, and then to
export. The literary parallel, of course, is concrete poetry, which ema-
nated from São Paulo, the industrial and technological center of the
nation. The new art form arose "in Brazilian conditions, living in an
urban reality (as national as the rural), where one could ponder the
machine, technical civilization, the relationship of men (workers) and
machines, the relationship of men (workers) and new architecture, and
respective contradictions, in conditions that could never occur, for ex-
ample, to a bearded artiste of the 'Left Bank' . . ." The linchpin in the
argument is that concrete poetry, "the most radical totalization of a
master line of poetics of our time, truly critical and committed to the
physiognomy of its time, was exported." The palpable pride here is paral-
lel to Mayakovsky's having exclaimed in 1922 that the Russian Con-
structivists for the first time had the latest word in art instead of the
French.[52] In the 1960s, with increasing international interest in Brazilian
concrete poetry, an innovative art was indeed exported, as Oswald had
theorized. Thus, the process of importation—the conventional flow of
information from metropolis to colony—was turned around. Whereas
in the industrial strategy for import substitution Brazil gained new
assembly-line production capabilities while the actual technological
knowledge remained in its countries of origin, in the case of concrete po-
etry, to take the comparison a step further, "we exported know-how."[53]

The aggressive argument put forward in the early sixties *Tendência*
paper was rearticulated in an oft-cited essay of the 1980s, in which
Haroldo adopts Bahktinian and poststructuralist critical language to
present Oswald's anthropophagy as a "solution" of sorts: the cannibal
devours the colonizer selectively and critically, producing a *dialogical*
upsetting, a *carnivalized* movement of native and foreign cast. Brazil's
distinctive traits—and this is certainly in the self-promoting spirit of
modernismo—are assigned positive values. Concretism, in turn, is por-
trayed as wanting to rethink Brazil as difference, as "an operative place of
a new synthesis of universal codes . . . authors of a supposedly peri-
pheric literature suddenly appropriated the whole code, reclaimed it as

their patrimony . . . to rethink its function in terms of a generalized, radical poetics of which the Brazilian case comes to be the differentiating optics and the condition of possibility."[54] Concrete poetry, in sum, effected a re-cannibalization of poetics, national and international, and projected, with profit, onto a universal plane.

The Phase of Invention: The Products

The diversified production of the phase of invention does not present a unified front comparable to the original collective with its utopian ideals. There is a mixture of continuations of late fifties concrete poetry, purposefully sociopolitical compositions, and pieces that moved away from verbality toward visuality. This sixties output anticipates stylistic aspects of the subsequent individual paths of Haroldo, Augusto, and Pignatari. Haroldo directly confronts *poesia pura* (pure poetry) and *poesia para* (poetry for [i.e., with a purpose]) in the spare verbal columns of "Servidão de passagem" ("Transient Servitude") and the permutational "Alea I- Semantic Variations." His vast experimental prose-poetry project — the densely alliterative, associative, and paronomastic blocks of text of the unique *Galáxias* — began in 1963.[55] For his part, Augusto elaborated on material and materialist elements in texts such as "greve" (strike) — a wax paper over backing-page text of solidarity with workers — and "cubagrama" — a multichromatic anti-imperialist graph incorporating the slogan "Cuba sí, Yankee no!" Urban awareness is an essential component of texts based on lexical coincidences: the wholly horizontal "cidade-cité-city," an alphabetic cityscape made of thirty word-roots and the trilingual suffix, and "LUXO-LIXO" (luxury-trash), an emphatic pseudo-elegant iteration of the first word made up of multiple reiterations of the second.[56] Augusto's series of *popcretos* (pop + concrete) are poeticized collages of newspaper clippings targeting modes of perception, multinational consumer society, and current affairs in postcoup Brazil (e.g., "SS" and "psiu!" [hush]). The most familiar piece is "olho por olho" (eye for eye), a pyramid-tower composed of semanticized photographic fragments displaying eyes (and one intrusive mouth) topped by "authoritarian" traffic semaphors.[57] This *popcreto* also falls, via the title phrase of biblical retribution (eye for an eye, tooth for a tooth . . .), into the anticliché paradigm posited above with respect to classical concrete poetry. Interplay of social factors and extraverbal artistry is also characteristic of Pignatari's early sixties pieces. Claims on the technocultural relevance of advertising, initiated with the satirical "beba coca cola," continued in "stèle pour vivre III- estela cubana," a verbal montage implementing commercial layout, and "disenfórmio," an actual ad for a pharmaceutical product whose textual effect of collapsing letters merited publication of the piece as creative writing. Another notable example of satire via a word-image mesh is a dollar bill with the inscription "Chri$t is the $olution" and the countenance of Jesus wearing the crown of thorns.[58]

Pignatari also teamed with Luiz Angelo Pinto to mold a variation called *poemas códigos* (code poems) or *poemas semióticos*. In these verbographic compositions, lexical keys connected simple words and/or categories (e.g., yes/no; male/female) to semaphoric designs (arrows, boxes, circles, diamonds, etc.) in series of different combinations.[59] After this brief experiment (only half a dozen pieces were produced), which, despite the lexical keys, Pignatari called "concrete without words," the ontology of the poem would have to be questioned in absolute terms. Standard concrete poetry was difficult enough for conventional readers to accept as a poetic endeavor. With the examples of "semiotic" poems (parodied in a "semi-idiotic" poem by Scottish poet Ian Hamilton Finley), there were further motivations to object to concrete based on the treatment of language. Other contributions to *Invenção* — such as Braga's *tatuagens* (tattoo poems) and some of Xisto's "logograms" — often embodied a literal, or nearly literal, visual materiality (drawings with words, graphic designs based on letters, etc.).[60] In these cases, the bounds of poetry conceived as verbal art may dissolve into the realm of graphic arts without explicit linguistic content or exemplify the significant contrast of "dirty" and "clean" concrete (i.e., organized words).[61] It is here that need arises for such further terms as "visual poems," with stress on the adjective and a "figurative" use of the noun. In historical terms, the experience of "semiotic poems" is the immediate and acknowledged forerunner of the *poema processo*, a vanguard proposal couched in communication theory, which is taken up at the end of this chapter.

Impact, Legacies, and Reception

If increasingly graphic realization of text raised serious questions about the status of such inventions as "poetry," the very exceeding of literary bounds in concretism led to a more appreciable contribution to contemporary Brazilian culture. Among the effects of the movement, especially in the "semiotic phase," was a general influence on visual programming in Brazil. Perhaps the greatest impact, a literary historian writes, was the exercise of an "influential force on any and all graphic and visual

schemes" (newspaper and magazine layout, advertisements, public sym-
bols, logotypes, etc.).[62] In a special issue of a leading North American
design publication, a cosmopolitan Brazilian stage director asserts an
even wider impact on the part of concrete poetry with the affirmation of
a liberating New World modernist function:

> it was through poets like Haroldo and Augusto de Campos and
> Décio Pignatari that an advertising language, as well as a graphic
> language, was found. The concrete poets were as important to the
> esthetics of Brazil as the Bauhaus was to Europe and Rodchenko to
> Russia. From that movement onwards, producing art in Brazil that
> was conspicuously Brazilian was almost on an equal footing with
> simply "responding" to the art of Europe and America. For the first
> time, film, poetry, and the visual arts had acquired an identity. . . .
> the concrete poets allowed Brazilians to play freely with their lan-
> guage for the first time and even dissect it when necessary. After
> centuries of colonization, this was the first indication of a cultural
> unblocking affecting all the arts.[63]

The presence of concrete poetry in artistic spheres and the urban
environment may be further tied to the poets' social consciousness. As
Rudolf Arnheim declared: "The maker of concrete poetry joins his fel-
low artists in their desire to escape from the social isolation that has
haunted the arts since they tore loose from their moorings during the
Renaissance. . . . the poet is disenchanted by the neutrality of the blank
paper and dreams of seeing his work as a sign or placard or icon in
the daily traffic of market, pilgrimage, and recreation."[64] Several such
"dreams" were realized in Brazil. Following intimations in the "pilot
plan" and other writings, Pignatari's poem-ads can be seen as manifesta-
tions of the desire Arnheim attributes to contemporary poet-artists.
Other instances of urban "feedback" of poetic information in São Paulo
include a display of "cidade-cité-city" on a huge electronic signboard
overlooking the central Paulista Avenue in São Paulo, a storefront sign
utilizing the designs of "LUXO-LIXO" (which was itself inspired by an ad
for high-end apartments), and a commercial borrowing (ad logo for
ready-to-wear stores) of the red and white "VIVA VAIA" (1972) (see
example 8), an inspirational "distich" that became the title of Augusto's
collected poems, as an embodiment of anagrammatic visual paronoma-
sia and as an "emblem of the confrontation between the artist and the
public."[65]

These last examples of specific visual impact actually occur years after
the main activities of the 1960s. In terms of concretism's development, it

Example 8

is instructive to see what legacy had been established by the time the final number of *Invenção* was published (1967) and the diversified movement had ceased militant action at home. One point to underscore in terms of public or audience is that concretism, with its different tacks and attacks, brought new sets of consumers to poetry from art, music, architecture, and graphic design, as suggested above in the appraisals of the movement's extraliterary impact. In creative terms, the Noigandres poets' pursuit of uniqueness and rigor led to alternative models with new expressive potential, especially the ability to affect verbal content via visual construct. Most notable on the side of lyric and imagination, of course, was the affirmation of a whole new take on making poetry, in effect the invention of a new poetic genre, variety, or modality. While lyric poetry continued on its established course, poets of various persuasions had shown interest in concrete poetry, and specifically focused concrete movements had sprung up in other states, most energetically in Ceará and Minas Gerais. Concretism's acknowledged advances in theory concern the study of literature in general. Brazil had been dominated by impressionistic criticism until Afrânio Coutinho introduced Anglo-American New Criticism in the 1950s. The Noigandres group brought a variety of additional perspectives and an unprecedented reliance on theoretical models. While many welcomed the serious proposals and challenges, others regarded the stress on theory as a negative, even intimidating, aspect. In any case, there can be little doubt that the maturing of Brazilian critical discourse at the conceptual level from the mid-fifties to the late sixties, and into the seventies, owes a considerable debt to the explorations and provocations undertaken to account for concrete poetry and to discuss related phenomena.[66]

Theory naturally figures prominently in a broad assessment by an active young poet of the late sixties significance of concretism: "[It] was a true schism in Brazilian aesthetic thought, especially in poetry. . . . Any analysis of today's best poetry is impossible without a broad consideration of concretism. . . . Only two historical moments of aesthetic renovation exist in twentieth-century Brazilian poetry: The Modern Art Week and concretism."[67] The basic contrast in the movement, from its inception, involves "an extremely well articulated virtuoso theoretical formulation with a precarious and deficient poetic production." Sparse creativity aside, there was a series of notable "immediate results": (1) the suspension of the influence of the Generation of '45 on the youngest poets and the assumption of national leadership; (2) a marked influence on well established poets (e.g., Drummond, Cassiano); (3) the general utilization of their supporting bibliography (i.e., those cited in the "pilot plan" plus such others as William Carlos Williams); (4) critical rereadings of neglected national authors; and (5) an internationalizing character. "The greatest virtue," the observer justifiably asserts, "was having put the poetic text in check, having amplified the conceptualization of what is poetic." He further affirms that there is no longer any discussion of whether "concretism is right, an exaggeration or alienated," but rather of how individuals can "use to their best advantage" the contributions and renovations of the movement. Given the continued resistance to concrete poetry, the point of leadership at that juncture (number 1 above) may be relative. But precisely because of such challenges, it would be hard to deny the conclusion that "Brazilian poetry today revolves referentially around the concretist movement." If one considers how other vanguard groups emerged from concrete poetry, how some proponents of sixties social verse defined themselves in opposition to concretism, and how responsible critical discourse had to address issues raised by the Noigandres group and absorb concepts they put into circulation, the assertion of concretism's central role is more than reasonable. To gauge concretism's influence beyond the sixties splinter groups, one must also take into account its part in the poetry of song and the postconcrete constructivist poetry of the 1960s–1990s.

It was already common, in the late sixties, for Brazilian critics of concrete poetry to note the preponderance of theory over actual poems. On this point, Augusto had already made the following Francophilic counterpoint: "Poetry has never been measured by the quantity of printed paper. The poetic work of Mallarmé fits in a small volume. Only eighteen poems of Arnaut Daniel remain. A few sonnets constitute the glory of Gérard de Nerval. Rimbaud fits in one pocketbook" ("Sem palavras," 88–89). In addition, one should bear in mind the level and density of original information in the concrete repertoire. On another count, even those with fundamentally hostile attitudes toward formalism and experimentalism in poetry grant the unsurpassed quality of the translations of the Noigandres group. Yet their poetic output has also been measured against the more impressive roles of their theoretical writings and translations, in effect to minimize their significance for lyric. Here it is worthwhile to recall that criticism and translations went hand in hand, and that the local critical editions of Pound and others weighed on poetry in general. Lyrical practice was indeed affected by concrete experimentalism, but, in the dialectic of artistic production, the provocations of such writing may have also encouraged and fostered discursivity by way of opposition and reaction.

All of the issues surrounding concrete poetry in the late sixties resurfaced forcefully during celebrations of the movement's thirtieth anniversary (1986), which occasioned numerous observances and much related commentary about *poesia concreta* per se, about the trajectory of concretism, and about the relevance of postmodernism, aspects of which will be confronted in chapter 6. A major difference in the evaluation of the poetry in the eighties was the level of exposure that had been achieved. By 1980, the collected poems of the Noigandres poets were available in commercial editions, and a popular-press pedagogical edition was a bestseller.[68] The previous charge that the theory was more widely available than the poetry no longer had any foundation. Among the aspects of the formulation and defense of concrete poetry that were (re-) discussed in the mid-1980s, some may have proved to be problematic — the virtual sanctification of certain critical references, e.g., Pound, or the elevation of rupture and textual radicalization to self-justified values — but the very fact that concretism was the object of such wide coverage and intense debate in the 1980s illustrates a vitality and a staying power unequaled by any other current of the foregoing thirty years.

The Noigandres group can fairly claim, as suggested above, the initiation of a major rethinking of structure, diction, and presentation in poetry. If in the late sixties the historic import of concretism was already evident, two decades later perspectives should naturally be clearer. Bypassing a construct so solidly in place as concrete poetry, one would imagine, should be rather questionable. Yet this is precisely what was done in some illustrative cases. In a Portuguese anthology of contemporary Brazilian poetry, the well-known Brazilian editors openly declare: "this collection deliberately stays away from the emptiness of experimental formalism and from all the -isms. . . . Thus the absence of so many avant-gardish experimentalisms today abandoned to every type of futuristic hallucination."[69] It is worth noting that Gullar and Chamie, both participants in the vanguard, do appear in the anthology cited. They figure in another national anthology that omits the Noigandres poets, without any disclaimer, despite their many more easily reproduceable poems. In this kind of presentation, contrariness simply interferes with balanced appreciation of contemporary poetry. The challenge to the fundamental lyrical impulses of Luso-Brazilian literature posed by concrete poetry, and its successes, may have occasioned a sort of national trauma, but the movement cannot in good conscience simply be dismissed. Explicit or implicit denial of the poetic feasibility of nonlinear approaches is founded in a concept of lyric that cannot accept anything but versemaking, the tradition of the image, or the pursuit of meaning. Exclusion of all concrete or concretelike poetry suggests inability to accept additions to the repertory of forms and is literarily reactionary. If that was more understandable in 1956, it was much less so in 1986.

The role of concretism has been continually fortified and modified by an often prominent international presence in exhibitions, related literature, and subsequent theoretical commentaries. The continued critical debate in Brazil parallels another sort of ambivalence toward concrete poetry in international responses involving Brazilian material.

Brazilian Concrete Poetry in International Context

Concrete poetry was more important in the reshaping of Brazilian lyric than it was in that of any other nation, and the central role of concretism in Brazilian literature — notwithstanding cited resistance and unresolved controversies — has no real parallel in other countries. These facts of local impact have naturally been of lesser concern to English-language students of concrete poetry, whose transnational motivations and interests are almost exclusively directed at theory, experimental qualities, and avant-garde action. While the original Noigandres contribution to the international movement of concrete poetry is for the most part acknowledged, one must also concede that where Brazilian participation is concerned, there is a dialectic of recognition and limitation (sometimes neglect) in the pertinent international bibliography. This has been especially so with the progressive growth of nonliterary traits in (what continued to use the name) concrete poetry worldwide. It would be useful from, if you will, a Lusocentric point of view, to pose questions about the breadth and understanding of Brazil-specific coverage in non-Brazilian literature regarding concrete poetry. Given the diversification of what was termed "concrete" in the 1960s, it would also be instructive to inquire how much the notion of "concrete" might have been affected (or even rejected) due to other factors overshadowing the late fifties verbivocovisual ideogram, which can be considered as the high point of concrete poetry as a poetic construction.

The main anthologies of concrete poetry, Williams and Solt, both firmly establish the Gomringer/Noigandres bases for concrete poetry and amply demonstrate the development of distance from linguistic and literary roots. British anthologist Stephen Bann, in turn, places the Brazilian group first in his introduction and presents the ideogram as the center of the program. Chicago editor Eugene Wildman, however, favors examples of anagrammatic dispersion and extreme iconoclasm, and gives comparatively little space to Brazilian efforts. This collection, more than anything else, illustrates expansion of nonverbal experiments in the sixties in the realm of "concretism."[70]

The focus of most of the considerable bibliography on concrete poetry that has appeared in the North American sphere since about 1970 (sometimes in conjunction with later related phenomena such as "visual literature") is decidedly more theoretical than critical. And as Caroline Bayard writes, "[t]he historian of concrete poetry would look upon the Brazilian theoretical texts as the richest and most articulate contribution" (22). Conceptual accounts, however, vary in their utilization of the Noigandres essays, "pilot plan," and high repertory. While Waldrop promotes the idea of a concrete poetry and appreciates its bases, R. P. Draper underplays the "clean" variety of words in spatial relations, and the whole of Brazilian theory.[71] In her important essay, Steiner forcefully rejoins the allegation that concrete poetry is a dead-end proposal, since poetry has always aspired to a visual state (204). Yet in her considerations of concrete theories she treats them somewhat as a block, making fewer distinctions than one might like between earliest uses of the term "concrete," *Teoria,* and subsequent Anglo-American interventions. With respect to creative repertories, Claus Clüver has been most concerned with noting differences between the apex of Brazilian concrete poetry and other production falling under the same rubric. As an eminently informed international reader of concrete poetry, he faces the established literary basis for concrete poetry and makes a telling comparison: "There is no real US-American equivalent to the Brazilian concrete ideogram."[72] In exceptional readings of media-age poetry in North America, Marjorie Perloff traverses the terrain of concrete poetry to arrive at one of her objects of analysis. In passage, she credits Noigandres, Gomringer, and related groups with establishing firmly the visual reception of all writing, especially modern poetry, which is "inevitably 'seen' as well as 'seen through' or heard." As a reader-critic, however, she shows a certain reluctance to meet concrete poetry squarely on its own terms, which always remains "open to the charges of a certain reductionism," not meaning purposeful minimalism but simplicity and, ultimately, deprivation. When Perloff, considering a noted poeticized logo from Brazil, asks whether it is all that different from witty California custom license plates, there is substantial reason to reply: yes![73] She favors, in conclusion, the "semantic complexity" and "cultural critique" of more extensive material texts without granting concrete's differential premises of condensation and structural content, nor the potential cumulative effects of sets of concrete texts.

A forceful example of the consequences of judging concrete poetry as a whole on the basis of limited evidence is seen in the position taken by the English poet and critic Veronica Forrest-Thomson. She saw concrete poetry as the extreme of "irrational obscurity," concentrating on the kind "seeking a point where language ceases to be language and becomes simply material, visual or aural, for making patterns." With this purely physical approach, she felt, it was difficult to "rise above the level of mere noise," and with her assumption that all "pretense to meaning [was] abandoned," one clearly could not achieve the kind of artifice she posited for modern poetry. While aware of some distinctions, she discarded concrete poetry as a rule because of an inherent lack of depth, a position that is defensible given her prime example.[74] But would the bases for this denial have been so clear if the critic had been exposed to what Bayard called the "exacting elegance" (163) and "well wrought urns" (22) of the Noigandres group, to their Poundian roots, and to the declared *rationality* of their orthodox phase?

Here, as in the case of borderline verbographic material, there is a need to specify *which* "concrete poetry" one is talking about, and at what stage. A relevant sidebar to the question of the consequences of delimitation concerns the Portuguese language itself. It has been said that if Portugal's renowned heteronymic poet Fernando Pessoa (1888–1935) had been English or French, he would have assumed his rightful place alongside Valéry, Eliot, and Pound as the major names of modernism. In the same way, one might wonder what the long-term consequences would have been if Brazilian *poesia concreta* and its theory had first been articulated in France or England, with commensurate force, rather than in the peripheral nation of Brazil, with its literary stock of relatively lesser value on the international market. Speculation aside, since the mid-fifties concrete poetry has indisputably aided the rise of Brazil's level of artistic recognition and, puns intended, visibility.

Other Poetic Vanguards in Brazil

Returning to the national arena, it is essential to remember that in Brazil, unlike in other countries, concrete poetry was the point of departure for a series of other avant-garde manifestations. The first dissident variation was that of Ferreira Gullar, who wrote a manifesto of neoconcretism two years after his rejection of the proposal of mathematical composition for concrete poetry. If from the point of view of poetry the brief splinter movement (1959–61) hardly existed, it was significant for the plastic arts, having involved such artists as Lygia Clark and Hélio Oiticica.[75] While desiring to maintain nonrepresentational and fundamentally constructivist positions, Gullar feared concrete poetry would be overly rationalist and mechanistic, alleging that it limited words to the status of visual signs in a graphic dimension. His proposed advance would make concrete "expressive" by taking words back to their condition of "verbs" and by reinstituting a syntax of temporality (i.e., nonsimultaneity) which was durational but not, in theory, linear. The application of these new ideas does not generate results that display clear-cut differences. In the section "poemas concretos/neoconcretos" in Gullar's collected poems, he himself does not indicate which might be which.[76] For him, the issue would soon be irrelevant, for once he dedicated himself to the politics of popular poetry, he abandoned all vanguard pretensions whatsoever.

Meshing of avant-garde and social intentions characterizes the second schism of the poetic vanguard, *poesia praxis*. Compared to neoconcretism, this group generated a considerable bibliography. The first "didactic manifesto" of what was called *instauração praxis* (establishing praxis) was appended to an inaugural book of poems (1962) by leader Mário Chamie.[77] The poetry was defined as that which "organizes and sets up aesthetically a situated reality, according to three conditions of action: a) the act of composing, b) the area to be surveyed by the composition, and c) the act of consumption."[78] In a later formulation, Chamie called his scheme *textor*, i.e., the sum of *autor+texto+leitor* (author-text-reader). Preferred textual situations involved rural conditions, labor, and economic exploitation. Formally, the poems were dominated by nominalism, multiple alliterations, parallelisms, and organization of semantic fields. It was not quite "watered down concrete," as an English editor chose to call it, but rather a separate proposal, semidiscursive and closer to the logic and mechanics of verse. To avoid backward appearances, however, Chamie coined the term *signos em conexão* (connected signs) to replace *verso* (line of verse); for his part, the sympathetic Cassiano Ricardo proffered the word *linossigno*.[79] Given the thematic foundation of *praxis*, semantics were more essential than in concrete poetry, with its greater dependence on intratextual dynamics. From the outset, the aims of *praxis* were complicated by Chamie's obsessive opposition to the theory of concrete poetry, whose tenets he attempted to invalidate and supersede without concession. He insisted, for instance, that his own notion of *espaço em preto* (black space), meaning the printed words on the page, had nothing to do with the *espaço em branco* (blank space) whose "signifying" function in the poem's overall graphic space had been asserted by the concrete poets. Chamie included concretism in what he called the "old vanguard" and offered his own "new vanguard" as a unique politically and artistically viable solution. His own theories and models of poetic communication, however, were too derivative, or simply tautological, to command sustained respect. Of the several young poets to associate with *poesia praxis,* the most enduring voice would prove to be Armando Freitas Filho (b. 1940), who followed an independent lyric path in the seventies and beyond.[80]

After *poesia praxis,* which placed great stress on sound strata and paronymous effects, the pictorial was favored by the self-styled avant-garde called *poema processo* (1967–1973), which signified the complete emptying of the poem as a literary construct. The group came to public attention with a dadaist demonstration-stunt on the steps of the Municipal Theater in Rio de Janeiro. Books of poetry by Drummond, Cassiano Ricardo, and others were torn up, and protestors carried signs with such messages as "Verse is a Drummondcide," "Uncle Scrooge is imperialism itself!" and "There's more poetry in a logotype than in all the poetry of J. G. de Araújo Jorge, Mário Chamie, and Vinícius de Moraes!" These noise-makers understood radicality as the ultimate virtue, and that meant a complete uprooting of the verbal. Guillermo de Torre, com-

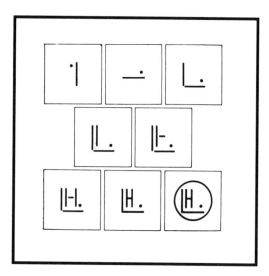

Example 9

menting on *lettrisme*, had called it "the reductio ad absurdum of all literary movements, their nihilist epilogue," and continued "[b]eyond the destruction of the word, one can only envision the barren land of the sign, noise and gestures, as the only means of communication."[81] With this observation, Torre unwittingly anticipated practices that literally do what he envisioned, such as *poema processo*. In this Brazilian activity, words soon gave way to various kinds of graphic constructs: lexically keyed sign fields, hieroglyphs, semaphoric codes, abstract animations, and collage. Some items would still be called "concrete poetry" in similar manifestations in other countries, though "visual poetry" might be more appropriate. Typical compositions of *poema processo* included boxed graphics with implied words or messages, wordless cartoons, nonsense diacritical and alphabetical sequences, and satirical paste-ups. With its dismantling of a word and its visual "theme," "olho" (eye) is an early symptomatic piece (example 9).[82]

The founders of this group acknowledge their clear origins in concrete poetry while stressing autonomy: "*poema processo* is not a mere or simple continuation of concretism: [it] is a radical continuity, implying a semiological unfolding of its own, of one of the directions of concrete poetry" (Cirne 45). That direction, clearly, was the "semiotic" repertory; specific models and inspirational sources were Pignatari's kinetic and code poems, Augusto's *popcretos*, cartoon-related material (e.g., the cover of *Teoria* [example 10], and Azeredo's "o sonho e o escravo" [the dream and the slave], a graphophotographic *poema-em-quadrinhos* [comic-strip-poem] in *Invenção 5*).

Example 10

With its numerous variations on such poses, Simon sees *poema processo* as an "exaggeration, but a politicized reading of concrete poetry" ("Esteticismo" 133). The content focus of adherents to the group is evident in an exhibition review saying that *"poema-processo,* by all indications, is only inclined to combat the political action of the United States in relation to underdeveloped countries."[83] Despite further appeals to popular protest and "mass" culture, however, the supporting documents of this enterprise can be abstract and scientifically toned to the point of distraction, as seen in this sample of the manifesto:

> PROPOSITION: QUANTITY + QUALITY/ONLY CONSUMPTION IS LOGIC . . . UTILITARIAN FORM/ NEW POSSIBILITIES FOR EACH NEW MATERIAL/ VISUALIZATION OF STRUCTURE/ READING OF THE PROCESS./ TECHNICAL LEVEL EQUAL TO EVOLUTION: THE DISUSE OF THE UNIQUE OBJECT . . . PROCESS: READING OF THE PROJECT/ 1. process: critical unleashing of always new structures. / Process is the necessary dynamic relationship between diverse structures or the components of a given structure, constituting concretization of the time-space continuum: movement ≈ to operate solutions. . . . 2. Process-poem: visualization of functionality : | : Discovery of reality / Consumption. There is no poetry / process. What there is is process-poem. . . . Movement or creative participation leads from structure (matrix) to the condition of process. . . . process/poem is that which, with each new experience, inaugurates informational processes . . . [it] is a radical position within vanguard poetry. It is necessary to frighten by radicality.

This excerpt comes from the last of a series of group manifestos of the poetic vanguard and, having bypassed words, necessarily closes the cycle.[84] The creative and conceptual production of *poema processo* may suggest (misguided) fixation on the notion of radicality, naive faith in technical solutions, or even a theoretical fetish, but in the censorial authoritarian context of the late 1960s, one must also consider the element of social commentary and reflection in the wordless processes. While the official movement was declared over in the early seventies, similar graphic practices continued in the work of such notable lyrico-satirists as Sebastião Nunes, as well as in some youth poetry of the seventies, and resurfaced in later, rather obscure, works of the original purveyors.[85] The collective vanguard spirit of innovation instituted with concrete poetry lasted only through the cycle of *poema processo.* Concretism, with its broader scope, continued to exercise greater influence on younger players throughout the following decades.

chapter three

The Social Imperative: *Violão de rua* and

the Politics of Poetry in the 1960s

Aos que pendegam entre o *eterno* e *a hora* pergunto: — E *agora?*
[To those who squabble about the eternal and the hour,
I ask: what about *now?*] — Geir Campos (1962)

In Western literature, examinations of poetry and politics inevitably hark
back to Plato's earliest comments about the roles of poets. The author of
the *Republic,* understanding the nonpragmatic spirit of lyric, advocated
state control of verse-makers and their material. Over the centuries, the
principal manifestation of politically motivated poetry was the eulogy of
rulers. In the twentieth century, discussions of literature and society
commonly revolve around artists' commitment to change. In his cele-
brated exposition of *engagement,* Jean-Paul Sartre distinguished between
the word-objects of poetry—which cannot by nature be utilitarian
or dedicated to causes—and the word-signs of prose, which can, and
should, be instruments of action.[1] Modern sociopolitical approaches to
literary study have largely depended on Marxist thought and refer almost
exclusively to narrative. Marx and Engels themselves did not treat po-
etry, nor did such important neo-Marxist theorists of fiction as Georg
Lukács.[2] Officials in socialist states or oppositional political organiza-
tions have not necessarily endorsed the exemption for poetic language
posited by Sartre but have, for the most part, shared with Plato the idea
that the state (party, or affiliated group) should be able to direct writers.
The classic examples of planned or directed literature in this century, of
course, are Soviet socialist realism and its off-shoots. Here again, fiction
and drama absolutely overshadow lyric, whose very constitution may
challenge the possibility of affiliation. Where history and poetry are con-
cerned, studies of political lyric in any epoch often "have done little more

than catalog judgments about the ideological stance of a given work according to a critic's fixed conception of which attitudes merit approval and which deserve censure," as a careful analyst has written.[3] Slippery questions of evaluation — confronting the transitory and relative nature of aesthetic values — ineluctably impinge on judgments about both the ideas expressed in poems and their artistic realizations. And, since in the general treatment of the politics of poetic value "*all* of the terms . . . are themselves historical in nature, functioning quite differently in the context and rhetoric of different eras, a series of individual studies is likely to prove far more profitable than any global claims." In accord with this affirmation of the usefulness of site-specific examinations, this chapter will treat the particular instance of political verse-making in Brazil in the turbulent 1960s and consider critiques of that episode as a manifestation of contemporary Brazilian poetry.

Populism and Participation

The sociopolitical function of art, and of poetry in particular, has never been more at issue in Brazil than it was during the period of populism, nationalism, and activism of the early 1960s. Orientation toward message and social involvement was evident in public discourse in the widespread employment of the verb *participar* (and its nominal and adjectival related forms). Beyond the evident sense of "to participate," dictionary meanings of this key word encompass "to inform, to communicate, to take part in, to associate oneself through thought or feeling, to have points in common." As far as poetry is concerned, authors' "participation" would comprise, in the words of a local poet-critic, "acts of communion and solidarity with their fellow creatures, and thus [be] perfectly valid and even imperative," and would normally be associated with politics of the Left.[4] Chroniclers of literature cannot but agree that historical and ideological factors profoundly affected the shape of lyric in the sixties. To indicate a recognizable and significant tendency, accounts of contemporary Brazilian poetry normally categorize via a modifier — such as "participatory," "committed," "*engagé*," or "sociopolitical" — or via other sorts of nominal locators, the prime example being a title emblematic of the trend: *Violão de rua* (Street guitar).[5] The present case study of the production and reception of poetry in politically charged circumstances focuses on the substance and character of that collective work. Guiding interests in cultural history and critical reception here underscore the rationale of aesthetic judgments of the lyrical material in question. Historical contexts, cultural projects, and varied commentary all confirm justifiable regard for extratextual factors.

Violão de rua is the title of a celebrated three-volume anthology published in Rio de Janeiro in 1962–63. While strictly speaking it does not designate a movement — *engagé* verse doesn't begin or end there, neither in terms of chronology nor of pertinent authors — it has served as a convenient synecdoche or purposeful appellation.[6] Since the *Violão de rua* compilations crystallized certain characteristic sensibilities and textual practices, they proved to be defining moments, and the title has been used to refer to organized manifestations of social poetry in the early sixties in general. Antônio Carlos Secchin, for example, is clear that *Violão de rua* offers "the most notable testimonial of that period."[7] The texts published in those modest vehicles were not especially numerous and, despite bright moments, for the most part have been harshly received on most conventional critical counts. Yet the poetry had quite an audience and remains an obligatory reference in chronicles of contemporary culture and national lyric. How was it that three small pocket books (of 100 to 150 pages), generally held to contain a preponderance of poetry of questionable quality, were such a success at the time of their publication and made a true mark in recent literary history? Beyond questions of literary taste, if not despite them, the reasons are various and revealing.

Violão de rua has been the object of telling critiques, both at the time of its release and in subsequent occasions. Its processes reflect scenes of the drama of Brazilian society of 1961 to 1964 and reveal passions of that historical period, especially the intense belief in the role of art in what some thought to be a (pre-) revolutionary stage. *Violão de rua* was, moreover, a direct challenge to established literary values based on aesthetic criteria and the assumption of the superiority of universality in literature. Brazilians were trying to institute locally a validation of a concept of literature stressing content and political rhetoric (generally Marxist-Leninist). In doing so, poets were answering to a declared necessity for the involvement of middle-class intellectuals and students with the working class and peasants. In the early sixties, concerned Brazilian artists faced a fundamental problem with respect to commitment: compulsions to involve others and to denounce had to be weighed against freedom of expression; in effect, individual perceptions had to be balanced with "correct" positions. Many acted according to perceptions of an ideal collective position. As a politico-cultural endeavor, *Violão de rua* bares an unprecedented faith in artistic purpose and in the efficacy of verse, as well as a series of difficulties inherent in ideologically driven literary practice. The sponsoring organization of *Violão de rua* fell short of its goals of broad-based consciousness-raising and mobilization. Still, their books were notable enough to be exhibited as "subversive literature" on television following the military coup that shook Brazilian society in 1964. Since then, the social concern that has lasted in poetry and related discussions, in critical awareness and debates, inevitably carries echos and residues of the specific early sixties experience. In sum, *Violão de rua* was a coagulator, a fulcrum for content-oriented poetry, and it remains an essential site to examine a social line of poetic production in Brazil.

The Social Heritage of Brazilian Lyric

The committed poets of the early 1960s were building on deep historical foundations. A current of social poetry begins with satirical verse in colonial days, strengthens during later romanticism (notably with the theme of abolition), and develops significantly during *modernismo,* with its governing regard for native populations and popular culture. To know the Brazilian people through poetry in the 1920s could well mean literarily confronting their status and living conditions. The social implications of the work of poet-ethnographer Mário de Andrade, for instance, are highlighted in a very deliberately topical study of modern lyric in Brazil.[8] In a later stage, the eruption of World War II was the impulse for Carlos Drummond de Andrade's collection *Sentimento do mundo* (Feeling of the world, 1940), which opened a social line of expression in the author's work that would peak with *A rosa do povo* (The rose of the people, 1945).[9] The aestheticist Generation of '45 was not noted for social discourse of any kind; what sparse relevant lyric existed was the exception. Yet several writers who began under the neo-Parnassian sign of '45 would later turn their attention to real-world issues. Geir Campos, Paulo Mendes Campos, and José Paulo Paes are among the pertinent names cited in a symptomatic sixties study of "participation."[10] While contemporaneous with the Generation of '45, João Cabral de Melo Neto is, again, an independent voice who charted an appreciably distinct course. Both his objective textual geometry and his treatment of Northeastern realities set him apart from the typical lines of '45 sophistication. Political climate increasingly affected views of literature in the course of the 1950s. Brazilian concrete poetry, as seen in chapter 2, emerged in a conscious context of developmentalism and nationalist sentiment. Innovation and ideology entered into the "critical nationalism" of the Tendência group in Minas Gerais, while the social concerns of writers around the country multiplied and reached unprecedented proportions in the early 1960s. Noigandres poet Décio Pignatari, faced with constant accusations of alienation and empty formalism, spoke of an imminent "participatory-semantic-content leap" in concretism. The alignment of his group with Tendência was intended to help carve out some space for creative participation. Having added Mayakovsky's phrase "without revolutionary form there is no revolutionary art" to the "pilot plan plan for concrete poetry," the Noigandres poets produced verbal inventions in instigating new formats but failed to convince most other sectors of their extraformal concerns. In the poetic arena, confrontation of experimentalism and discursive verse of a social tenor was a prime feature of the years when *Violão de rua* appeared.[11]

The Climate of Mobilization and Judgment

In Brazil, as elsewhere in Latin America, the Cuban Revolution emphatically brought to the fore such issues as Third World identity, self-determination, and anti-imperialism, the playing out of which affected all kinds of public discourse. Benedito Nunes, in a retrospective mode, synthesizes the significance of Fidel Castro's victory for his generation of thinkers and artists: "Cuba awakened political hopes because our horizon of expectation was utopian: the renovation of art and the renovation of life corresponded with each other . . ."[12] The impact of that Cuban example is immediately tangible in the words of an enthusiastic "participant," who asserts that Brazilian intellectuals and artists "from one moment to the next, found themselves faced with a radical option, on which depended the very continuation of their creative activities: either to carry on serving a minority to the detriment of an oppressed and crushed majority, or to stand beside them in their strategy of emancipation. In other words: either to resign from history or to place oneself squarely in it, by making it" (Pontual 65). This strong declaration exemplifies a radical position that, while exaggerating the historical situation, sets the tone for discussions of art and society by rhetorically suggesting commitment as the central aspect of intellectual atmosphere prior to the military coup. The populist government of João Goulart (1961–1964) witnessed great agitation on numerous fronts. Mobilization for social transformation included cultural projects with explicitly political ideals.

In terms of literature and youth involvement, a visit by neo-Marxist Jean-Paul Sartre to Brazil in 1961 was a key event. The respected thinker's main address emphasized a need to pay attention to "popular art" and "expressions of the common people" and influenced many admirers who were attuned to existentialist thought and literature.[13] For a host of reasons, the traditional cultivation of literature came to be viewed suspiciously; as a representative young essayist of the day wrote, "Belles-lettres are, today, literary indignity. For intellectuals to become bourgeois is desertion, an act of treason."[14] Following Cuba, Sartre, and continuing shifts in attitude, the vogue in Brazil was social art, which came to be measured by its levels of participation and integration into social reality.

Critics and commentators also ought to demonstrate their concern and commitment. Youthful enthusiasm or revolutionary zeal could sometimes translate, however, into self-righteous reviews or disparaging, holier-than-thou attitudes. The following extended definition of *participar,* for example, verges on editorial policing and demonstrates the eminently political poetics that some espoused:

> A correlative task to the production of participatory poetry is the unmasking of false participatory poetry. One of the functions of the *engagé* poet, [who is] obliged by his engagement, is to denounce all alienated practices, especially those which, under a revolutionary guise, offer the people inadequate, false, or sometimes counter-revolutionary information. Almost always reformist. Correct and objective information is the first trait of participatory poems. . . . Participatory poetry is not a return to anything; it is the integration of cultural production into the space-time of Brazil (i.e., the pre-revolution we are living) . . . Participatory poetry is culture thought of . . . in terms of dialectical materialism . . . critical poems, informed by the structure of Brazilian society and dialectically critical of it.[15]

These kinds of values were most prevalent among university students moving toward or already holding socialist or communist positions. For such youth, the true issues for poetry were functional and thematic rather than aesthetic per se, corresponding to those of general concern: anti-imperialism, agrarian reform, peasant leagues, workers movements, etc. Such matters concerned the membership of a noted student organization for cultural education, the Centro Popular de Cultura, or CPC. This center was founded in 1962 in Rio de Janeiro as an autonomous group within the UNE (National Union of Students), a long-constituted body of some nationwide impact. The CPC worked to make and disseminate "popular revolutionary art," aiming to de-alienate the people and to foster social change. Affiliated centers were soon founded in other cities around the country.

The CPC elaborated projects in theater, popular music, and film. As part of their *agitprop* (agitation and propaganda), they also cooperated with a politically oriented commercial publishing house in the organization and dissemination of a book series featuring *Cadernos do povo,* pedagogical little "notebooks of the people," with such titles as *What are the peasant leagues?, Who are the people in Brazil?, Why don't the rich go on strike?,* and *Who will lead the coup in Brazil?* It was as "special editions" of this series, and with the same didactic intent at heart, that the issues of *Violão de rua* were released, as were individual titles by Ferreira Gullar.[16] The position papers of the center's leaders demonstrate clearly the kind of rhetoric that guided CPC activities and anticipate the nature of associated lyrical output. The overall express ideal was to communicate through artistic means ideology that would aid in changing society. In his manifesto, founding director Carlos Estevam Martins posits three options for artists: to be conformist (alienated), nonconformist (sympathetic to change), or revolutionary (in the struggle), as the CPC expected to be. Martins establishes differences between the bases of traditional forms, held to be flawed, and the principles of real "popular" art, which must be governed not just by identification with the common people but by a political spirit of transformation as well.[17] Creative guidelines based on such assumptions led to inevitable conflicts and problems, as seen below. The last director of Rio's CPC was the reformed experimental poet Ferreira Gullar, one of the featured writers in *Violão de rua* and, from a literary point of view, the most visible personality in the group. His polemical positions included definition of *popular culture* as a "new phenomenon" in Brazilian life, as "achieving consciousness of Brazilian reality," and as comprising (directly or indirectly) didactic works that act upon that reality, in short, as tools of transformation. In this scheme, *popular* does not mean of or emanating from the people but rather imbued with correct political consciousness.[18] Anything not so endowed must be alienated or alienating. For both Martins and Gullar, traditional (folk) modes of expression, if not admirable in and of themselves, were strategically useful, and could be altered for CPC purposes.

These positions manifest, at many turns, mechanistic application of Marxist tenets, and an abiding radicality throughout. Rather than theoretical persuasion per se, what should be emphasized in this situation, for a broader humanistic understanding of the ambience and artistic output of the period, is the intensity of the emotion and belief involved.

CPC participants acted with strong and sustained personal investment, literally taking performances to the people in efforts to organize and raise consciousness. As filmmaker Arnaldo Jabor summarized it: "Never has anyone believed so much in art as a political force in the world!"[19] One can hardly talk about CPC activities without being taken by the fervor and faith of organizers and writers, and by the deadly serious tone of creative and analytical language. Dedicated makers might regard germane poetry not just as simple denunciation, protest, or outcry but also as a true aesthetic weapon. A student of Gullar's trajectory, for example, calls specific attention to his "firm conviction that his poetic words can aid in changing society."[20] The CPC was thought of internally as one of the political arms of a struggle that could lead to the seizure of power. For its part, poetry was not an ornament but a forceful tool. There was an orienting belief in the "revolutionary efficacy of the poetic word, which . . . was represented as very powerful and even as an instrument of projects to take power" (Hollanda 15). Without the existence of the myth of the revolutionary reach of the poetic word, *Violão de rua* could not have been as successful as it was in student sectors. Lafetá assigns no less importance to attitudinal factors in a later reading of Martins's post-facto defense of CPC, finding the document to be replete with *certainty*. Excessive confidence characterizes both the political action and the associated poetry, which is guided by "an almost magical belief in the verbal" (111–112). In keeping with this persuasion, there could be similar accompanying senses about the objects of outreach efforts. As one absorbed voice claimed: "In the present-day phase of plunder, under external command, even the most advanced workers in the country and the city need, in a primordial way, the elements of content of social poetry" (Castro 242). From a distance it might seem self-generous or presumptuous for poets to assert workers' necessity for the content of verse, but it was essential that writers whose activities might include dramatic presentations or distribution (or sale) of readings to workers maintain belief in what they were doing.

Books, Makers, and Contents

Given this contextualization, it should be clarified that the actual editing of *Violão de rua* was done outside the confines of the center and that not all the participants in the books shared such extreme political and strategic views. The makeup of the publication itself, in any case, soon reveals some of the consequences of assuming CPC positions. The three little books carry the subtitle *Poemas para a liberdade,* or poems for liberty, with all the clear and desired overtones. The "street guitar" of the main title conveys a public, out-of-the-ivory-tower stance, nonelitist in nature, communicative like song. A straightforward statement of purpose appears on the copyright page of volume 1, which "aims to make known poets who use their instruments of labor to participate in a more direct fashion in the ongoing struggles of the Brazilian people, revolutionarily attuned to demands for a better and more human world." These poets chosen to "participate" more directly do not form a homogeneous group. In fact, the collection has no real generational, geographical, or stylistic criteria. Participants come from many different states and include modernists, refugees from the Generation of '45, others who began at the same time without sharing the neo-Parnassian bias, and college-age individuals, including cpc members. Volume 1 (September 1962) showcases eight poets, while volumes 2 (also 1962) and 3 (1963) have more numerous and diverse contributors. In total, there are twenty-eight poets, more than half of whom were born between 1921 and 1939, placing them in the twenty to forty age range. There were more contributors from the Northeast than from Rio de Janeiro and São Paulo combined, which is in keeping with democratic principles and a concern for representing voices of the stricken Northeastern region, seen as home to peasant populations in semifeudal conditions. (The inspiration for the cpc had come, incidentally, from the state-sponsored literacy campaign Movimento Popular de Cultura in Pernambuco.) In addition to original material, *Violão de rua* took advantage to reprint (with permission) appropriate texts by such recognized names as Vinícius de Morais, Cassiano Ricardo, and the noted modernist poet of the Northeast, Joaquim Cardozo.

The introduction to volume 3 has been taken as the manifesto of *Violão de rua*. Editor and contributor Moacyr Félix delineates six main interrelated objectives: to affirm poetry as a consciousness-raising form of knowledge; to stand against the "ivory tower," with which are associated any formalism or mechanistic approach to verse; to assert that truth is to be found in the people and in resistance to the evils of capitalism and imperialism; to help end "pointless" poetry by fostering verse-making driven by worldview rather than individualism or mere artistry; to affirm poetry as a humanistic endeavor; and to make a natural alignment with the proletariat and the peasantry. Though not specifically elaborated upon in this introduction, experimental writing is generally viewed with strong suspicion, even as an enemy to target. Poets of this tendency were generally anti–concrete poetry and remained unconvinced by the concrete poets' recognition of current realities and participation in timely events.[21] For their part, poets of radical dissent might regard themselves as "vanguard," in the sense of representing the cutting edge or frontline of attack on literary convention.

The collected poems of *Violão de rua* embody Félix's principles to varying degrees, without ever contradicting them. Texts address such expected topics as oppression, poverty, imperialism, latifundiary privilege, and future redemption. Although materialist outlooks dominate, structuring moods and tones are most often determined by emotion and feeling: hope, anger, indignation, guilt, pity, or sorrow. Poetic spaces are, for the most part, exterior; frames of operation and reference include the city, the countryside, and the nation. There are some Latin American references (especially to Cuba) and a few international examples (anti-colonialism in Algeria, South Africa, the Congo, Hiroshima, and the Cold War). There is an abundance, naturally, of musical titles, speakers, and motifs. Indicative titles include Ferreira Gullar's "Quatro mortos por minuto" (Four dead per minute) and "Canto menor com final heróico" (Minor song with heroic end) by Reynaldo Jardim, from the inaugural volume; "Canto angustiado aos plantadores de cana" (Anguished song to the cane planters) by J. J. Paes Loureiro, from the second volume; and Oscar Niemeyer's unique "O que você fez, arquiteto?" (What have you done, architect?) and "Canção do guerrilheiro torturado" (Song of the tortured warrior) by Ruy G. Barata, from the third volume. In terms of form, it has been asserted with frequency that *Violão de rua* (and social verse in general) was modeled on the common measures of Brazil's chapbook folk verse, *literatura de cordel*, especially since Gullar does pointedly use the narrative frames of that popular form.[22] It is not strictly true, however, that the educated, urban poets purveyed by the CPC generally followed traditionalist dictates. Folk-inspired quatrains and sextains may seem dominant overall, but there is a liberal mix of free verse as well, with occasional nonconventional techniques. Such stylistic mixes should be kept in mind in overall assessments of the project. The weight of popular forms is sufficient enough that pieces which are deviant in any way do stand out.

The best instance of mixture is Félix de Atahyde's ten-part "Arenga" (Harangue) (vol. 3, 45–51). The first and recurring verse "félix fúria foice martelo" (felix fury scythe hammer) establishes a sense of sound-aware rhythm and suggests appropriate adaptation of language to intended tone and mood, as the writer assumes the (his own) persona of an inflamed poet speaking to the people in their midst. Some fragmentation and spatialization further fortify the poem. Facts, statistics, journalistically styled quotes and slogans are interjected into the text, making for some interesting juxtapositions. The informational aspect — as opposed to the linguistic — eventually comes to dominate and questions the lyrical vehicle itself. The option (requirement) to give the people (literally) correct information and political perspective edges out the poet's appreciable urban awareness and the potential for irony that might substantiate greater poeticity in the eyes of readers attuned to the *making* of the poem as protest. Another good example of what was imagined to be suitable (relevant, useful, participatory) is "Cortiço" (Tenement) by Cassiano Ricardo (vol. 3, 38–41). The poetic voice here does not speak to the oppressed, but rather offers a litany of their ills, appealing to a well-off readership to insist that people in "brutal misery . . . are beings like us." This separation and comparison of assumed audience and subjects unwittingly hints at some of the problematic aspects of *Violão de rua* treated below.

Moacyr Félix addresses the political and artistic adversaries of protest writing in "A fala irritada" (Irritated speech) (vol. 3, 92–102), another harangue that serves as a sort of platform from which to situate *Violão de rua* among movements in poetry.[23] In this poem, as well as in Félix's introduction, there are different measures of attitude toward the status of social verse. This ambivalence reflects on *Violão de rua* in a general way and impinges on judgments of the products. The project wanted to distance itself from academic definitions of lyric and aesthetic standards and to set up nonelite directions of operation. Yet in practice established literary values were never really left behind, even in folk-affected modes. Notions of the poet as an endowed being and of poetry as a "privileged" activity were maintained. Notwithstanding stated political and organizational goals, Félix and colleagues did not renounce citizenship in the local province of letters; they still sought legitimacy there and made claims on artistry. Though they sought to readjust the scale of values for poetry in favor of communicability and construction of worldview, they wanted recognition as artists of the word. The poets of *Violão de rua* are not somehow immune from textual criticism because of their political idealism.

In terms of governing outlook and lyrical practice, "Poética" by Geir Campos proves to be symptomatic of the collection:

> Eu quisera ser claro de tal forma
> que ao dizer
>   — rosa!

todos soubessem o que haviam de pensar.
Mais: quisera ser claro de tal forma
que ao dizer
    —já!
todos soubessem o que haviam de fazer.*
(vol. 1, 40)

The ideals of effective communication and appropriate (implied revolutionary) action are expressed here in a clear parallelism. However, by positing a utilitarian instrument gauged by referential and imperative modes of language, the poem leaves itself open to be read as a statement against an essential aspect of lyric. To the degree that the speaker yearns for clarity, he is opposed to ambiguity, and his utterance runs counter to the conventional position that the polyvalence of language sustains artful verse. Geir Campos displays awareness of literary devices here but uses them in a fashion that suggests fear of abstraction, of even minimal indeterminacy, of failing to go the right way. What occurs, in the long run, wholly lacks discovery, surprise, and provocation. The treatment given this text anticipates challenges to openly political poetry, with or without specific reference to *Violão de rua,* by different readers whose judgments are based on other than a preprogrammed system of partisan valuation.

Reception, Rejection, and Critique

The reception and critiques of *Violão de rua* since the time of its appearance disclose user enthusiasm, debate among Left intellectuals, established literary standards at odds with ideological motivations, and the wisdom of critical distance. Brazilian criticism has been nearly unanimous in its questioning of the poetic value of *Violão de rua* and, in retrospect, of its efficacy or contribution to CPC campaigns. If the ultimate value of the undertaking proves to be largely sociocultural, it is worthwhile to examine various facts and critical opinions for what they divulge about the "populist" approach and its potential in poetry. As far as exposure is concerned, it must be said that *Violão de rua* achieved much wider repercussions than most poetry. By one account, ten thousand copies of one title were sold, quite a significant figure in Brazil in

---

*[I should like to be so clear / that when I said "rose" / everyone would know what they ought to think / What's more: I should like to be so clear / that when I said "now!" / everyone would know what they ought to do]

the early 1960s. While there is evidence that student activists did get the books into the hands of working people, the consumption of this production was, for the most part, in student communities, where users "sought it out and consumed it not for artistic reasons but for ideological motives" (Bilharinho 25). This is an example of the common implication that the favoring of ideological motives adversely affects artistic merit. Such opinions are still normally accompanied by an assumption of goodwill. In one early case, a curious reviewer of CPC publications wonders how to reconcile the subtitle (*Poemas para a liberdade*) with the ideology of most of the verse, which is tied to "other new idolatries that, like all idolatry, lead to slavery" (Reis 81). While the issue of liberty is raised here, the implied villains (communism, totalitarianism, atheism) are not cited.

Conventional Brazilian commentators, whether contemporaneous with *Violão de rua* or more recent, may share internationally expressed sentiments about the limiting of poetry's potential by virtue of existential circumscription. These "poems for liberty" and like material may be regarded as innately referential and programmatic, and if one takes "lyric" to imply private, personal tones, the "presumptive deficiency" of political poetry would be its very public concern.[24] In this respect, one must be careful not to confuse expressions of aesthetic "standards" with any supposed political neutrality. Hans Magnus Enzenberger, while skeptical of Left demands on figurative language of poetry, was careful to note:

> But too often the champions of inwardness and sensibility are reactionaries. . . . They advise poetry to stick to such models as they have devised for it, in other words, to high aspirations and eternal values. The promised reward for this continence is timeless validity. Behind these high-sounding proclamations lurks a contempt for poetry no less profound than that of vulgar Marxism. For a political quarantine placed on poetry in the name of eternal values itself serves political ends. (75)

Such reservations help to maintain balance when working through questions of partisanship, ideology, and their consequences where evaluation of such poetry as *Violão de rua* is concerned. Underlying attitudes of paternalism have been denounced, without hostility, in CPC position papers and adaptations of folk literature alike. A recurring complaint about the poems is echoed by Turchi (94), who cites them for the same "manichean, axiomatic, pedagogical tone of the booklets," that is, the topical CPC pamphlets. Overall problems for the verse qua lyric emerge from several factors that tend to narrow concepts of social poetry. As already suggested, there is a seeming sense of obligation to denounce in somewhat obvious fashion; thus there may be, for instance, a perception of historical allusion as insufficient or a reluctance to rely on subtle personae or semantics. Limitation of horizons may lead to rejection of profoundly human but nonsectarian expressions. Artistic criteria were also impugned from politically sympathetic perspectives. *Violão de rua* was seen by one vocal contemporary as "static monotone" and as a confusion of "subliterature, terrorism, and committed literature . . ."[25] Another sixties critic reiterates objections to stereotypes and detects a sentimentalization of social facts in the poems. While the tendency to heroicize situations and standardized types is problematic in its own right, the fundamental problem is the lack of inventiveness in the language (Uchoa Leite 102).

The potential for "aesthetic" problems in the CPC poetry is indeed enormous if the linguistic ethics of Martins' above-cited manifesto are applied. The director had proposed that artists should "never go beyond the limits that are imposed upon them by the capacity that the spectators may (not) have to translate, in terms of their own existence, that which the symbolic speech of the artist intends to transmit." This position not only underestimates the ken of the people but leaves artists open to both condemnation from zealots and complaints from anyone interested in things other than brute content or more appreciative of symbolic language. While the CPC manifesto refers to other genres, it is poetry, of course, that stands to suffer most from precepts on language, especially where class differences also come into play. A fundamental question is whether it is even possible for middle-class creators to make "popular" language their own. Citing an admonition of Adorno's, Hollanda notes that a key CPC manifesto phrase—"laborious training effort of mass syntax"—itself embodies distance from the population at large. Attempts at adapting language to mass mentality led to exaggeration and stylized regression to rural folk forms of expression. If there is an express mission to emulate the common people, "[p]oetically this option translates into a celebratory, ritualized, exhortative and pacifying language . . . which does not take into account the level of symbolic production in that same popular poetics" (Hollanda 19). This last sentiment is shared even by an admiring analyst of Gullar, whose ideas are seen to reflect the authoritarian stance of the intellectual who arrogates the competence to decide what common people will understand or not. CPC verse, moreover, reduces the rich world of folk poetry to schematic and metaphorically poor formulas (Turchi 93). A most apropos appraisal of early sixties manipulation of popular verse, from a poetic point of view, was made by Augusto de Campos:

> One of the lessons to be gained from the experiment a few urban poets conducted — when they tried to avail themselves of the external form and the typical language of folk [*cordel*] poetry in order to give it a participatory content, to "correct" it ideologically and at the same time take advantage of its theoretical mass penetration — is that authentic popular poetry cannot be imitated or corrected.[26]

In this appraisal, the critic shifts attention away from the dominant narrative type of *cordel* toward another modality of folk chapbooks, the register of poetic duels (*desafio*) in Northeastern song cycles. It is indeed appropriate to set the value of the lyrical playfulness and gamesomeness of *desafio* over the story-telling function of most *cordel,* in which message can be highlighted but syntagmatic logic exercises control and, ultimately, simplifies.

The simplification of language is precisely one of the points of departure for João Luis Lafetá in his critique of artistic nationalism and *Violão de rua.* Self-proclaimed populist verse was overly direct and colloquial, overloaded the text with passages dominated by the emotive function, and simply made political harangues. Poets may have sought communication with a wider public but their means included marking off certain thematic areas and cutting off, in effect, linguistic resources (110). With notable exceptions, the poets in question did not problematize language — lexically, syntactically, or semantically. Instead, they fell into easy rhetorical patterns, tending to "reify" or "fetishize" such terms as "people," "worker," or "revolution," without a hint of irony. From their own viewpoint, committed poets themselves could also be sensitive to less-than-careful manipulation of vocabulary.[27] Lafetá goes on to conclude that populist poets' use of stereotypes actually ends up reproducing mental structures of their supposed adversaries, to wit, an ideology of force, action, and individual heroism (nineteenth-century bourgeois values) (113–114). This critic refers specifically to Paulo Mendes Campos's "Poema para ser cantado" (Poem to be sung) (vol. 1), which demonstrates the mystical faith and unwavering attitudes that govern this kind of expression. The principal evidence is the insistent refrain "Sei que o povo reinará" (I know the people shall reign). As do many items in *Violão de rua,* this poem also illustrates what would appear to be a poetic application of a tenet of socialist realism, usually thought of in terms of fiction, that calls for the (eventual) victory of the people to be portrayed, or at least visible, in all works of literature.[28]

This example invites consideration of how desired transference of Marxist beliefs may affect the making of poetry. For any poet to invent a mythology in the secular modern world is a tough job, poet-essayist Stephen Spender writes, and the difficulties of such a creative task in lyric can only be compounded with the demands of a system of thought. Secular communist poetry intending to correspond, for instance, to a religious metaphysical poetry is a blurred project, because Marxism, "in common with other analytical and scientific systems, cannot be taken outside its method and terms, and interpreted imagistically, or converted into a mystique without in the process losing its mechanical or scientific precision."[29] These, it should be emphasized, are indispensable in the domain of materialist ideology, socialist realism, and, to judge by position papers cited above, Brazil's CPC-backed verse. In addition, one ought to consider the relationship of real-world discourse and literary renderings. "The temptation for the poet," Spender continues, "is to take over the rhetoric of political will and action and translate it into the rhetoric of poetry." Common to many who write strong-willed poems "is that the poet has allowed his scrupulous poet's rhetoric of the study of 'minute particulars' to be overwhelmed by the secret yearning for a heroic public rhetoric of historic action" (66). While this judgment is made vis-à-vis English-language poems for the Spanish Civil War and other circumstances, its relevance to the early sixties Brazilian case has been made clear in various circumstances.

When assessing the political and artistic aims of the CPC poetry project, it should be reiterated that some regarded it as a "vanguard," as participating in an advanced politico-cultural front. In his retrospective outline of twentieth-century Brazilian poetry, one former participant does not hesitate to present *Violão de rua* as one in a series of vanguard moments (1956–1968), characterizing it as an attempt to maintain an avant-garde (i.e., forward, ground-breaking) position but without any compromise with aesthetic formalism, guided by a belief that poets should participate actively in the historical process (Sant'Anna 152). Given the revolutionary projections and the political affiliation of CPC, the original military sense of "vanguard" as frontline is more applicable to *Violão de rua* than the acquired sense of "avant-garde" applied to art of change. In Jorge Wanderley's pertinent critique of *Violão de rua*, in contrast, the vanguard in literature is conceived of as the leading attack on constituted power, on horizons of expectation, on textual predictability. CPC poetry is seen to belong, in the long run, to social or historical spheres rather than to those of art or literature, because it represents no real literary movement or style, which is evidenced by the lack of any diluting of individuality in the common concerns of the group. The antiestablishment poets "while rising up against constituted power, did not rise up against the constituted code—language—whereby they lost their vanguardist intentions."[30]

Legacy, Lessons, Impact, and Continuity

If, following this argument, any avant-garde intentions of *Violão de rua* can be dismissed, and if, as has been asserted, ideological bias so interfered with potential artistic contributions, what was the value of the poetic arm of the CPC? What was the positive legacy of the *Violão de rua* enterprise? The CPC and *Violão de rua* as had been constituted were dissolved by the military following the coup d'état of 1964. The headquarters of the UNE were, in fact, invaded and destroyed. The four additional volumes of *Violão de rua* that were ready to go to press never did. Social poetry would continue without the community connections or original dissemination scheme, and with new overall perspective. Events naturally brought home political and literary lessons to disillusioned participants, and varied commentary has since reinforced certain outcomes. The educated middle class could not, for example, simply will to merge with the target *povo*, nor to communicate with their language. Organizational and artistic activity further revealed the differences of the urban working class and the rural underclass. The belief that had held together the CPC's activities, including literary, was, of course, shaken. If literature was to be considered as an instrument of empowerment, it could only be so in very subtle and slow ways. Poetry was not for proselytizing nor could it institute class affinity. In broader terms, CPC may have failed to affect widely the masses, but it had some measure of impact and was certainly inspirational. *Violão de rua* retains a place in the history and established tradition of political poetry in the West. Especially with its musical metaphors, the movement had an emotional value, as suggested in the words of other poets of the Americas: "Still another aspect of the tradition of political poetry is the way in which, just as songs do, it can express and heighten a shared emotion, intensifying morale rather than making converts. 'To have embodied hope for many people, even for one minute,' said Neruda, 'is something unforgettable and profoundly touching for any poet.'"[31] Brazil's CPC cultural projects, furthermore, helped to raise middle-class consciousness. The overall mobilization of writers, intellectuals, and students, as well as the discussion of cultural issues—notwithstanding dogmas and orthodoxies—had not been negligible; groundwork was established for debates that continued through the

1960s and into the 1980s.[32] The CPC outlook on popular art, albeit pater-
nalistic or unrealistic, as well as the task of engagement through poetry,
also aided in a rediscovery of folk culture, which had been de-emphasized
lyrically since the first phase of *modernismo* in the 1920s. Whether that
rediscovery was regressive or progressive, the impulse was provided.

It has also been suggested that in a very general way, sociopolitical
verse helped to recuperate a realist side of poetry that had been disarticu-
lated by the experimental vanguards.[33] From the reverse angle, political
climate did affect developments in concrete poetry, as suggested above,
as well as the emergence of *poesia praxis,* the self-proclaimed "alternative"
vanguard with social pretensions. Mário Chamie declared that his mate-
rial sought to be "linguistic experience associated with social preoccupa-
tions, especially the conflict of country and city."[34] In his essays, however,
political or committed elements never equal the theoretical preoccupa-
tion with display, technique, and innovation, which results from an
obsessive need to respond to all aspects of concrete poetry. Still, at its
inception, *praxis* could be conceived of as a third option for younger
poets dissatisfied with both the formal emphases of concrete poetry and
the limitations of tradition-bound *Violão de rua.*[35]

Most of the CPC-anthologized authors had published socially relevant
material before 1962 or would do so in the course of the decade. As for
continuity, the *Revista civilização brasileira* was founded soon after the
coup to offer intellectual responses to the military regime. In this new
publication, poetry was considered an important topic alongside politics
and economics, because of a perceived link with the people. Writers
adopted careful approaches to reflect on pre-coup practices and to ex-
press hope in light of current events, as in this discussion of "Poesia
brasileira, 1964":

> The "street guitars" were optimistic, trusting, euphoric, believing
> in the transformations of Brazilian life; today, stowed away, they
> will resurface with the first waters, cleansed, purified by suffering, a
> determinant of obligatory silences, that, at times, is fear, but for that
> very reason, is a fecund silence, of germination.[36]

The subsequent numbers of this review have a section, "Poets speak
about poetry," in which carryovers from *Violão de rua,* other older names
with a certain respectability, and young voices respond to a question-
naire. The committed line of Gullar and Félix appears consciously toned
down and metaphorical, and other responses are more lyrical and ro-
mantic in their identification of social issues in art. Fernando Mendes

Vianna, for example, says: "poetry should be a form of liberation from the residues of theology and metaphysics, and should collaborate with the sciences in making matter dignified . . . in the struggle for a more just (true and useful) world and for a universal consciousness of that justice."[37] The poet also underlines the need to talk about the struggle for sexual freedom as an ethical act. To make poetry of the body is humanizing, here meaning to free the body and to free women from the inequality of entrenched ideas. With the expression of ideas in this fashion, Vianna's voice marks a transition in Brazilian poetry. He was one of those later anthologized by the same publisher in *Poesia viva 2*, a continuation of a salient collection of social verse in the sixties, itself a bibliographical extension of *Violão de rua*.[38]

A complete account of the sociopolitical orientation of contemporary lyric would follow, through the sixties to the nineties, the trajectories of the editor of *Violão de rua*, of the consistently involved Thiago de Mello, and of Ferreira Gullar, whose late sixties output contains several emblematic metapoetical texts.[39] In assessing such production on an individual basis and as a developing or continuing trend, one should consider carefully how much of the criticism of the original *Violão de rua* would be applicable to the bulk of similar production of the period. Most of the best social poetry of the decade appeared in non-CPC vehicles. While many of the enthusiastic works of the time surely exhibit some of the limitations discussed above, one can acknowledge both the uneven qualities of such books and their collective importance as illustrations of "one of the central components of the literary climate of the sixties," as Alfredo Bosi does.[40] His compilation of relevant titles includes three by the innovation-minded Affonso Ávila and the collected poems of José Paulo Paes. Among the book-length collections published subsequently by contributors to *Violão de rua*, one of the most distinguished is the image-rich *Inquisitorial* by poet-lyricist José Carlos Capinan, which merited the critical attention of both Barata, who says the poet "inquires and meditates rather than appeal to action" (72), and José Guilherme Merquior.[41] Dialectical without platitudes of historical materialism, Capinan's poetry is significantly less immediate than that of other participants, as seen in "Poema intencional":

Há em cada substância a sua negativa
e a possibilidade de processo.

Processo inexorável a ir ao fim
meta a ser de pão e flores:

a rosa será uma outra rosa
e nós já não seremos

vejo nos olhos tristes
um filho possível

vejo na árvore antiga do parque
uma cadeira, uma muleta, mas sobretudo um aríete . . .*

A Final Cadence

Though the social preoccupation in contemporary Brazilian lyric emerges from the nationalism of the 1950s and spans the 1960s, studies of commitment have focused on *Violão de rua* because "participation" has never been so much in the foreground as the historical circumstances of the populist period allowed in the early 1960s. Despite the shortcomings of the political-action cultural programs that backed *Violão de rua,* its fragile aesthetic contribution, and all manner of associated discouragements (e.g., the authoritarian regime's repression of free speech), early sixties *engagé* poetry still echoes in the artistic arena in Brazil. Transnational issues of political poetry—from Plato to contemporary Latin America—found forceful expression, moreover, in this Brazilian experience. *Violão de rua* remains, whether as object of critique or of affirmation, an emphatic point of reference in cultural history.

*[There is in every substance its negative / and the possibility of process / Inexorable process to go to the end / a goal to be of bread and flowers / the rose will be another rose / and we will no longer be / I see in the sad eyes / a possible son / I see in the old tree in the park / a chair, a crutch, but above all a battering ram]

chapter four

The Orphic Imperative: Lyric, Lyrics,

and the Poetry of Song

If literary compendiums wish to understand this extremely complex period of our culture, they will have to come to terms with the realm of discography. In the new chapter of Brazilian poetry that began in 1967, everything, or almost everything, ends up on records. —Augusto de Campos (1972)

A singular aspect of the contemporary culture of Brazil is the recognition of urban popular music as one of the nation's richest artistic manifestations.[1] Among the reasons cultural analysts have been drawn to songwriting of the 1960s, and beyond, is its lyrical sophistication. The remarkable craft of songwriters and lyricists has made "the poetry of song" a frame of reference for critics of music and literature alike. For many, there is no question whether figures of popular music have made a contribution to national poetry, only to what extent they have. In the late sixties, the ever attentive Augusto de Campos proclaimed that the most inventive new Brazilian poetry was being produced in the realm of song.[2] This idea was seconded by literary critics of the stature of Antonio Candido, Haroldo de Campos, and Afrânio Coutinho, from their respective vantage points, and numerous others have addressed the textual qualities of the work of leading songwriters. While some hold that the dominant poetic mode of song lasted only through the early seventies, the extraordinary flourishing of lyrically distinctive popular music continued throughout that decade, and, in some cases, into the eighties.[3] Keeping ever present the natural limitations that the print medium imposes on musical phenomena, this chapter will explore the dimensions of song in Brazil's contemporary poetry. The two most prominent names of the current of post–Bossa Nova popular music known as MPB (*música popular brasileira*), Chico Buarque (b. 1944) and Caetano Veloso (b. 1942), have often been regarded not only as Brazil's leading performing songwriters but also as the major poetic voices of their generation; accordingly, the present chapter will feature their work. Further attention will be paid to other songwriters with poetic inclinations and select lyricists. As a prelude to this, we will consider precedents in Brazilian cultural history to the poets of popular music of the 1960s and raise necessary questions of approach to song, its text, and the history of poetry.

Ars Lyrica: Lyrics (Song Text) as Lyric (Poetry)

With few exceptions, academic studies of the interrelations of music and poetry are concerned with classical or so-called art music.[4] Historically, this orientation is linked to the institutionalization of concepts of high art and low art. Such distinctions are often justified in studies of word-music relations, because lyrical elaboration in the popular sphere — in Europe and the Americas alike — has been so limited, both by tradition and commercial circumstances. Central to considerations of song text in any category is the unending debate about the relative importance of sound and the verbal in vocal music. Steven Scher has provided an excellent overview and bibliography of such musico-literary issues.[5] He establishes three broad divisions of orientation: (1) "Music in literature," which considers writers' use of musical structures and the sound qualities of verse; (2) "Literature in music," which considers program music and literary sources of composition; and (3) "Music and literature," covering vocal music and art song with texts drawn from literature. Entirely absent from this account is the potential role of song lyrics in the domain of poetry of a given nation. To assign a place to the discourse of popular music in accounts of contemporary poetry in Brazil is, then, like the song texts that motivate such a position, innovative. Linking modern song to the category of poetry, generally considered part of the domain of literature, always brings with it numerous problems of appraisal.

After the troubadours of Provence and Iberia, the separation of music and poetry, and the poet-composers of the English Renaissance, it is quite rare that songwriters or lyricists should be considered as contributors to Western poetry. In the 1960s, with the sui generis Bob Dylan at the fore, there was in the Anglo-American realm a so-called "poetry of rock," which was significant enough to merit an entry in the *Princeton Encyclopedia of Poetry and Poetics*. While rock's overall cultural impact has been massive and pervasive, rock text never really came to be regarded, by either the public or critics, as an important manifestation of lyric. With the nearly absolute triumph of commercialism in popular music in the 1970s, little additional thought was given to the poetry of rock.[6] By contrast, in Brazil, the world's second largest musical system, the 1960s witnessed the emergence of a series of poet-composers who made the topic of popular music and poetry a real and lasting issue for music-makers, their public, and critics. In assessments of contemporary Brazilian poetry, the place of song, like that of concrete poetry, is simply much greater than in North American or European literatures.

Treating song text as a kind of poetry, and by extension as literature, requires, of course, appropriate modifications of analytical perspective. As soon as Brazilian literary critics began to discuss song discourse, the need for distinctions became evident. One might have to make a fundamental clarification of limits — that the poetry of song is not all inclusive but a tendency *within* the field of popular music — or establish some ground rules of operation. Questions that arise when evaluating the poetic character of song include those of quality, technique, transmission, including print transcription of lyrics, and reception by public and critics. Admonitions about the dangers of "reading" the text of vocal music are wholly necessary, but cannot be taken to absolute extremes. Lyrics (song texts) can in some ways be treated as "literary" items (a particular kind of poetry) without losing sight of the natural musical dimension or of the debate about the relative weight of words in music. One's first concern must be song's occurrence in acoustic, real time, which makes song less accessible than a written text, which can be consulted indefinitely. Yet compensation may come with repetition, memory (a mental text), and/or transcription of words, often for publication. A print register of a song text fulfills a secondary function, which may become significant, as suggested below. One ought to hear performative vocal effects and consider how musical features (melody, harmony, tempo) may relate to mood or verbal tones of the text. In any case, if page poetry has an implicit "speaker," the lyric self or poetic "I" of song lyrics can be thought of as a "singer." Discussion of the fictive singer's "qualities of mind" should involve, to use the words of a philosopher of art, "musical substance."[7]

Compositional complexity also impinges on judgments, since music intervenes to varying degrees in song. From a literary point of view, Northrop Frye wrote that "in modern combinations of music and poetry one art regularly absorbs the other," with art song being an example of musical dominance and folk song of verbal strength.[8] Contemporary popular music comes in diverse molds and can lean either way, or fall somewhere in between. When considering song texts (not canonized poems selected by a composer to be set), one should be less concerned with whether musical form inherently precludes poetization, and more with what *actually happens* in song. It is, after all, the strength of textual evidence that has driven the discussion of the poetry of popular music in Brazil. Convention and marketing attitudes have impoverished lyrical aspects of most popular song everywhere, but this is not necessarily due to any *ontology* of form.[9] Given the broad range of possibilities for its consumption, a certain mode of song ought to be able to be taken as a medium of communication with literary potential, especially if it can be shown that listeners are intent on hearing, consciously choosing to focus on words as they are sung, as historical circumstances determined in contemporary Brazil. Moreover, if tension and rhetorical control mark songs' verbal structures, some literary parameters may well be called for to understand them. A complete, integral appreciation in the acoustic dimension is achieved through such concepts as "performed litera-ture."[10] It is further imperative to avoid the "imperialism" of comparing out-of-context lyrics to poems.[11] If given songs provoke poetic re-sponses, and if "literary" claims are made for a portion of songs, the discourse of popular music in general certainly cannot be evaluated by such standards.

   Textual evaluation of song invariably leads to the thorny issue of song lyric in written manifestations. As Bertrand Bronson says of the work of the lutenist songwriters, their verses can be read with delight but only fully experienced in the musical setting.[12] But if a given song text, be-yond its musical function, indeed enjoys "readability," is there any reason to deny this? What must be avoided is judgmental negativity or rejection of song texts based on reading alone. On another level, the lyric sheet or published song text does have bearing on lyrics as a literary manifesta-tion. Song texts in print may be a secondary mode of artistic communi-cation with literary pertinence. In the United States, David Pichaske points to the printing of song lyrics and poems with records as evidence of the widening cultural significance of popular music in the 1960s.[13] The same and more can be argued for the Brazilian case. Beginning in the late sixties, the lyrics of Buarque, and of many others to follow, were regularly made available as reading on record jackets, on show programs, in songbooks, in literary magazines, and as selections in anthologies. Shifting cultural attitudes are further seen in the symbiosis of sound and print transmission of lyrics. In many instances, Brazilian songwriters and lyricists demonstrate writerly intentions when they put their words on jackets or inserts. One encounters customized structuring of verses and lyrical layout with concern for visual effects. Typographical devices are employed in deliberate fashion, and epigraphs or commentary often accompany the lyrics. Record albums, then, may be a source for poetic production in two senses: first, as registers of performed (recorded) lyrics, and second, as the primary site of the printed versions of song texts, which are by-products of the sound recordings. The publication of lyrics separate from LPs is also directly relevant to the proposal of incorporating song into the study of lyric. Many Brazilian songwriters have published books of musical texts, and many lyricists have included their song texts in books of poetry. In such cases, words to songs are published not as sing-along aids but to give value to the text itself in a context other than singing. The frequent publication of song texts also provides biographical evidence of the intersection of the cultural orders of music and literature.

The Poetization of Brazilian Song

In what specific ways did MPB exhibit an artful complexity that turned the heads of critics usually attuned to literature alone and that convinced other cultural critics of the validity of speaking of "the poetry of song"? In a general sense, there was sustained concern with the manipulation of formal features (meter, rhyme, etc.) and with the structuring of ideas. Complex wordplay and constructs were common. Subtlety of phrase, ambiguity, metaphor, and allegory were part of an effort to enhance the level of song, which was encouraged by historical conditions. After the 1964 military coup and the 1968 institution of total dictatorship, censorship became a severe problem. The Brazilian public, especially politically committed university youth, looked to music to express sentiments and ideas prohibited in truncated political discourse. Figurative language was a necessary strategy to sidestep censors. From an affective viewpoint, lyrics also elaborated on the anguish and sense of loss experienced by many in collective repressive circumstances. The lyrical surrealism of sixties hallucinogenic culture in North America also became evident in Brazil.

From the viewpoint of literature, one of the most significant aspects of MPB has been intertextuality, in a broad sense encompassing musicalizations, partial settings, structural allusion, homage, rewritings, and parody of literary sources.[14] Settings of well-known poems do not contribute, since the texts are not new, to the poetry of song per se and thus are less significant for a nontraditional literary history, but they do change the channel of communication and help establish a literary ambience in the musical context. Sociocultural commentary in original Brazilian songs was based on different literary eras and styles — the baroque, romantic, Parnassian, symbolist, and, especially, modernist, and beyond. By turning to literature for inspiration, songwriters sought increased legitimation. They further enhanced humor, particular meaning, and points of comparison with the present.

A good example of the intertextual approach in popular music is Chico Buarque's lyric "Sabiá" (Songbird) (1968), a reformulation of Gonçalves Dias's "The Song of Exile" (1843), a classic romantic poem of longing for the homeland in exile, and one of the most parodied of all Brazilian poems. Many other lyricists have alluded to the poem in a vein of literary parody or to mock antiquated aesthetic values in general. Such song texts contribute to an ongoing literary paradigm; and a mapping of the topos would be incomplete without the musical instances. At the same time, a full comprehension of related songs is unthinkable without a grasp of the literary information alluded to therein.

Many contemporary Brazilian songs echo literary heritage with texts that implement other epochal styles or show close affinities. Lyricists have bordered on symbolist modes of expression by relying on suggestive imagery and lush alliteration in contemplations of self or the pursuit of transcendence. A good number of recent songs are reminiscent of the free verse, iconoclasm, and ironic stances of *modernismo*. Lyricists who worked with the internationally acclaimed vocalist-composer Milton Nascimento often developed retrospective or introspective song texts based on key modernist referents, as seen later in this chapter. Veloso's juxtapositions of primitive and modern phenomena in parodic or visionary songs relive Oswald de Andrade's tropical cubism. Other lyric writers have explored the sonority of the indigenous strain in Brazilian Portuguese, as the dean of modernist poets, Manuel Bandeira, had done decades earlier. This musico-literary affinity can be heard in the following two excerpts. The first, in the nationalist spirit of *modernismo,* is from Bandeira's mellifluous "Berimbau" (1924), inspired in folk legend (the title is the name of an Afro-Brazilian bow-and-gourd musical instrument) and built with words of indigenous origin (not in European Portuguese dictionaries). Sound patterns are central here; no translation is necessary to perceive visually and imagine the auditory aims of the first strophe:

Os aguapés dos aguaçais
nos igapós dos Japurás
bolem, bolem, bolem.
Chama o saci: — Si si si si!
— Ui ui ui ui ui! uiva a iara.
Nos aguaçais dos Igapós
dos Japurás e dos Purus . . .

And in a late seventies song by a leading MPB artist one finds much the
same approach:

. . . Suco de suru rucu / diga lá jacu / cutia comadre
posta de pira rucu / diga lá caju / barata cascuda
carangue jeira / saúva coruja / rastro de/jara rucu
jarara coral / piranha colunga . . . purus jurua . . .[15]

Again, the text is left in the original, since meaning is clearly subordinated to observable formal features: alliterative continuity, variety of
rhyme, and verbal melodics. Some of the words are actually neologisms,
variations, or derivatives, crafted for the sake of intensity of sound.

On another front, visual and experimental values of MPB are revealed
in the impact that concrete poetry had on popular music in terms of
attitude, actual text, and overall organization. In the wake of concretism,
songwriters attuned to the (neo-) avant-garde tried out nonlinear syntax, geometric textual designs, and techniques such as verbal decomposition, morphemic juxtaposition, or phonemic concatenations. Superimposition of voices or interplay of voice and instruments paralleled similar
structural effects of page-poetry.[16]

Given that literary connections in MPB stretch from the baroque to the
very modern, a key clarification about musical lyricism is in order. Lest it
be thought that song came under critical scrutiny solely because so much
literary material was used, it should be emphasized that song repertories
revealed many poetic innovations of their own and that this sui generis
creativity was largely responsible for the critical attention paid to popular music. Some argued that poets had *chosen* music as a vehicle since
electronic media (sound recording, radio, TV) offered much greater
exposure. This argument is fallacious, since it assumes that a poet can
simply conjure up musical ability or a composer partner/cowriter at
will. The most significant cases of musical lyricism in Brazil involve
songwriters with a fundamentally musical vocation, not poets who saw
greater opportunities in music.

Precedents: Portuguese Roots to the Musical Stage

There were notable precedents to the forceful emergence of musical lyricism in the sixties. Discussions of the relations of music and poetry naturally revert to the later Middle Ages, when all poetry was still made as song. Historical accounts of European literature generally cite the art of the troubadours of Provence and the *trouvères* of northern France as the first manifestations of lyric poetry. The initial chapters of any history of Portuguese literature deal with medieval *trovadores,* whose songs received the strong influence of the courtly masters of Provence. The first collections of poetry in the Iberian Peninsula were the songbooks — *cancioneiros/cancioneros* — organized by royalty to preserve oral traditions of sung poetry. During the Renaissance, poetry began to develop as an art independent of musical accompaniment, but the birth of literature in colonial Brazil is marked by the continuing presence of medieval tradition. As a leading chronicler wrote: "From the Middle Ages came our old poetic yardstick, in the form of popular lyrics and courtly versions of troubadour ballads . . . the importance of the medieval legacy is broad, because sixteenth-century Brazil . . . is a continuation of the Middle Ages."[17]

The principal poet of the baroque period in Brazil, Gregório de Matos (1623–1696), cultivated Iberian *conceptismo* and serious religious poetry but was also an avid troubadour of sensual love lyrics and satirical songs. One of the first historians of Brazilian literature called the bard "The Homer of the Lundu" (an early Afro-Brazilian song form), noting his application of poetic skills in nascent forms of popular music.[18] There were no printing presses in the Portuguese colony of Brazil, and Matos's work was not published in his lifetime. His lyrics circulated in manuscript copies, some of which were likely texts of songs he performed accompanying himself on the guitarlike instrument, the *viola.* The caustic "Boca do Inferno" (Mouth from Hell), as the poet was nicknamed, moved in both aristocratic and popular circles, which is reflected in his verse. Matos authored "Triste Bahia," a sonnet that Veloso appropriated for musical use, and the editor of the baroque figure's complete works has pointedly compared his social roles and poetic attitudes to those of that key figure of MPB.[19]

During the pre-romantic Arcadian period, the Brazilian mulatto Domingos Caldas Barbosa (1738–1800) made a splash in the court of Lisbon by introducing the sentimental and sensual song types of *modinha* and *lundu.* Although this poet-performer was one of the founders of the resurrected literary academy in the Portuguese capital, the *Nova*

Arcadia (1790), usually thought of as a place for stiff neoclassical formalism, he also brought an emollient, affected note into verse of the day. The instrument he used when singing his texts is reflected in the title of his collected poetic works, *Viola de Lereno* (2 vols., 1798–1823), alongside the pen name he adopted.[20]

Brazil's romantic poets of the nineteenth century found that the sentimentality of the *modinha* form, popularized by the success of Caldas Barbosa, blended well with their concern for increased appeal to individual emotion. The language of the *modinha* and that of early romantic poetry have much in common, and a noted musical scholar believes that the verbosity of midcentury songs designed for performance in aristocratic salons can be attributed to a transference of literary standards.[21] Among the recognized poets of the second romantic generation, Laurindo Rabelo (1826–1864) maintained the closest relations with popular music, penning both literary verse and lyrics for his own songs. His *modinha* texts were included in his complete works. A leading historian of Brazilian literature likens Rabelo to Catulo da Paixão Cearense (1863–1946), a noted performer of the early twentieth century who revitalized the *modinha* in Rio de Janeiro and pompously dressed the folk verse of the backlands in literary publications.[22]

There are occasional instances of participation in urban popular music by literary poets of the first quarter of the twentieth century. Some late Parnassian writers composed song texts, as did a few early adherents to *modernismo*. The most important example of a practicing poet who crossed lines in the twenties and thirties is Orestes Barbosa (1893–1966), who, while being recognized as a columnist and poet, is best remembered for his musical lyrics. Manuel Bandeira once cited a line of his from the song "Chão de estrelas"—"tu pisavas os astros distraída" (inattentive you went stepping on the stars)—as one of the most beautiful in the Portuguese language.

Songwriter-lyricist Noel Rosa (1910–1937), unlike the authors mentioned above, had no connection to the literary world, yet he has been discussed as an example of "literary quality" in song. He is one of the outstanding figures in the emergence of samba as the dominant genre in early urban popular music. Rosa gained the nickname "The Philosopher of Samba" for the contemplative character of much of his verse and for his subtle powers of sociocultural observation. To give an indication of the respect he maintains in Brazil, he has been included in educational publications about literary figures.[23] The controlled colloquial language of Rosa's sambas corresponds in some ways to contemporaneous developments in *modernismo,* but this rough equivalence is instinctive rather than deliberate. This songwriter's verbal agility, wit, and wisdom were isolated instances in his time, and his true legacy came to be realized with the emergence of the poet-musicians of the sixties.

The transition to that generation is marked by the prominent participation of Vinícius de Morais in music. He was one of the noteworthy poets of the second, less nationalistic generation of *modernismo* beginning in the 1930s. In the 1950s, as his most popular books were appearing, he turned his talents to songwriting, teaming most notably with Antônio Carlos Jobim (1927–1994). They wrote the lead song for the award-winning French film *Black Orpheus,* which was based on Morais's verse-play *Orfeu da Conceição,* a re-creation of the Orpheus myth in the midst of Brazilian *carnaval.* From the beginning of the Bossa Nova movement (1958), Morais was the most prolific and successful lyricist of the style he helped to define, producing some two hundred titles. The poet's musical lyricism, for the most part, stayed within conventional linguistic and thematic bounds (emotional experience and courtship), with some significant exceptions. Morais had some part in the early sixties movement of *engagé* poetry anthologized in *Violão de rua,* a title with special regard for the musical vehicle. Songs of the second phase of Bossa Nova, in turn, often showed close stylistic and ideological affinities with the poetry of social commitment. The closest Morais came to such a mind-set was the series of "afro-sambas" he wrote with composer-guitarist Baden Powell (the best known of which is "Berimbau," not related to Bandeira's above-cited poem).

As a lyricist, Morais exhibited certain literary tones, careful diction, controlled exposition, and technical precision in coordinating words and melody. His song verse is, however, not noted for any innovative use of language or structuring.[24] What was most important in terms of the relationship of poetry and music was his professional example. The testimony of lyricists and songwriters alike has confirmed that Morais was an inspiration and a challenge for the younger generation. In the 1960s, as a recognized poet and former career diplomat, he brought a previously unthinkable dignity and status to popular music. In the 1960s and 1970s, poets neither avoided the field of music nor felt any associated inferiority. On the contrary, songwriters were now able to enjoy a sort of artistic prestige, in addition to the admiration afforded entertainers. Morais himself began to perform in the 1960s, and his stage appearances (and recordings) included recitations and musical versions of his best-loved poems. The poet Vinícius de Morais, in sum, adapted music to verse, brought a new sophistication to songwriting, stimulated audience response to performed poetry, and provided a general model of musical

expressivity to be emulated. He built a stage of musico-poetic communi-
cation in Brazil on which many figures would subsequently perform.

Chico Buarque: Banding Poetry and Music

No contemporary songwriter has garnered wider critical acclaim in Bra-
zil than Francisco "Chico" Buarque de Holanda (b. 1944, Rio de Ja-
neiro). Songs represent the greater part of the artist's output, which also
encompasses drama and fiction, including a short novel translated into
several languages.[25] One of the best analysts of Buarque's work believes
that poetic impulses underlie the entirety of his output:

> all his multiple activities can be reduced to a common denominator:
> songwriter, dramatist, and fiction writer meet, knocking down bar-
> riers of genre and form, under the sign of the *poet*. Chico Buarque is
> an artisan of language. With him, words acquire in their fluidity,
> something of alchemy, something magical.[26]

From the outset, Buarque's carefully crafted song texts were rich in
rhyme, rhythm, and sound effects. A poetically coherent lexical selection
and structuring of text was complemented by functional imagery and
symbols. While fundamentally traditional in approach and language,
Buarque used diverse personae, and his particular use of feminine voices
distinguished his uncommon psychological insight. His early songs
(1965–1969) expressed what might be termed a "mytho-magical" con-
cept of song, and numerous other works proved to be true masterpieces
of social criticism. In both instances, the songwriter demonstrated a
special capacity for reflection on his artistic self, the creative process, and
the evolution of MPB. One aspect of his contribution is the dramatic
mode of performed literature. In fact, Buarque's partial setting of João
Cabral de Melo Neto's "Morte e vida severina" marked the beginning of
a musical career that would have constant literary overtones. For exam-
ple, Buarque's metaphorically rich and socially relevant "Rosa dos
ventos" (Weathervane, 1969) can be illuminated via its textual and stylis-
tic links with a historical sequence by the neosymbolist modernist poet
Cecília Meireles. Throughout, Buarque has blended linguistic and musi-
cal effects to intensify mood, to create nuances, and to produce irony.

Music and song in themselves are recurring themes in Buarque's
sixties production. The word *samba* takes on multiple meanings in a
series of compositions, signifying — in addition to the typical Brazilian
rhythm, music, and dance — song itself, the plenitude of experience, or
the material or object of poetry. This is evident in the songwriter's first

ars poetica, "Tem mais samba" (There's more samba, 1966), whose lyric is constructed as a string of defining comparative metaphors and a pair of optimistic conclusions tied to musical changes (see *MCBS,* 8–10). In contrast, other songs of the period create a poetic space of loss and disillusionment. Anxiety, want of comprehension, and exclusion from shared intimacy resonate in symbolic setups that fortify sung laments and complaints.

Buarque's adroitness is demonstrated in his fitting of words to the melody of Jobim in the ballad "Retrato em branco e preto" (Portrait in black and white, 1968). The lyric — reminiscent of the romantic poems of Vinícius de Morais — is sonnetlike with its two stanzas of fourteen lines of varying length (according to the extension of melodic phrases). The rhyme scheme is challenging (AABCCBDDDDEFFE), and there is no exact repetition of syllabic design in the second strophe. The beauty of the lyric has much to do with Portuguese sound features, the frequency of sibilants at the outset, and the ("o" dominant) vocalic ring at the beginning of the second part:

> Já conheço os passos dessa estrada
> Sei que não vai dar em nada
> Seus segredos sei de cor
> Já conheço as pedras do caminho
> E sei também que ali sozinho
> Eu vou ficar, tanto pior
> O que é que eu posso contra o encanto
> Desse amor que nego tanto
> Evito tanto
> E que no entanto
> Volta sempre a enfeitiçar
> Com seus mesmos tristes velhos fatos
> Que num álbum de retratos
> Eu teimo em colecionar.
>
> Lá vou eu de novo como um tolo
> Procurar o desconsolo
> Que cansei de conhecer
> Novos dias tristes, noites claras
> Versos, cartas, minha cara
> Ainda volto a lhe escrever
> Pra lhe dizer que isso é pecado
> Eu trago o peito tão marcado
> De lembranças do passado

E você sabe a razão
Vou colecionar mais um soneto
Outro retrato em branco e preto
A maltratar meu coração.[27]*

What is interesting in the second part, from a musico-literary point of view, is the connection between the anticipation of further distress and the emotional release through writing. The lyric voice foresees a continuing interpretation of experience through poetry and visual artifacts. The word "sonnet" is associated with photographs through rhyme, syntactical juxtaposition, reiteration of "collect," and, in vocal performance, the fusion of *soneto* and *outro* (another). The black-and-white photo image underlies the symmetry of the text and the emotive conflict the singer embodies (empirical knowledge of suffering vs. inability to resist involvement). Thus, the song is a successful reworking of a time-honored amorous theme and an implicit portrait of an artistic self as well. Several other of Buarque's own sixties songs reveal a central meta-musico-linguistic character with both individual and social implications.

The key social paradigm in Buarque's repertory begins with the song "Pedro Pedreiro" (1965), a remarkable samba–Bossa Nova whose text, with a unique sound fabric, depicts the revealing ruminations of a common worker (see *MCBS,* 13–16). The character of the song, a bricklayer/construction worker, is written into the conclusion of the preface of a songbook that the young Buarque published the year of his first LP:

E este livro é bem meu samba (não samba-ritmo- mas samba no seu sentido mais largo). O samba que uma criança andou cantarolando. E que um pedreiro pendurado num andaime, mesmo assim achou de assobiar . . .[28]**

---

*[I already know the steps of this road / I know it won't lead anywhere / I know its secret by heart / I know the stones in the roadway / and I know too that alone there / It's only going to get worse for me / How can I fight the enchantment / of this love that I so deny / So avoid and that yet / always comes back to bewitch me / With the same old sad facts / that I keep on collecting / in a photo album

There I go again like a fool / looking for the distress / I'm so tired of knowing / More sad days, clear nights / Verses, letters, my dear / I shall still write you / To tell you that this is sin / And my breast is marked / by the memories of the past / and you know the reason / I'm going to collect another sonnet / another black-and-white portrait / to mistreat my heart]

**[And this book is really my samba (not samba-rhythm — but samba in its wider sense). The samba that a kid was humming. And that a bricklayer, hanging off a scaffolding, still thought he would whistle]

This image of a precariously perched construction worker recurs, subtlely, in a pair of interconnected titles that show Buarque's compositional dexterity and intensely social discourse: "Deus lhe pague" (May God reward you, 1970) and "Construção" (Construction, 1970), a piece of musical architecture built on multiple word shifts. Antiregime and democratic sentiment is further poeticized in such songs as "Cotidiano" (Quotidian) and the surreptitious "Corrente" (Chain). In terms of lyrical extension, figurative language, and conceptual provocation, no song of Buarque's matches "O que será" (What could it be, 1976), whose singular text stands firmly on its own.

The pace of Buarque's output of song decreased in the 1980s, and the overriding sensation of poeticity in his music slackens somewhat. Still, the fundamental linguistic consciousness that permeates his songwriting is never lost. There is no better testimony to this than the composition "Uma palavra" (A word, 1989), where Buarque muses:

> Palavra prima / Uma palavra só, a crua palavra
> Que quer dizer / Tudo / Anterior ao entendimento, palavra
> Palavra viva / Palavra com temperatura, palavra
> Que se produz / Muda / Feira de luz, mais que de vento, palavra
>
> . . . .
>
> Palavra minha / Matéria, minha criatura, palavra
> Que me conduz / Mudo / E que me escreve desatento, palavra
>
> Talvez, à noite / Quase-palavra que um de nós murmura
> Que ela mistura as letras, que eu invento
> Outras pronúncias do prazer, palavra[29]*
>
> . . . .

The pleasure of "wordwork" that Buarque expresses here is undeniable as a central facet of his work; it surfaces with still greater intensity in the music of another poet-songwriter of Buarque's generation, with whom he is often compared.

From Modernism to Samba-Rap: Other Words of Caetano Veloso

Since the mid-1960s the leading innovator in Brazilian popular music has been Caetano Veloso. His contributions to the domain of song en-

---

*[Prime word cousin / a sole word, raw word / that means / everything / Before understanding, word / Live word / Word with temperature, word / that is produced / mute /

compass new performative designs, multifarious sound frames, and tire-
less pursuit of conceptual composition, often involving distinctive tex-
tual approaches. In this regard, Veloso is, for many, not just the poet
laureate of song but the most compelling poetic voice of his generation
in any medium. As far as lyrical aspects are concerned, his varied output
includes mellifluous amorous pieces, spiritual contemplations, philo-
sophical expressions in a "pop" vein, brief epiphanical pieces, nonlinear
experiments, longer visionary accounts of experience, numerous titles
drawn from literature, and a series of metalinguistic works. Throughout
this select repertory, there is an artistic tension of striking imagery and
harmonized, or dissonant, turns of phrase. Veloso, in addition, has pub-
lished a few items that help establish his stature as a poet and illuminate
his musical lyricism.

At the beginning of his career, the songwriter indicated that he was
trying to develop poetic consciousness in his first songs in the Bossa
Nova vein, which is evident in such titles as "Coração vagabundo" (Vag-
abond heart, 1967).[30] After these early compositions within contained
sentimental frames, a constant dialectic of emotive affirmation and de-
nial tinges Veloso's poetry of song. There is an overarching competition
between the "romantic" and more technically aware and ludic impulses.
The poet-composer gives voice to this counterposition in an early light-
rock dare "Não identificado" (Unidentified, 1969) and in the later, sig-
nificantly open, declaration of principles, "Outras Palavras" (Other
words, 1981). In the former, Veloso casually interjects a rare and reveal-
ing rhyme: "Eu vou fazer/ um iê-iê-iê romântico/ um antico/ mputa-
dor . . ." (I'm going to make/ a romantic yeah-yeah-yeah/ an antico/
mputer . . .), while in the latter song, Veloso's self-retort is: "Tinjo-me
romântico mas sou vadio computador" (I paint myself romantic but I'm
a vagrant computer).[31]

This sort of demythification of conventional affective discourse also
emerges in the unusual verbal harmonies of "Clara" (1968), in which
images of light, clarity, and color structure a none too evident cubistlike
narration of a separation of lovers. Additive rhymes, anagrams, and par-
onymous forms interrelate in a context of dispersion. Truncated state-
ments, phrases from imaginary monologues, and isolated flashes are

---

a fair of light, more than of wind, word. . . . My word / Matter, my creature, word / that
leads me / mute / and that writes me unmindful, word / Maybe at night / Quasi-word that
one of us murmurs / that she mixes up the letters, that I invent / Other pronunciations of
pleasure, word. . . .]

strung together in a sonorous spatialization, as suggested in this intentional transcription (*Balanço* 175) by Augusto de Campos:

quando a manhã madrugava
calma
alta
clara
clara morria de amor.
    faca de ponta flor e flor
    cambraia branca sob o sol
    cravina branca amor
    cravina amor
    cravina e sonha
    a moça chamada clara
água
alma
lava
alva cambraia no sol . . .*

In historical terms, this poetically "illuminating" song figured on an album that proved to be the foundational document of a popular musical movement of quite wide-ranging effect.

In the late 1960s, Veloso was the most provocative voice of a short-lived but extremely influential vanguard called *tropicalismo* or, after an allegorical and manifesto-like song of his, "Tropicália." The Tropicalists — Veloso; fellow singer-songwriters from Bahia, Gilberto Gil (b. 1942) and Tom Zé (b. 1936); poet-lyricists Torquato Neto (1944–1972) and José Carlos Capinan (b. 1941); and other performers and arrangers — collectively effected a critical revision of Brazilian culture through music and instituted new paradigms of plurality. Their work is concentrated in one collection, the concept album, *Tropicália ou panis et circensis*.[32] Building a "neo-anthropophagic" strategy of contrast and appropriation, indebted to the modernist projects of Oswald de Andrade, as well as to concretism, the young poet-musicians availed themselves of diverse sources — national and international, musical and nonmusical — to revitalize Brazilian popular music and its discourse. The open-ended designs of Tropicalism made for a curious "intellectualization" of popu-

---

*[when the morning dawned / calm / high / clear / Clara was dying of love / pointed knife flower and flower / white cambric beneath the sun / white grass pink love / grass pink love / grass pink and dreams / the maiden called Clara / water / soul / lava (washes) / white dawn cambric in the sun . . .]

lar music, permitting links with folk verse and vanguard poetics alike. Among the contributions of Veloso's group was the infusion of substantial literary material into song, whether for parodic or otherwise provocative purposes. Tropicalist colleagues introduced significant fragmentation and plurisignification into musical poetics, seeking to get beyond the linearity of most socially committed ("protest") song and poetry (i.e., *Violão de rua*), as well as the simple emotional appeal of traditional musical lyricism, as seen above in "Clara." Tropicalism meant a more complex and sophisticated notion of song, which became a vehicle to exercise refined parody, sociocultural allegory, and different nondiscursive approaches.

Following the official phase of Tropicalism (1968–69), an unmistakable avant-garde imprint is evident in the work of Caetano Veloso. He recorded some performed poems (e.g., "Acrilírico," 1969) and did not shy away from risks, especially in one extremely controversial early seventies collection.[33] In the same period, Veloso made some symptomatic contributions to arts journals, explored in the next chapter as vehicles of youth poetry. The following lines of Veloso's, the lyrical opening of an extended mixed piece, reveal notions of contrast, fusion, and visual representation found in contemporaneous songs:

> sais eram (espelho) maresias
> eram olhe (pés, mãos) onde   anda
>   nada
>   do
> ainda   soam doen
> no meu coração de poeta   romântico
> antigo amor
> (sempre o mar e aquilo que o mar espelha)
> as palavras . . .[34]*

The most fundamental of all the encounters in Veloso's art—poetic expression and singing—is explored in another untitled poem with a fundamental graphic element, triangulated photos of a human bust (head/throat) which balance, reflect, and echo the similarly shaped text shown in example 11. The double repetition of the text—suggested in the seventh line and as if in a round song or refrain—evokes actual singing,

---

*[salts were (mirror) sea breezes / they were look! (feet, hands) where goes
    nothing   -of -still   they sound ach[-ing]
    in my heart of a romantic poet   old love
    (always the sea and that which the sea mirrors) words]

ar
o ar
continuar
antes do sopro
cantar
cantar e o momento:
a uma só vez, três, nós
e sofro o sim do silêncio
desde o a do canto até o z da voz

ar
o ar
continuar
antes do sopro
cantar
cantar e o momento:
a uma só vez, três, nós
e sofro o sim do silêncio
desde o a do canto até o z da voz

ar
o ar
continuar
antes do sopro
cantar
cantar e o momento:
a uma só vez, três, nós
e sofro o sim do silêncio
desde o a do canto até o z da voz

Example 11*

*[air / the air / to continue / before (the) breath / to sing / to sing and the moment / at once, three, we / and I suffer the yes of silence / from the *a* of *canto* (song) to the *z* of *voz* (voice)]

relating it to writing with use of the first and last characters of the alphabet. The letter *a* begins the spelling of *ar* (air), which connotes the making of sound through the vocal cords. The letter *z,* final graph of the alphabet and the text, completes articulation of the word *voz* (voice). This symbolic treatment of vocal production in print actualizes an intersemiotic theme and helps to keep in focus the poetic fabric of Veloso's songwriting.

That consistently realized potential is one of many issues raised in a pair of unusual press releases Veloso wrote for the complementary albums *Jóia* (Gem) and *Qualquer Coisa* (Any old thing).[35] The writings are mock manifestos that, while intended to play a trick on critics avid for "movements" since the demise of Tropicalism, belong to the artist's poetic repertory. In the seemingly contradictory documents, juxtaposition and playfulness are central, as they are in the musical projects that they accompany. While the twin declarations are not to be taken as serious proposals, they do reflect the role of literary concepts in Veloso's songwriting. In particular, they suggest the key avant-garde element. Issuing manifestos is characteristic of vanguard mentality and practice, and Veloso's case is no exception. The apparent chaos in his texts is reminiscent of dadaism, which is consistent with the poet-songwriter's concern for innovation and vitalization of the musical arts. With their reliance on humor, fragmentation, and paradoxical language, the dual manifestos further revive the spirit of Oswald de Andrade and the declarations of his two movements. One of his poetic fragments is in fact set to music as a samba on one of the albums. Beyond this gesture, Veloso's publications of prose and poetry, while relatively few, prove to be a significant facet of his artistic edifice in the 1970s.

Into the 1980s, Veloso sustained various modes of melodious expressivity in his poetry of song. He continued to cultivate a broad-based musical lyricism of mystical, cosmological, and existential weight. Considering this thematic, often intertextual, breadth, the ever insightful José Miguel Wisnik summarizes the depth of Veloso's poetic vision:

> Caetano reads destiny through the labyrinth of language, the labyrinth of songs, he knows how to come and go through that labyrinth; and when he comes back to the beginning, in solitude/ solidarity, he indicates what exists *there.* It is in this way that he penetrates deeply into existence.[36]

Veloso's conceptually informed musicality involves linguistically focused, experimental compositions throughout his career. One of the most outstanding is "Língua" (Tongue, 1983), a philological samba-rap whose main theme is evolution and variation of language. This song, with its extensive text, helps form a recurring pattern on the artist's albums since the early eighties: the feature of a long, discursive, and poetically involved composition.

That function is fulfilled on the evocative *Estrangeiro* (Foreigner/ stranger, 1989) by the title track, which makes the "other" from abroad the operative image of the collection. The presentation of the album (produced in New York) may suggest the topos of the estranged or alienated Latin American artist in the metropolis, but a domestic Brazilian focus proves to be central. The quasi-recitative opens with different impressions of a national symbol — Rio de Janeiro's Guanabara Bay:

> O pintor Paul Gauguin amou a luz da Baía de Guanabara
> O compositor Cole Porter adorou as luzes na noite dela . . .
> O antropólogo Claude Lévi-Strauss detestou a Baía de Guanabara
> Pareceu-lhe uma boca banguela . . . *

In concert with these reported views, the album's cover art depicts the panoramic bay in a photo reproduction of a painting used for the live performance of *Estrangeiro,* a multicolored backdrop made for the 1967 staging of Oswald de Andrade's drama *O rei da vela* (The candle king), directed by José Celso Martinez Correa, whose wild production of the acrid antibourgeois farce was a major event of Tropicalism. The vanguard spirit of that movement is relived in Veloso's selection of the visual artifact and in his new image-laden songs. On a more metaphorical level, "O estrangeiro" refers to the vagaries of vision (blindness vs. insight) and perception itself. The song text plays out as a colorful dream sequence with apocalyptic strains that both questions touristic images of Rio and constructs a lyric self at odds with conventional interpretations of the city, the nation, and its guiding values.

At the song's conclusion Veloso sings, in English, "some may like a soft Brazilian singer/ but I've given up all attempts at perfection," rephrasing a Bob Dylan line to give it new contextual meaning. On the jacket of *Bringing It All Back Home* (Columbia CS 9128, 1967), Dylan wrote "my songs're written with the kettledrum in mind/ a touch of any anxious color. obvious. an' people perhaps like a soft brazilian singer . . . i have given up at making any attempt at perfection." Veloso's paraphrase aligns him with the early Dylan and suggests parallels with the initially

---

* [The painter Paul Gauguin loved the light of Guanabara Bay / the songwriter Cole Porter adored the light of her nights . . . / the anthropologist Claude Lévi-Strauss detested Guanabara Bay / To him it seemed like a toothless mouth . . .][37]

rebellious poet-songwriter, who was noted for literary leanings and for contrariness with literal-minded critics and followers expecting reportable coherence or a certain kind of established production. As a coda to an unsettling and "foreign" (rock-driven) song, Veloso's allusion is ironically "bringing it all back home," anticipating (negative) reactions to a particular vision and, in the context of Brazilian popular music in the U.S. market or of antirock sentiment in Brazil, affirming the individual course of the persona/composer, who follows aesthetic instinct rather than fashion or proscriptive values.

Since the days of Dylan and transitional Bossa Nova, such intertextuality has enriched Veloso's poetry of song. In 1991, he recorded another notable setting — "Circuladô de fulô" (Circulatin' flower-fan), an excerpt from Haroldo de Campos's massive prose-poetry project *Galáxias* — and had another notable encounter in music and literature with "A terceira margem do rio" (The third bank of the river), with music by Milton Nascimento and words by Veloso himself.[38] The composition is based on both songwriters' admiration for Brazil's renowned novelist João Guimarães Rosa. The song title is that of one of his best short stories, which heads an English-language collection of his short fiction.[39] In the speculative story, narrated by a son, the father of a backlands family ends up spending his life in a canoe in the middle of a river, without returning to either shore. Veloso's tightly structured lyric suggests both the expansive poeticity of Rosa's prose fiction (citing his last name) and the mystical qualities of the designated vocal interpreter.

Oco de pau que diz: / Eu sou madeira, beira / Boa, dá vau, tristriz
Risca certeira / Meio a meio o rio ri / Silencioso sério
Nosso pai não diz, diz: Risca terceira
Água da palavra / Água calada pura
Água da palavra / Água de rosa dura
Proa da palavra / Duro silêncio, nosso pai.
Margem da palavra / Entre as escuras duas
Margens da palavra / Clareira, luz madura
Rosa da palavra / Puro silêncio, nosso pai.
Meio a meio o rio ri / Por entre as árvores da vida
O rio riu, ri / Por sob a risca da canoa
O rio viu, vi / O que ninguém jamais olvida
Ouvi ouvi ouvi / A voz das águas
Asa da palavra / Asa parada agora
Casa da palavra / Onde o silêncio mora
Brasa da palavra / A hora clara, nosso pai.

Hora da palavra / Quando não se diz nada
Fora da palavra / Quando mais dentro aflora
Tora da palavra / Rio, pau enorme, nosso pai*

While designed for vocalist Nascimento and as a homage to a power-
ful story and writer, the poem-for-musical performance stands alone —
with its verbal rhythm, sound fabric, and images of the word — as testi-
monial to Veloso's "passion" for the tasks of the wordsmith and to the
figurative realm he creates and modifies with each new musical experi-
ence. His contribution to the poetry — of Brazil, of the contemporary
period, of song — remains continuous.

Completing the Chorus: A Generation of Poet-Composers

The songbooks of Veloso and Buarque are the source of the most salient
("literary quality") lyricism of Brazilian popular music since the 1960s.
Yet there are numerous other songwriters and lyricists of their genera-
tion whose work further defines the poetry of MPB as a cultural phenom-
enon of the sixties, seventies, and beyond. In the work of poet-com-
posers and authors of song texts from several regions of the country, and
representative of different styles, one finds ample material that is signifi-
cant in a musico-literary context. Diverse song repertories include wide-
ranging examples of lyrical craft, from the contemplative, the spiritual,
and the aesthetic to the ethical, the satirical, and the experimental.

    Among the most engaging compositions of Gilberto Gil are his musi-
cal inquiries into spiritual and epistemological questions. His interest in
Oriental religion, mysticism, androgyny, and euthenics has yielded curi-
ous lyrical explorations that test the limits of popular music. On a meta-
linguistic level, an outstanding instance of poetic consciousness in song is
Gil's "Metáfora" (Metaphor, 1982), whose text plays out as an elucida-

---

*[Hollow of timber that says: / I am wood, a shore / Good, river crossing / zigzag / stripe
hits the mark / half and half the river laughs / Serious silent one / Our father doesn't say, he
says: Third stripe / Water of the word / Pure quiet water / Water of the word / Water of
hard rose / Bow of the word / Hard silence, our father / River bank of the word / Among
the dark two / Margins of the word / Clearing, ripe light / Rose (Rosa) of the word / Pure
silence, our father / Half and half the river laughs / Between the trees of life / the river
laughed, it laughs / Beneath the canoe's stripe / the river saw, it sees / what no one ever
forgets / I heard heard heard / the voice of the waters / Wing of the word / Wings stopped
now / Home of the word / where silence resides / Embers of the word / The clearing hour,
our father / Time for words / when nothing is said / Outside of words / when deeper
down blossoms / Log of the word / River, enormous wood, our father]

```
A     DEUS
DEUS     A
AFRODITE
DE       TI
TI       VE
VI       DA
DA       DA
A     DEUS
```

Example 12

tion of figurative language and verbal interrelations, and as an apology for artful abstraction. On the theme of artistic inspiration, in the 1970s Gil composed a series of songs that feature (in titles and texts) the prefix *re-* and embody notions of renewal, renovation, reformulation, renaissance, etc. This concern encompasses Gil's cultivation of African-Brazilian legacies and a contemporary negritude, as well as his occasional experimentation with vanguardist techniques. All of these elements are reflected in a lyric Gil wrote for a collaboration with Veloso for *Tropicália 2,* their quarter-century commemoration of the Tropicalist experience (example 12). The text for vocal performance depends on double meanings, fractures, and fusions, which are complemented and given other nuances in the print register. On one level, the sung syllables combine to produce a meaningful string: good-bye goddess Aphrodite, from thee I had life, given, good-bye. Other possibilities — based on fragments and extrapolations — diversify the field: to God, God to, Afro, I saw thee / of the, Dada, to God. The meshing of religious, mythological, erotic, and ethnic elements reminds one, in a general sense, of the contrastive approach of Tropicalism. Links with concretism are evident in the geometry of the song and in the micromanipulations of words, splits, and pairings, which multiply their suggestions. The avant-garde spirit, of course, is realized in the citation of "Dada," which is the title of the song. The exaltation of life and the wild approach of that historical avant-garde are invoked here, opening, in one considered analysis, a dimension of "creative liberty in an act of giving" (Lucchesi and Dieguez 230). With all these factors, this composition reflects well several of Gil's guiding pre-occupations, including his frequent desire to pursue poeticity through music.

While not as prolific or widely known as his colleagues Gil and Veloso, another original of Tropicalism from Bahia state, Tom Zé, developed, from both musical and lyrical vantage points, a sophisticated and pro-vocative repertory. A contemporaneous poet-critic coined the term *poemúsica* to describe the songwriter's work.[40] For his part, Augusto de Campos recognized him as: "a troubador dedicated, in his best mo-ments, to the difficult art of whipping good tones into shape and of blending *motz el som* (words and sound), as desired by the Provençals, those Bahians of the XIIth century" (*Balanço* 335). Tom Zé's albums include experimental pieces of clear concretist influence (spatializations, verbal decomposition), alongside satirical material and lyrical pieces of dense metaphorical content. With the surge of interest in world music at the turn of the decade of the 1990s, Tom Zé received some attention in the North American sphere as an unusual musician with idiosyncratic verbal approaches.[41]

Early in his career, performing songwriter Belchior (b. 1946), from the Northeastern state of Ceará, consciously chose the musical vehicle to make his poetry known. He called himself a *cancioneiro,* meaning not a songbook but a maker of songs in the medieval sense. Noting the ety-mology of *lyricism* (from *lyre*), Belchior referred to his electronic art as *guitarrismo* (from the Brazilian Portuguese word used for electric guitar).[42] In his first recordings, Belchior was openly preoccupied with novelty ("the new") and vanguard poses. Oddly shaped transcriptions of lyrics adorn album jackets, reflecting the acoustic designs of guitar-driven experimental compositions. These cases exemplify the songwrit-er's dual intentions. For subsequent albums, Belchior did not create songs in concrete molds but did continue to embellish lyric sheets with graphic ideas (shapes, use of nonverbal signs, highlighting, etc.). In his discursive, subjective lyrics, Belchior explored sentimentalism and tran-sitions to modernity. From a literary perspective, the most fascinating aspect of his songbook was the constant, and sometimes ingenious, re-course to allusion, whether through direct citation of other texts (songs, poems, fiction, foreign and national) or incorporated references. An outstanding example of quotation came in the title of "Divina comédia humana" and its text, in which the songwriter inserts verses of a classic of Brazilian poetry, Olavo Bilac's "Via Láctea" (Milky Way): "Ora direis ouvir estrelas! Certo perdeste o senso/ E eu vos direi, no entanto, en-quanto houver . . ." (Now you will say to hear stars. Surely you have lost your mind/ and I will tell you still as long as there is). This example is quite indicative of the mind-set of the seventies and early eighties that drove Belchior's poetry of song.

Several contemporary poet-composers have made artistic contributions in different genres, often out of the limelight. Such is the case of Marcus Vinícius (b. 1949), whose activities as a page-poet and a playwright established a literary stature that was reinforced in song. He was one of the principal poets of the regional Grupo Sanhauá, who explored neoconcrete and *praxis* poetry in independent productions characteristic of the 1970s, as seen in the next chapter. In addition, he received three awards from the National Theatre Service for dramatic literature.[43] While careful to distinguish print poetry from song lyrics, Marcus Vinícius declared that select compositions of his "fit fully well in the frame of the recent poetic intentions of MPB."[44] In his songwriting, this artist has shown concern with making verse of careful sound design, metaphorical weight, and a frequently intertextual flavor. As he writes on an early album: "há que re-inventar a cada instante o labirinto do lábio, desenrolando sempre o carretel da linguagem" (one must reinvent at every moment the labyrinth of the lip, always unwinding the spool of language). This statement emerges from his most verbally intense song, "Dédalus" (Daedalus), a sophisticated *embolada,* a folk form characterized by tongue-twisting verbal strings and combinations. The highly alliterative verses of the song carve intertwined images of oral language:

> Carretel desenrolado/ No labirinto do lábio
> Na boca dessa embolada/ Dedo dédalus de nada . . .
> A direção do destino . . .
> O dito pelo não dito/ E o mundo sem cadeado . . .
> Perigo sobre perigo/ Tramela tranca e trancado
> Na trama do trava língua . . . *

Having developed a singular style based on the popular verse-making of the Northeast, singer-songwriter Zé Ramalho (b. 1949) also merits inclusion in the role of Brazil's contemporary poets of song in the 1970s and 1980s. His work — including a few chapbooks and a print volume — is largely derived from *cantoria,* the regional system of sung traditional poetry highlighting *desafios,* poetic exchanges or duels. As in his model,

---

* [Spool unwound / in the labyrinth of the lip / in the mouth of this song / Digit Daedalus of naught . . . the direction of destiny . . . the unsaid says / and the world without locks . . . Danger over danger / tongue-latch bar and locked / woven in the plot of tongue-ties]

Ramalho's hybrid lyrics often comprise prophetic visions of fantastic symbolism or mythological constructs. In other cases, his contemplations of self are founded on abstract or surreal imagery.

In a more urban vein, another poetic facet of MPB was revealed in the experimental rock of Walter Franco (b. 1945) in the seventies. The themes he pursued in musical texts included language itself, thought, and the nature of knowledge. Discovery seemed imminent, for instance, in the aggressive recording of "Mixturação" (Mixture), in a terse series of nouns leading to an edge: "O raciocínio lento / O poço e o pensamento / O olho o orifício/ O passo o precipício . . ." (The slow ratiocination / the well and thought / the eye the orifice / the step the precipice). In another representative early composition, the lyric voice sings of mental dimensions — " . . . meu barco / que muito/navega no espaço do verso / no uni-verso da mente . . ." (my ship / that navigates so in the space of verse / in the uni-verse of the mind) — and censures the limits of discourse of popular music.[45] With pointed concision and synthesis of form and idea, Franco generated evocative sono-verbal tensions, and a slippery poetic dimension in his music. On the formal level, he showed a true propensity toward phonemic and morphemic playfulness, intensified by performance designs, as well as structural audacity in shaped or multisectional compositions, whose concretist transcriptions comprise poetic by-products.[46] Such intersemiotic interests will be further illustrated with published examples in chapter 5.

Select titles by several other Brazilian singer-songwriters would merit inclusion in an anthology of contemporary musical lyricism. In the songs of samba artist Paulinho da Viola (b. 1942), for example, there are interesting symbolist strains in the context of pensive constraint. Many lyrics of Jorge Ben (b. 1942) comprise a unique expressionistic declamatory prose-poetry. Luiz Gonzaga Júnior (1945–1992) depicted struggle and distress in long "I" lyrics enriched by an analytical dimension, as did the early Fátima Guedes (b. 1958). Among the early compositions of Djavan (b. 1945), some careful manipulations of sound and figurative language show an admirable lyrical imagination. From a comprehensive point of view, no single poetic approach is dominant among poet-composers in the sixties and seventies. This stylistic and thematic variety attests to the vitality of song as a vehicle for poetry.

Literato Cantabile: The Craft of the Lyricist

The poetic dimension of MPB is energized further with the contribution of noted lyricists, who fit words to composed music or author texts for later setting. As seen above, the model of modernist poet Vinícius de Morais was crucial in modifying attitudes toward the profession of lyricist. Young poets José Carlos Capinan and Torquato Neto were instrumental in making late-sixties *tropicalismo* a musical movement with literary overtones. During the seventies, several lyricists of MPB emerged with offerings of notably poetic character. The foremost name in this camp is Aldir Blanc (b. 1946), longtime partner of vocalist-guitarist João Bosco. As a writer, Blanc has published collections of *crônicas* (journalistic stories, sketches), and some of his extended song texts are akin to this narrative prose. He is more often a linguistically oddball satirist or musical purveyor of unsettling imagery or allusive constructs. In one noted instance, Blanc reworked an esoteric symbolist sonnet in a samba setting to portray degradation in modern urban media culture.[47] Authors of song texts who work with Milton Nascimento (and other musicians of the Minas Gerais popular music collective) have also contributed to the celebrated lyricism of MPB, whether through abstraction, as in the words of Márcio Borges (b. 194?), or allusion, as is often the case with Fernando Brant (b. 1946).[48] In his repertory, confluence of stone and roadway imagery keys such songs as "Itamarandiba": "No meio do meu caminho/ Sempre haverá uma pedra/ plantarei a minha casa/ numa cidade de pedra . . ." (In the middle of my road / there will always be a stone / I will plant my home / in a city of stone). This and other lyrics sung by Milton clearly depend on intertextual gestures toward Carlos Drummond de Andrade and his celebrated "In the Middle of the Road."

The signature poem of the modernist master, "Poema de sete faces," in turn, was reworked by Torquato Neto as an offbeat lyric for the ludic "Let's Play That":

quando eu nasci
um anjo louco muito louco
veio ler a minha mão

. . . .

eis que esse anjo me disse
apertando a minha mão
com um sorriso entre dentes
vai bicho desafinar
o coros dos contentes[49]*

* [When I was born / a crazy very crazy angel / came to read my hand . . . behold the angel said unto me / gripping my hand / with a smile between teeth / go on man untune / the chorus of the contented]

There is a double allusion here, as the concluding line is taken from the "Inferno de Wall Street" by the anomalous Brazilian romantic Joaquim de Sousândrade.[50] With these "antiestablishment" literary borrowings, the poet of popular music aligns himself with Sousândrade's extremism in the romantic context and with Drummond's modernism of rupture. The lyric becomes an attitudinal stance, a cultural posture, an apology for audacity, challenge, and novelty.

Torquato Neto was one of many lyricists from the sixties to the eighties who were published authors. Artists of the word often operated on two fronts — page and stage — and the practice of including song texts in books of creative writing, or of making whole books of lyrics, suggests the literary trappings of much Brazilian songwriting. Several of the young poets discussed in the next chapter — Cacaso, Chacal, Geraldo Carneiro, Waly Salomão, Paulo Leminski, and others — participated, to greater or lesser degrees, in the sphere of popular music as well. This is consistent with, on one hand, the development of a "counterculture" with poetic reflections, and, on the other, of the cross-disciplinary nature of alternative production in the seventies.

In the eighties, after new strains of national rock had assumed a prominent position in middle-class urban popular music and the general phenomenon of the poetry of song had diminished, there emerged one singular case of association of verbal artistry and popular music: Arnaldo Antunes (b. 1958). He first established himself as a vocalist, songwriter, and lyricist with the rock ensemble Os Titãs (The titans). He later invested in publication projects involving very nominative minimalist verse and nondiscursive verbo-graphic art, moving on to visual poetry, ludic calligraphy, and computer-generated word images.[51] Such production, again, rightly belongs to the category of "intersemiotic creation," to be taken up in chapter 5. After embarking on a solo career, Antunes established his place in the poetry of song most firmly with a wholly unique multimedia work presented as video text, sound recording, and book.[52] Most of the thirty compositions are presented as "words and music," but some are labeled "poems," including some that appeared in Antunes's previous books. The video takes the poetic experience a step further with shifting colors, moving script, letter animation, objectified contrasts, and myriad computer effects done, unlike nearly all commercial music videos, with the poetic function of language in mind. Among these rock vignettes, only the last track is a more conventional song. It is the first and title track "Nome" (Name) — with his rough verbal attack, and the terse diction, interchanges, and permutations of its word field — that best characterizes the collection (see examples 13 and 14).

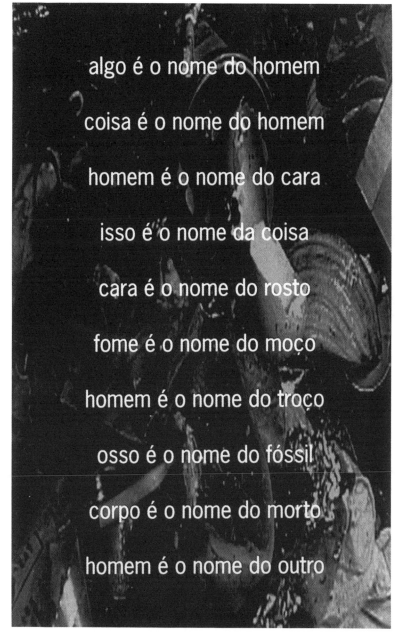

algo é o nome do homem

coisa é o nome do homem

homem é o nome do cara

isso é o nome da coisa

cara é o nome do rosto

fome é o nome do moço

homem é o nome do troço

osso é o nome do fóssil

corpo é o nome do morto

homem é o nome do outro

Example 13*

*[something is the name of the man / thing is the name of the man / man is the name of the guy / that is the name of the thing / face is the name of the face / hunger is the name of the mister / man is the name of the item / bone is the name of the fossil / body is the name of the dead man / man is the name of the other]

Example 14

Da Capo al Fine

The legacies of radical *modernismo,* concrete poetry, Tropicália, and the most creative MPB are all evident in the work-in-progress of Arnaldo Antunes. While he is a singular figure in the final decade of the century, from the late sixties to the early eighties in Brazil a generation of acoustic and electronic erudite poet-composers grew up within the confines of popular music. So much of the work of Chico Buarque, Caetano Veloso, numerous other adept songwriters, and outstanding lyricists expanded the meaning of "lyric" in this contemporary period. Countless fusions of melody and poetry comprised a contemporary revival of the art of the troubadors. This renaissance forcefully attests to the lyrical vitality of Brazil's diversified arts.

chapter five

Margins and Marginals: New Brazilian

Poetry of the 1970s

Diante de tudo isto, / os beletristas / hão de censurar,

no mínimo, / a minha falta / de estilo.

[In view of all this / men of letters / will censure

at the very least / my lack / of style][1]

Varied poetic generations found themselves at a crossroads in the 1970s in Brazil. The last great voice of *modernismo,* the widely read and influential Carlos Drummond de Andrade, pondered progress and his own longevity and completed his serial lyrical reminiscence.[2] The classically toned Generation of '45 still wrote, albeit with relatively little acceptance, and found some echo in the work of such conventional lyrical poets as Carlos Néjar (b. 1939).[3] The acknowledged master of the second half of the twentieth century, João Cabral de Melo Neto, who set himself apart from contemporaries of '45 with his textual geometry and integration of social and regional phenomena, earned increasing acclaim and published his collected poems. Ferreira Gullar, the penitent experimentalist of the 1950s and outspoken political poet of the 1960s, gave voice to antiregime sentiment and, with Affonso Romano de Sant'Anna, helped establish a neo-epical mode.[4] The internationally recognized Noigandres group of concrete poetry further diversified, increasing both their visibility and opportunities for discussion with the publication of their respective collected poems in the latter part of the decade.

New Brazilian poetry of the 1970s comprises the output of poets born, for the most part, from the mid-1940s to the mid-1950s who represent emergent stylistic tendencies. Their decade was marked by deviations and contrasts. Young writers took many individual approaches to lyrical expression and text-making, exhibiting different common habits, to greater and lesser degrees. Overall practice, in broad terms, operated between two poles. On one extreme, there was the informality of what came to be known as *poesia marginal,* or marginal poetry, with its related extraliterary interests. On the other, there was what was termed *criação intersemiótica,* or intersemiotic creation, encompassing postconcretist visual poetry and "constructivist" verse. Irrespective of positioning between the poles, certain traits are shared by young writers of the seventies. Across the spread of the spectrum, though with divergent motivations, there were stylistic mixtures and a thrust toward resubjectivization in lyric. The unfolding fan of seventies phenomena was built on a series of contrastive features and conceptual oppositions between *poesia marginal* and other youth poetry. The former — on the axis of subjectivity / objectivity — declared neoromantic preferences, while nonmarginals acted on modified classical impulses. Where spontaneity and actual experience interested one, elaboration and applied imagination were more important to the other. Colloquialism was a primary aspect of *poesia marginal,* often in a literal empirical sense, while counterparts sought more literary or aesthetic solutions. In this sense, oral qualities contrasted with desires for writerly textuality. In conjunction, *poesia marginal* can be seen as a form of handicraft next to the more carefully manufactured products of the other sector. While having sparked new interest in poetry as cultural practice, received more critical (including journalistic) notice, and, in effect, shaped views of poetry in the seventies, *poesia marginal,* qua trend, proved to be ephemeral and limiting. Those who superseded or challenged the limitations, in turn, merit well-contextualized attention.

Discussions of the varied production of the seventies invariably involve, whether by affirmation or denial, two key facets of modern Brazilian poetry: the iconoclastic phase of *modernismo* of the 1920s and early 1930s, and the contemporary influence of concretism, in the wider sense including both vanguard texts of the Noigandres poets and their critical campaign in favor of select authors representing values of "invention." Relating to both facets are the widely cited poetics of Oswald de Andrade, in creative texts and manifestos alike. The experimentalism of splinter vanguard groups, the political poetry of the sixties, and the poetry of song are also points of reference for new seventies poetry. The parameters of literary tradition and renewal do not alone suffice to come to terms with new manifestations in their productive environments. In this chapter, then, recurrent criticisms of informal youth poetry are necessarily balanced with other factors of broader sociocultural interest.

The Airs and Adventures of *Poesia Marginal*

The term *poesia marginal* does not designate an articulated literary move-
ment but rather the sum of heterogenous activities involved in noncom-
mercial networks of poetry. The "marginality" of this phenomenon was
determined from two angles: that of form, in a literal sense, of the physi-
cal making and dissemination of products, and that of content, of the
texts themselves, with their constituent language and attitudes. On the
first count, this kind of seventies poetry was characterized by nonconven-
tional, alternative modes of production and distribution, removed from
the "center" constituted by established publishing businesses. Indepen-
dent ventures began early in the decade, under the sign of the harshest
repression of civil society by the military regime. Frustrated by lack
of access to publishers, and/or taken with the idea of self-production,
young poets in Rio de Janeiro and São Paulo—and soon after other
urban centers—took matters into their own hands. Rather than enter
standard commercial schemes, they published their own works, individ-
ually or in groups, availing themselves of all manner of printing and
reproduction to create an independent non- to mini- to small-press cir-
cuit. Texts were often produced in rudimentary fashion—mimeograph,
ditto, photocopy, chapbooks, pamphlets, etc.—and professional design
was often freely sacrificed for the sake of printing at any cost, no matter
how small. Until late in the decade, bookstore sales of broadsides and
little books were generally bypassed. Many young authors considered
actual personal contact with potential readers to be part of the process of
communication; thus they would sell (or hand out) their titles in public,
at cafés, schools, theaters, declamations preceding shows of popular mu-
sic (especially rock), or performance happenings. In this way, a new
reading public was created among urban middle-class youth.

   Questions of audience, readership, and reception are particularly
significant here. The introduction to the commercial anthology that
brought the "underground" poets of Rio de Janeiro into brighter public
light opens: "At present, curiously enough, the article of the day is po-
etry."[5] The adverb of mode was noteworthy, implying as it did an un-
common or unexpected interest in poetry. In the age of television, lyric is
naturally thought of as the least empowered genre among the suffering
literary arts. That so many young people should have gone to so much
effort to put their poetry into circulation, albeit in mostly rudimentary
forms, and that they should have struck such a responsive chord, was
indeed unusual in the age of ever-increasing technology and the hege-
mony of mass media. Yet while a popularization of poetry among urban

youth indeed occurred, it came at the price, in the words of a concerned observer, of an evident "penury of the word and concepts," implications of which impinge on most aspects of the present chapter.[6]

The amateur nature of production of early marginal poets spawned the term *mimeograph generation*, which was used with some frequency in reference to underground youth poetry of the seventies. Precarious conditions of manufacture — with little care for the quality of paper, page design, typography, and overall appearance of the print document — also led to such derogatory descriptive terms as *lixeratura*, which conveniently translates as "litterature." Applying Marshall McLuhan's dictum "the medium is the message" to the case of the bulk of *poesia marginal*, the makeup of text vehicles would imply the very trashiness of the text, its throwaway value, the largely unrefined discourse, and the flaunting of prosaic language. From a broader sociocultural angle, one can see the substantive poverty of publications embodying a rejection of established institutional frameworks, literary and social alike, as seen below. By the mid-1970s, some groups established cooperatives, imprints, or small presses that produced books of simple but comparatively higher quality, in both material and poetic terms. In such cases, independence from mainstream publishing houses was still maintained. Self-production by authors is nothing new in Brazilian literature; from *modernismo* to the neovanguards and to the present, poets have financed and designed their own editions. It is known that João Cabral distributed small books made on a vintage home press. What distinguished the *samizdat* of Brazilian *poesia marginal* were the strikingly high levels of tolerance and the personal involvement of the makers at each stage.

The poor or nonindustrial production values of such new poetry combined with factors of content in the characterization of *poesia marginal*, which for the most part lay on the fringe of literary standards. A low-filtered, subjective, discursive approach was most common. Dominant tones were largely casual, often apparently anti-intellectual. In many cases, the language might have seemed simply superficial, facile, light, or cute. As poets relied on colloquial language in somewhat brute expressions of experience, poorly mediated story-telling or confessionalism resulted. Problematic relations — of words, the self, or society — might be avoided, and development of sound structures, imagery, or symbolic options could be rather sparse. In such free-form verse of the 1970s, high value was given to currency and personal, authorial affectivity, as distinguished from the creation of lyric selves or personae. One of the comprehensive driving principles was what has been called "the abandonment, if not the scorn, of the modern tradition," which left critics perplexed by verbal instruments that fell, despite any mitigating circumstances, "this side of poetic language."[7]

Such unprestigious and unpretentious marginal production has been portrayed as a reaction against the non-orality and extreme intellectualization of concretism and other neo-avant-garde projects. Ingenuous, neo-romantic employment of a very subjective poetry has been seen by interested critics as comprising opposition to the vanguards, whose "clean" art was allegedly rejected in favor of a "dirty" art.[8] José Guilherme Merquior aired his own admitted reservations with experimentalism by affirming: "the 'uncultured' disarray of so-called marginal poetry was born in good measure of the desire to break with the ritualism, the sterility of the laboratorial vanguard."[9] In this statement, any "break" would seem to assume previous affiliation, which is dubious in any wide sense. Positing instead a desire simply not to follow experimental models, what Merquior says may have been true of such individual poets as Cacaso, pen name of Antônio Carlos de Brito (1944–1987), who had been involved with poetry before the emergence of alternative activity. Still, most "marginals" did not articulate rupture with any "ritualism." As Hollanda observed: "despite being systematically presented as a front of opposition to the vanguards, that opposition is not made explicitly conscious."[10] Young informal poets were, for the most part, clearly disinterested in any sort of classical discipline or restraint — including Cabral's measured rationality — but most either had no real problem with the creative side of the vanguards or were simply ignorant of them.

If marginal manifestations were not consistently or expressly anti-vanguard, they did offer stark contrasts with the theoretical weight, recourses to visuality, and artful purposefulness associated with concretism and other such manifestations. Early seventies poetic registers normally revealed "a critical sense independent of programmatic commitments" (Hollanda, *Impressões* 98). Unlike with the concrete poets, the proponents of the neo-avant-garde projects of *poesia praxis* and *poema processo,* as well as the *engagé* writers of *Violão de rua,* all of whom dedicated themselves to organization and pursuit of agendas, the practices of young marginal poets began spontaneously, without manifestos, statements of goals, or missionary objectives. Some marginal publications in the course of the decade did appear with editorial introductions, but none truly comprised a platform or theoretical framework.[11]

While some names affiliated with *poesia marginal* had previous publication records or advanced academic training — primarily those who issued a series called Coleção Frenesi (Frenzy collection): Francisco Alvim (b. 1938), Cacaso, Roberto Schwarz (b. 1938), Geraldo Carneiro

(b. 1952) — numerous others seemed to reject "serious" forms of knowledge. Just as they discarded established notions of good taste in production, many rebellious young poets displayed lack of belief or confidence in the university and academic circles in general. If not as conscious or resolved acts of rupture, they did turn away from, even scoff at, the languages of linguistic science and intellectual endeavor. Adding lack of literary preparation to a sometimes adolescent playfulness, they developed an ironic "hedonistic taste for playing with the disqualification of their own sensibility."[12] In fact, from the point of view of an urban anthropologist, the three keys to understanding marginal poets in Rio de Janeiro were their *anti-technicism, anti-intellectualism,* and *politicization of the quotidian.*[13] In these seventies practices, then, a whole new set of attitudes about making and communicating poetry came into play.

In many respects, the operative principles of *poesia marginal* were not founded on literature but experience. The empirical base brought with it, as suggested above, natural problems of judgment. Flashes of daily life, recounting of personal incidents, and simple observations all reached the page without appreciable detachment or the kind of aesthetic monitoring traditionally expected in poetic art. Marginal poets might mistake informality for stylization and real-life events for literarily usable material. As the lines between art and life became blurred, any reaction to any situation might qualify as poetic expression. An abundance of circumstantial, spur-of-the-moment texts appeared, especially after *poesia marginal* exceeded its initial quasi-literary bounds and became fashionable after 1975. The spontaneity and informality were such that, as an involved observer reasoned, any and all might ultimately be considered apt to make art; everyone could be promoted to the status of artist, which was the same as "extinguishing the species."[14] From the point of view of underground artisans of the word themselves, however, the blessing of traditional or academic criticism did not matter. What was important was the opportunity to express themselves and the young public's reception of their products.

One of the key aspects of experience in the world of modern urban youth that got expression in *poesia marginal* was neoromantic nonconformity. An antiestablishment stance for the 1970s was taken via recasting of a nineteenth-century *maudit* pose. A characteristic participant emphasized vital links in an account of the rise of underground poetry: "Reestablishing a dialogue with Rimbaud and swashbucklers of that quality as a point of departure, [poetry] tears up once and for all theoretical and intellectual costumes and goes ahead to transform *life*. Changing life: — poets, unite!"[15] One notes here the centrality of lifestyle, community, and the anti-intellectuallism noted above. The allusion to Rimbaud (which would likely have escaped many "lesser" marginal poets), appropriately, seems to emphasize combative behavior rather than antinormative text. Where seventies urban middle-class youth demeanor is concerned, an important defining idea in cultural manifestations such as *poesia marginal* was *desbunde:* to trip out, act wild, without rational or productive objectives. In a retrospective on his transgressive role, one of the most typical marginal voices, using the pen name Chacal (b. 1951), reiterating the reference to Rimbaud, gave the triadic call of hippie counterculture and affirmed sensual and hedonistic elements: "Sex, drugs and rock and roll began to spin in my life as all powerful elements. Like Rimbaud, I went in search of my 'déreglement de tous les sens' . . . hence my verse could only be expressive and true in those delirious states of mind. . . . Poetry for me only existed as momentary *flash,* portrait of the times. I always preferred the free humor of Oswald to the 'straightjacket' of Cabral's metrics."[16] In addition to delineating behavorial questions, this declaration provides a link with three key points for evaluation of Chacal and the tendency he represents: common technique (flash), the notion of epochal portrait, and the connection with Oswald de Andrade, whose overarching pertinence will continue to be developed below. At this point, for purposes of illustration of several relevant points, Chacal's "My Generation" (original title) functions well:

> aquela guitarrinha ranheta
> debochada desbocada
> my generation
> satisfaction
>
> aquela mina felina
> cuba sarro cocaína
> do you wanna dance
> don't let me down
>
> aquele clima da pesada
> cheiro de porrada no ar
> street fighting man
> jumping jack flash*
> (*Drops* 42)

---

*[that brash little guitar / debauched foul-mouthed / my generation / satisfaction / that feline dame / cuba [libre] get it on cocaine / do you wanna dance / don't let me down / that heavy climate / smell of shit-kickin' in the air / street fighting man / jumping jack flash]

In several ways, this modest adolescent text fits the prototype of early seventies youth poem suggested by a curious observer: short, epigrammatic, ironic, colloquial, attitudinal, valuing real-life experience, and targeting a more common reader.[17] More specifically, the final quatrain's climate of conflict integrates additional behavioral (musical) references (citations of songs by the Rolling Stones), while the last word conveniently echoes the favored approach mentioned in the above-cited testimonial: *flash*. This typical take also leads to further questions about literary value in *poesia marginal*. A well-made photographic analogy structures a pertinent observation about stylistic limits: "the Brazilian poetry that in *modernismo* appealed to the Kodak to discover snapshots of life, today makes the 'Polaroid-poem,' with instantaneous development, and 'elaborates' a style and an aesthetic of the unfinished, of that which is 'surprised' by the chance interference of the poet" (Freitas Filho 113). Following this view, one might say that fascination on the part of the makers of *poesia marginal* with flash, immediacy, and the surprise of potentially revealing moments may have simply signified lack of time and willingness to develop the image, to labor in the darkroom, to sort out situations of impact from the merely circumstantial.

If Chacal's little generational portrait again underscores the literary shortcomings of *poesia marginal,* it also underlines its importance as a vehicle of attitude and as a sociocultural manifestation. Most observers have necessarily considered extraliterary functions when approaching the youth movement in seventies poetry. In an account of an exhibition of "alternative" forms of poetry in the early 1970s, two involved parties stipulated outright that in some cases literary values were relegated to a secondary plane and that such phenomena had above all attitudinal and sociopsychological value: "A form of preservation of individuality, this scattered poetry is much more a search for recognition and identity, a precarious way of saying we are alive, than a 'literary' event."[18] Young citizens, prevented from participating in national affairs by the repressive circumstances of military dictatorship (e.g., "that heavy climate" in the above text), sought release in the self-expression or introspection of poetry, which was more an act of resistance than literature. In marginal collectives that have been subjected to scrutiny, identified paramount aims were going against the grain of manufacturing convention and participating in socializing processes.[19] Local groups in Rio acted upon the means of production, in a "subversion of established relations for production of culture." The realization of little books as "integrated" products—from writing to taking to press to hawking—had a central affective dimension and involved maker and receiver in dialogue (Hollanda, *Impressões* 96–97). It was no accident that the most complete study of *poesia marginal* was posited as a "case study" and undertaken by an urban anthropologist, who noted that poetry was lived "as a totalizing experience, with a logic of its own, and a strong dose of incompatibility with different aspects of the dominant institutional order" (Pereira 63). Those different aspects are literary, cultural, historical, economic, and political.

In the context of a perceived editorial blockade and of the reigning authoritarianism that restricted real political expression, *poesia marginal* can also be taken as a symbolic "democratization." Through the facilities of graphic reproduction and the lowering of limiting literary standards, conditions were created for egalitarian opportunity and freedom of speech. However valid such a sociopolitical symbolism may have been, there is little question that links to historical conjuncture are central in a general appreciation of informal verse and its antisystem sentiments. At the outer limits, the scope of the epithet *marginal* could be considered, much beyond the sector of underground poetry, to encompass any enunciation countering the military government's version of national affairs. Symptomatically, an involved writer quoted a colleague and filmmaker to the effect that the category of *marginal* included anyone speaking in humanitarian, antiregime terms. The military rulers' self-investiture with dictatorial powers in late 1968 also immediately implied "the emergence of the concept of marginality in Brazilian culture, when lie upon lie made an outlaw of the slightest intention of truth. Equally repudiated by those [poets] coming up, the label of *marginal* simply characterized, as it still does, the entire national situation since 1964, when by force of threat of annihilation they were able to render useless the path that society was following in search of its life and human dignity" (Henriques Neto 43). Though it clearly stretches the concept of marginality, this account can be credited, for rhetorical effect, with giving valid generational perspective and depicting the turn of the decade in seventies poetry.

The statement in *poesia marginal* against repression and historical conditions was, to an appreciable degree, abstracted into the act of writing as behavioral deviance, as suggested earlier. Where literary evaluation is concerned, if the protest aspect of marginal experiences gave them importance, they were then only valid as long as political repression, censorship, and the interdiction of public space necessitated alternative channels. The historical conjuncture, in sum, lent *poesia marginal* "a symbolic value much greater than its poetic content" (Simon and Dantas

53). When some poets actually addressed perpetrators or wrote about the repressive situation known as *sufoco,* or the "suffocation" of the dark days, the results were dubious, as in Chacal's "S.O.S.":

> tem gente morrendo de medo
> tem gente morrendo de esquistossomose
> tem gente morrendo de hepatite meningite sifilite
> tem gente morrendo de fome
> tem gente morrendo por muitas causas
>
> nós que não somos médicos, psiquiatras
> nem ao menos bons cristãos,
> nos dedicamos a salvar as pessoas
> que como nós
> sofrem de um mal misterioso:
> o sufoco*
> (*Drops* 46)

This second citation of the emblematic Chacal leads back to his invocation of Oswald de Andrade, whose legacy links youth poetry and its critiques with historical situations and with *modernismo* as a measure for comparison. In the early seventies, *modernismo* was entering a more popular and less literary dimension, in some sense due to "the fiftieth anniversary of the Modern Art Week, festively commemorated by the military dictatorship." The name of Oswald de Andrade gave off an aura of nonconformity that acted as an antidote to censorship, official culture, and the lack of political and cultural perspectives.[20] In terms of tone, Oswald's sarcasm and irreverence were admired and emulated. As for style, *poesia marginal* involved multiple attempts at aphorism and *poesia minuto* in the manner of Oswald, preferences that prove to offer revealing opportunities to consider similarities.

Those who have sought to place *poesia marginal* in some sort of literary perspective have asserted parallels with modernist rupture. The informality of youth verse, for instance, can be held up as a return to the antinormative colloquialism of the poets of the 1920s who penned tirades against the strictures of Parnassianism and created the so-called "joke poem." Other aspects of *modernismo* relevant to the seventies

---

*[people are dying of fear / . . . schistosomiasis / . . . hepatitis meningitis . . . syphillis / . . . hunger / people are dying for many causes / we who are not doctors, psychiatrists / not even good Christians / dedicate ourselves to saving those who / like us / suffer from a mysterious sickness / the "suffocation"]

would include energetic insistence on nonacademic language and the valuing of "real-life" sources. In addition to the insolent Oswald, models would be found in such consecrated authors as the early Carlos Drummond de Andrade and Manuel Bandeira. With reference to the former, a spokesman of a characteristic seventies poetry collective stated that Drummond's work transcended classification, solidly affirming its validity via allusions to the constituents of the last strophe of the "Seven-Sided Poem": " . . . that brandy he speaks of in a classic poem, that moon, both the brandy and the moon are still the same . . . we continue to drink the brandy and the moon alike . . . There would never be a denial."[21] The pertinent Bandeira is the one who voiced the following proposal:[22]

> Vou lançar a teoria do poeta sórdido.
> Poeta sórdido:
> Aquele em cuja poesia há a marca suja da vida.
> Vai um sujeito,
> Sai um sujeito de sua casa com a roupa de brim branco muito
>   bem engomada, e na primeira esquina passa
>   um caminhão, salpica-lhe o paletó ou a calça
>   de uma nódoa de lama:
> É a vida.
>
> O poema deve ser com a nódoa de brim:
> Fazer o leitor satisfeito de si dar o desespero.
>
> Sei que a poesia é também orvalho.
> Mas este fica para as menininhas, as estrelas alfas,
>   as virgens cem por cento e as amadas que
>   envelheceram sem maldade.*

Surface aspects of this poem — sordid poet, dirty marks, and underscoring "life" — certainly make sense for unrefined *poesia marginal*. The parallels, however, are less likely at another level involving theory, conceptualizations of poetic practice, and reader response. Here and in a broad general sense, equivalencies between marginality in seventies lyric

*[I'm going to launch the theory of the sordid poet / the sordid poet / he in whose poetry there is the dirty mark of life / some guy goes out / he leaves his house with his white linen suit very / well starched, and on the first corner a truck / passes, splashes and stains his jacket or trousers with mud / That's life. / Poems should be like the linen stain: making the self-satisfied reader despair. / I know that poetry is also dew / But that's for the little girls, the alpha stars / the 100% virgins and the lovers who / grew old without malice]

and strains of *modernismo* do not stand up under closer examination. The purported model's free-verse familiarity involved a more conscious literary elaboration and stylization that superseded the directness or confessional sense at the heart of much *poesia marginal*. As a key contemporary poet and an aware participant in a roundtable exchange about new poetry put it, the colloquialism of Bandeira, Drummond, and Oswald had "a very strong sense of objectivity," while the young poets of the mid-1970s had a corresponding "keynote of subjectivity."[23] For her part, the organizer of *26 poetas hoje,* rethinking an earlier position on the "binomial life / art," noted that Oswald's colloquialism was a literary process par excellence, while for a typical marginal poet, such use constituted poetization of actual daily experience (Hollanda, *Impressões* 101). That difference in mediation is palpable in the bulk of informal seventies verse.

The Oswald connection provides additional valuable perspective on positive and negative aspects of *poesia marginal*. "Papo de índio" (Injun talk) by Chacal was a noteworthy moment for its actualization of anthropophagy, Oswald's elaborate metaphor of cultural cannibalism in literature:

> Veiu uns ómi de saia preta
> cheiu di caixinha e pó branco
> qui eles disserum qui chamava açúcri.
> aí eles falarum e nós fechamu a cara.
> depois eles arrepetirum e nós fechamu o corpo.
> aí eles insistirum e nós comemu eles.*
>
> (*Drops* 20)

Dissonant humor and sure antiauthoritarian stance are achieved here in a linguistically consistent position. Rather than apply the Oswald-inspired orientation of popular (here, primitive) speech to his own private world, the poet steps outside of himself into the *persona* of an aggressive native (a future victim of colonization), which has effective historical, anthropological, and literary overtones. However, this poem proves to be unique in the output of Chacal, and the novelty of this text reinforces necessary critiques of *poesia marginal,* especially vis-à-vis Oswaldian parameters.

The informal young poets of the seventies rarely lived up to the standard implicit in "Papo de índio." Points already established here help to

---

*[Some mens in black skirt come / full of little box and white powder / dat dey call sugary / then dey talk and we red-face mad / then dey repeat and we put a spell on to protect our body / then dey insist and we eat 'um]

explain how Oswald was given an incomplete reading and how his vision was transferred partially. Elements of daily life or ready-made material entered Oswald's lyrical domain through a process of selection and internal naturalization (i.e., in the fictional logic of the text). That process broke down in the practice of aspiring poets who relied on external (i.e., real-world naturalization, or "explanation"). Dantas has usefully elaborated on the differences between Oswald as source and Chacal as representative of *poesia marginal*. The latter's uninhibited spontaneity resulted from a naive application of the model of *Poesia Pau-Brasil* to his own experience. Foundational strategies of Oswald's poetry — metonymic observation, cubist cut-and-paste montage — became mundane and ceased to constitute, as components of the poet's own spontaneity, stylistic processes of estrangement. Such naturalizing treatment of the quotidian, with its populist flavor, has the grave disadvantage of expelling the utopian element of Oswald's constructivism. The beauty of Oswald's regressive (infantile) poetry, Dantas perceives, resides in his having placed process — techniques of making and constructing — ahead of observations of the real in a world where those techniques are not known and whose modernity seems eccentric. The artifice of *Poesia Pau-Brasil* allowed for presentation of the archaic enchantments of a picturesque Brazil to idealize a playful and virtual modernity, which, born of shock and contrast, both revealed a mythopoetics and projected utopian liberation. Brazil, to use the Russian formalist term, was defamiliarized or made strange, and Oswald found (local) modern traits better than those of the metropolis. What Oswald called in his first manifesto "the millionaire contribution of all the errors" in national language was not a stumbling block but "a liberating desire, a program of life and beauty, a positive ideal" (Dantas 47–48).

Against this backdrop, Chacal and contemporaries, unlike the modernist master, did not reveal the world through technique. If they used fragments, truncated phrases, or montage, the motive was mimetic; it was because the world *was* cut and pasted. Having simply given themselves over, to borrow the above-cited critic's words, "to the materiality of lived or recorded data" (Dantas 47–48), the marginal poets lacked, it can be concluded, an ideal comparable to Oswald's. Chacal and company tended to go straight to data — speech, attitudes, things — rather than filter phenomena or engage in any intellectual or ideological reflection. Marginal discourse, with its emphasis on deflated language in individual instances, was not posed to equal one of the keys to Oswald's poetics: the *systemization* of short takes, flashes, citations, etc., into organized sequences. The integrated circuits of the manifestos and of *Poesia Pau-*

Brasil — be they historical, geographical, or developmental — carry much more current than the sum of isolated passages and poems. None of the young seventies poets had an overall scheme or poetic construct comparable to Oswald's pointed fashioning of intellectual and literary history.

While *poesia marginal* invited critical negativity — such as the identification of its tonic notes as "regressive sense," "de-literarization," and "literary disqualification" (Simon and Dantas 49) — questioning of its literary value has been based on a wide-angle view of uneven phenomena and on selective focus on specific examples. The sociocultural interest of networks of informal youth poetry has been justifiably asserted, but while it marks the cultural landscape of the 1970s, there are dangers in over-estimating the significance of *poesia marginal* for literature. Stressing the tendency as dominant, with its concomitant weaknesses, may in fact lead to confusion about the period as a whole and make a holistic view difficult. The aesthetically "peripheral" traits of *poesia marginal* as trend should not limit the expected and admirable exceptions to the rule of "disqualification." Precisely because of negative connotations, it would not be "fair" to consider all young contemporaries under the rubric of *marginal*. Several poets who appeared in *26 poetas hoje* are independent voices, notably Antônio Carlos Secchin (b. 1952), of a more cerebral post-Cabral orientation. Others have garnered attention for motives of poetic form and expression. Ana Cristina César (1952–1983) — a most significant name for contemporary women's literature — was noted, on one hand, for an unusual, self-conscious quasi-confessional approach, and on the other, for "leafing through traditions," including glosses of Baudelaire and imagery drawn from Rimbaud.[24] Adélia Prado (b. 1936) has been associated with the seventies generation because of the date of publication of her first book (1976), though she does not take a particularly "youthful" approach. Unassuming and accessible, her free verse is frequently spiritual (traditional monotheistic) in preoccupation or has strong feminist overtones. In another context of opposition, her "Com licença poética" / "With Poetic License" rekindles dialogue with Drummond's "Poema de sete faces" to ironize the shouldering of burden:

> Quando nasci um anjo esbelto,
> desses que tocam trombeta, anunciou:
> vai carregar bandeira.
> Cargo muito pesado pra mulher,
> esta espécie ainda envergonhada.

Aceito os subterfúgios que me cabem,
sem precisar mentir.
. . . .
Vai ser coxo, é maldição pra homem.
Mulher é desdobrável. Eu sou.

When I was born, one of those svelte angels
who plays a trumpet proclaimed:
this one will carry a flag.
A heavy load for a woman,
even nowadays such a bashful species.
I accept the subterfuges that fit;
no need to lie.
. . . . . .
It's man's curse to be lame in life,
woman's to unfold. I do.[25]

The most frequently cited lyrical voice associated with seventies "youth poetry" is Francisco Alvim. While he also belongs chronologically to an earlier generation, his verse is indeed symptomatic of the "marginal" period in terms of relaxed diction and of certain neo-Oswaldian traits in a mixed style. Merquior perceives such representation and representativity in a central text: " 'Paralaxe' is a poem in multiple planes, where a more accentuated confessional tone comes alongside magical, cosmic, anthropophagous allusions and objective flashes directly imported from the headstrong chapter of vices and customs of Brazil."[26] On another front, Geraldo Carneiro achieved some unusual blends of popular perspectives into a universal sphere of literature, as in the English original "decolonization of myself":

I wish I could write parodies
as dubliner bards lull a bye-bye blackbird
singin' in the dread of flight
or dreaming for Gold sake a spiritual rag
under the milkshakespearean wood of symbols
but, as poor Camoens said,
my indiom is portugeese
and returned to write
his songs of hymnonsense[27]

These and numerous other poets surpassed transitory modes related to epochal factors and sustained individual poetic diction beyond the informal adventures of the seventies.

The vogue of *poesia marginal* tended toward dissolution in the early 1980s. The general climate of fear diminished with gradual political opening and redemocratization, and cycles of youth culture ran their natural courses, as suggested in the title *A velhice do poeta marginal* (The old-age of the marginal poet, 1983) by the ever-satirical graphic poet Sebastião Nunes. Patterns of activity and publication allow the period of the seventies to be extended to about 1983. The appearance of critical material on marginal phenomena, as well as the "reprint" editions of individual poets (e.g., Chacal, Alvim, César, Cacaso) by established publishing houses, also marked a transition. Emergent and continuing poets of the eighties, in contrast, were increasingly attuned to literary heritage and vitalization through discipline and reflection. Benedito Nunes establishes (179ff.) four constants or characteristic lines for poetry of the 1980s which, by proximity and continuity, naturally relate to emergence in the 1970s: (1) self-reflexive or metapoetic gestures, (2) techniques of fragmentation, (3) epigrammatic configuration, and (4) neo-rhetorical (i.e., neo-epical) composition. This last reference, as seen at the outset of this chapter, had been instituted in works by Gullar and Sant'Anna. Categories two and three, as illustrated above, are most relevant to *poesia marginal;* they are shared, though approached differently, by nonmarginals, one of whose distinguishing features is precisely the first constant.

In the Margins, Between the Lines, Signs of the Times

The other orientation of new Brazilian poetry of the 1970s encompassed postconcretist output of "constructivist" verse-makers and practices of visual poetry. These types of production, while involving more literary or conceptual issues per se, have been the object of considerably less critical treatment in Brazil than *poesia marginal.* The two spheres overlapped somewhat, especially in the first half of the decade, since certain seemingly anarchic attitudes informed some nonmarginal material. This other orientation did not fully assert itself until the effective end of the period (i.e., the early eighties).[28] For this and other reasons, due distinctions between the two camps have not been uniformly made. For instance, writing about the domain of poetry in the seventies, a respected chronicler of Brazilian literature underscored the "anthropophagical climate of Oswald de Andrade," the modernist atmosphere of '22, colloquialism, and the "marginal."[29] The exemplary publications he cited, however, were *Navilouca* (1974), *Código* (first issue 1974), *Muda* (1977), and *Corpo estranho* (1975–1981), which were not vehicles of the kind of informal verse critiqued above, but rather of intersemiotic creation, as indicated by their frequent inclusion of graphic arts and of the later works of the concrete poets. The veteran literary historian's assignment of neocolloquialism as the centerpiece of seventies poetry demonstrates the results of critical overemphasis on *poesia marginal* and, consequently, the necessity for a broader view of youth poetry of the period.

The other-than-marginal character of new poetry in the seventies was often revealed in the production values of its vehicles. In contrast to the catch-as-catch-can approach of most *poesia marginal,* its counterpart appeared in carefully produced art journals, special-issue magazines, anthologies, and individual editions. In addition to those cited above, representative titles included *Polem* (1974) and *Artéria* (1976–1977). The umbrella term *intersemiotic creation,* subtitle of the arts journal *Corpo estranho* 2, accounts for the interplay of varied sign languages: the printed word in multiple typographic and spatial representations, illustrated verse, graphics, photography, and mixtures thereof. Where poetry was concerned, writers often repudiated linear syntax and were highly concerned with the materiality of language and *mise-en-page*. Essentially lyrical voices showed renewed interest in both empirical sources and extraverbal aspects of text, in aspects of orality and the public language of advertising. Combinatory approaches were tried in a search for new inventive ground, and ambivalences resulted. In this arena, natural tensions arose between subjective expressivity and objective optical concerns. Régis Bonvicino (b. 1955) symptomatically called himself "a signic reporter" and "a concretist who didn't know what to do with his heart."[30] Like poets tended to subordinate existential elements to linguistic exploration and elaboration on textual structures and/or graphic elements. Diverse works comprise reactions to the power of the cultural industry (film, cartoons, etc.) and to the circulation of structuralist theory. With or without visual elements per se, engagement with aesthetic issues and literary legacies were valued. In typical journals, guiding preoccupation with having theoretical and cultural information was reflected in creative and critical texts, as well as in the frequent publication of translations of poetry. The variety of textual solutions there suggests that informed makers responded to the competitive appeals of self-projection, impersonality, and media awareness.

The terms *construtiva* (constructive) and *construtivista* (constructivist) were employed by young writers to disassociate their work from undisciplined *poesia marginal* and to align with a position of conscious internationalism. For instance, it was argued — via Paul de Man and the Jakobsonian specificity of poetic language — that *poesia marginal* was not even poetry, but rather verbal posturing and expression of attitude; the antagonist would be poetic work having "constructivist character."[31] In the account of another representative voice, a variety of "de-automatized" individual dictions and languages was posited in opposition to informal youth verse. Here too there was an admitted "recuperation of the colloquial," but in a reworking quite unlike the passive and conventional *poesia marginal*. What characterized such informed production were a consciousness of making, a postconcrete semantic opening, and, emerging from the synthesis of concrete poetry, verbal economy and constructive rigor.[32] If, in a fundamental way, most *poesia marginal* was steeped in immediacy and experience, those with constructivist interests sought to draw on a legacy of language-oriented poetry.

In their own work, such new seventies poets restricted and consciously controlled discursivity and referential functions of language. Semantics were often tied to graphic space and/or manipulations of linguistic coincidences. Carlos Ávila (b. 1955), for instance, sets in white letters on a black field the following lines: "o terceiro mundo / vai explodir / no quarto escuro / um segundo / e o primeiro tiro" (the third world / is going to explode / in the (forth) dark room / one second / and the first shot).[33] In this example, verbal ambivalences (of words for ordinal numbers) serve to empower notions of contention, imminence, and compacting to the point of explosion in a gesture of sociohistorical awareness.

Spontaneity could be countered via the Cabral model of metrical construction, material symbols, and topicalizing of rational measurement, as in this "definição de poesia" (definition of poetry) by Nelson Ascher (b. 1958):

> Poesia, ponte em cima
> de abismos não abertos
> ainda ou flor que anima
> a pedra no deserto
>
> e a deixa logo prenha,
> é régua que calcula a
> linguagem e lhe engenha
> modelos de medula.[34]*

---

*[Poetry, bridge over / still unopened abysses / or a flower that animates / stone in the desert / and soon leaves it pregnant, / is a ruler that calculates / language and designs for it / models of medulla]

```
L  R         E
             O
H  M  M      O  E
C  M         O  U
   M         I     O
S  GN




        E              V  R
   O                   N
        O  E           H  M  M
        O  O           C  M  M
   U                   S  GN
        I     O
```

Example 15*

More common than this "calculated" model were fragmentation and extreme concision. Adoption of minimalist modes led to a legion of epigrams, aphorisms, highlighted statements, and sensorial flashes, exemplified in the neologistic self-revelation of Duda Machado (b. 1944) in "breakfast":[35]

manhã azulcrinando o céu de meus sentidos

Other productive factors in constructivist poetry were sharp awareness of phonetics, alphabetic qualities, and textual shape. Semiotics grew in Brazil in the 1970s and concerns with signification affected creativity itself.[36] Semiosis could be stressed over emotivity and referentiation to the point of becoming a self-sufficient theme, as illustrated in Ávila's extraction and reclustering of vowels (example 15).[37]

The inheritance of concrete poetry in intersemiotic creation is clear

* [to read man like a sign / to see in man like a sign]

como é que é meu caro ezra pound? vou acender
um cigarro daqueles para ver se consigo lhe dizer isto.
andei fazendo um pouco de tudo aquilo que você
aconselhou para desenvolver a capacidade de bem escre-
ver. estudei Homero; li o livro de Fenollosa sobre o
ideograma chinês, tornei-me capaz de dedilhar um alaú-
de; todos os meus amigos agora são pessoas que têm o
hábito de fazer boa música; pratiquei diversos exercícios
de melopéia, fanopéia e logopéia, analisei criações de
vários dos integrantes do seu paideuma.
continuo, no entanto, a sentir a mesma dificuldade do
início. uma grande confusão na cabeça tão infinitamente
grande confusão um vasto emaranhado de pensamentos
misturados com as possíveis variantes que se completam
antiteticamente.

rogério duarte

Example 16*

but not oppressive or obsessive. Where seventies production is con-
cerned, manifestations reminiscent of the original "organic" concrete
poetry and "inventive" variations were numerous. The more program-
matic "orthodox" models were admired, and in spirit absorbed, but
rarely imitated. However influential concrete poetry is judged to have
been in the 1970s, the term "postconcrete," rather than designating
any stylistic parameter, is judged to have an essentially chronological
value.[38]

The marks of concretism—concrete poetry itself, as well as criticism,
theory, and translations of the Noigandres group—were varied in the
seventies arena. Augusto de Campos's interest in innovative popular
music was, as seen in chapter 4, a key factor in the recognition of song as

---

*[How's it goin' my dear Ezra Pound? I'm going to light / one of those cigarettes to see if I
can manage to tell you this / I was doing a little of everything you / suggested to develop
the ability to write / well. I studied Homer; I read Fenollosa's book on / Chinese ideo-
grams; I became able to finger a lute / all my friends now are people who have the / habit of
making good music; I practiced diverse exercises / of melopeia, phanopeia and logopeia; I
analyzed creations of / several of those who form your paideuma / yet I continue to feel the
same beginning difficulty / a great confusion in my head such an infinitely / great confu-
sion, a vast mesh of thoughts / mixed with possible variants that complement each other /
antithetically]

a channel of poetry in the late 1960s. His involvement prompted further musical experiments inspired in concretist models, which is but one of the aspects of the multifaceted poetry of song that outlasted the seventies. Among the concretists' creative and critical references in world literature, Ezra Pound perhaps elicited the greatest response. The imperative of "make it new" influenced both those concerned with lyrical expression and, via the "ideogrammic" concepts of concrete poetry as well, those interested in visuality. Though in an ultimately negative frame, a curious prose-poem by Rogério Duarte (b. 194?) illustrates the purposeful attention paid to Poundian parameters (example 16).[39]

This confessional apostrophe, revealing an individual groping for a literary voice, depicts intertwined threads of seventies poetry: musico-literary affinities, some of the subjective discursive qualities of *poesia marginal,* perhaps even a hint of its anti-intellectual stance. If the speaker's confused disillusionment may suggest fissure within would-be constructivist ranks, the very premise of critical concern is a distinguishing feature that links the youthful text to the agenda of concretism.

The prime poetic influence of the Noigandres poets was seen in a propensity toward brevity, linked in origin to reductive concrete principles and to the revival of the bare-boned *poesia-minuto* of Oswald de Andrade, whose related cultural critiques were also part of the overall concretist project. As seen with *poesia marginal,* the brazen modernist was a model for contestatory stances in the authoritarian seventies. He had the further advantage of being, as Dantas (47) says, "the official and officiating vanguardist totem." Since he was a prime reference point for marginal poets, however, their reading of him had to be questioned by those who sought to dissociate themselves from that trend. Hence the following expression of reservations by a contemporary poet: " . . . POESIA MARGINAL, establishes as a paradigm of poetic making, facility and dilution, reading the work of Oswald de Andrade in a reduced and facilitated form. . . . The 'marginal' does not exist as a movement of rupture, setting up new models of sensibility." The facilitators in question are held—playing on Oswald's central metaphor—to have practiced "a toothless [*banguela*] anthropophagy."[40] The reasons for the lack of bite in informal youth poetry having been established above, this critical reference illustrates again how self-conceived nonmarginal poets perceived a need to define their efforts against the more publicized phenomenon. In terms of actual lyric, Bonvicino displays a characteristic open admiration for Oswald, operating via homage, controlled stylemes, and intertextuality. For example, he interprets a moment in the "Cannibalist Manifesto" in search of more contemporary insight:

```
oswald de andrade
sugere
no manifesto antropofágico
(ó lua nova)
a idéia
de um mundo não datado
minuto mútuo
tempo composto
gema gêmea
de um outro*
```

In a contiguous derivative poem, "vingança de português" (Portuguese revenge), the anecdotal manner and evolutionary nativism of *Poesia Pau-Brasil* are adopted in a self-proclaimed palinode:

```
o português plantou
um pé de ipê
na calçada do prédio

no dia seguinte
os transeúntes desfolharam o ipê

indignado
o português não teve dúvida
— é coisa de índio!41**
```

While these examples are purely verbal, their author, like many other young voices of the 1970s, in many other instances depended on nonverbal elements in the construction of new texts. The poetry of intersemiotic creation is largely about establishing "difference," about asserting aversion to standard poetic props and speech-act lyric. Efforts at estrangement may be embodied in typography — the use of bold or raised characters, photocopy amplifications, difficult fonts that add enigma to texts — or in a kind of "semiotic synesthesia" whereby different senses and artistic practices are juxtaposed or joined. Take example 17, for instance. This fractured text appeared on a white card as one of many inserts into a large envelope lining a clear plastic shopping bag (with resealable handle) that comprised the second number of *Arteria,* orga-

---

*[Oswald de Andrade suggests / in the cannibalist manifesto / oh new moon / the idea / of an undated world / mutual minute / composed time / twin yolk / of an other]

**[the Portuguese planted / a native tree / on the sidewalk of the building / the next day / passersby de-leafed the tree / incensed / the Portuguese had no doubts / "It was Indians!"]

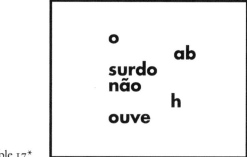

Example 17*

nized by Omar Khouri. Co-author Walter Franco, a composer in the rock idiom, plays with the senses of sight and hearing, in a homographic conceit that includes preemptive response to any questioning of its coherence, i.e., there is no absurdity in this gesture. Thus from the micro level of textual detail to the macro level of vessel, this example projects multiple connections and illustrates perfectly the "intersemiotic" face of new seventies poetry.

As exemplified in *Arteria,* the designs of new poetry could in many cases be determined by its methods of presentation and "marketing," i.e., being divulged in conjunction with visual arts or in graphic schemes. Thus the self-declared "feminist manifesto" of Alice Ruiz (b. 1946) — maker of haiku-like verse of contained wit — is built as a fan of phrase-spokes emanating from a nautilus shell. This vivacious design empowers the series of ironic statements of the feminine condition, double standards, stereotypes, clichés, etc., that gathers steam as it is rotated and read.[42] The title — "o que é a que é" (what is it that / what is the one [she] who) — is posed as a riddle with a feminine subject (example 18).

In a more metatextual mode, intentional testings of the page extended to the probing of the book format itself and to the fabrication of alternative "containers" for text. A notable early experiment by Eliane Zagury (b. 1945) is the humoristic "mercado" (1970) (example 19), six overlaid concentric word-wheels with do-it-yourself instructions for more-than-a-book's-worth of combinations.

Numerous seventies page-poet-artists offered assorted works in different paper sizes and colors, in folders, binders, bags, or even cardboard cans with "text chips." In such cases, physical variations allow for individuality or particularity within the context of an ad hoc collective (group) or of a collection (of the same author). Such assertions of the

---

*[the deaf man does not hear / there was no absurdity]

Example 18

interrelations and limitations of lyric were continual during the youthful rediscovery of poetry.

Display of instrument, often linked to a structuring ludic approach, was a notable constant in typical pieces of "intersemiotic" or "constructivist" poets, who reacted to technological expansion as they pondered the boundaries of poetry. Extraverbal materials were transferred to the page as expressionistic devices, as well as in phatic or metalinguistic functions. Juxtaposition of codes (form) is as purposeful as words (content), for instance, in the *babilaques* (ID cards) of Waly Salomão (b. 1944), which comprised color photos of diverse handwritten diaries and writer's scrapbooks.[43] Image was also tied to words to act as "inspiration." For his part, Carlos Ávila attached a kitsch aphorism to a suggestive image (example 20). Choosing an old cursive font and a hand holding an antiquity of calligraphy (the quill pen) — a visual component from an eighteenth-century volume on reading and writing — the poet touches on anachronism and sentimentalism while framing an intersemiotic question.[44] A similar procedure was effected by Antônio Risério (b. 1953), who interlocked image — the custom Oriental topography of the words, and, especially, two photos of an infant emerging from a giant eggshell — with a poetically topical quatrain: laughter cracks good sense / rivers change plumage / when from the ashes is reborn / the kamikaze of language.[45]

A later example of the reach of technology into verbal page art is a work by Philadelpho Menezes (b. 1960) which comprises a pair of photos of calculator digits (612309) whose flipped negative spells *poesia*.[46] This invocation of lyric through computer chip embodies an ambivalence shared by numerous poets of his generation and outlook: a concern for poetry per se but with a certain aversion to the standard props of lyrical convention. Such examples seek to establish their difference to answer to the imperative of invention inherited from concretism and the other vanguards. These later "intersemiotic" experiments imply acceptance of the mid-fifties declaration of the demise of verse, carry a sense that the manipulation of visuality represents in itself an "advanced" practice, and uncover a belief that experimental avenues opened by concrete poetry are still worth pursuing. Recent poetic history, cultural journalism, and mass cultural industry informed the interdisciplinary parodies of Glauco Mattoso, who between 1977 and 1981 edited a mock, typewriter-produced, arts journal, *Jornal Dobrabil* (a title that resembles that of the leading daily *Jornal do Brasil* and forges a pseudo-word for "foldable"). Mattoso's comic-strip sequence "O Marginal," in collaboration with Angeli, depicted a mugging and an arrest couched in terms of avant-garde experiments — *poesia concreta, poema processo* — and youthful "intervention."[47] While beyond the realm of lyric, this graphic narrative is more than a humorous episode; it incorporates and represents a determining factor for the "constructivist" sector, to wit, operating with constant consciousness of contemporary critical parameters and foregrounded issues of genre and kinship.

The Instructive Case of Paulo Leminski

In terms of individual production, the most representative poetic voice of the 1970s and 1980s was Paulo Leminski (1944–1989). His multiform prose and poetry directly participated in, or alluded to, the central man-

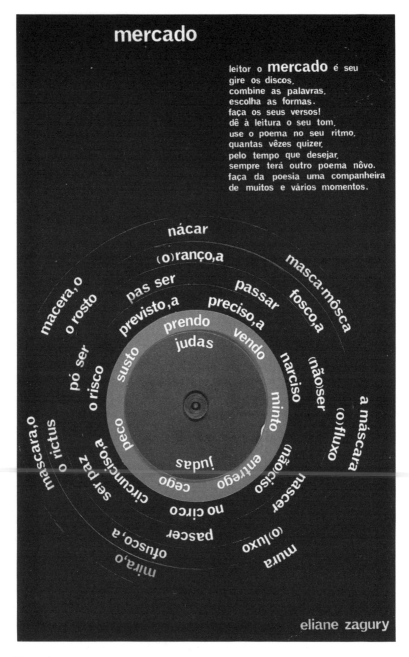

Example 19

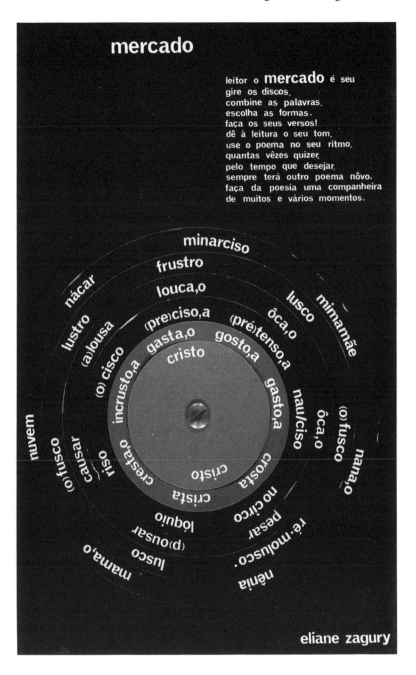

mercado

leitor o **mercado** é seu
gire os discos.
combine as palavras.
escolha as formas.
faça os seus versos!
dê à leitura o seu tom.
use o poema no seu ritmo.
quantas vêzes quizer.
pelo tempo que desejar.
sempre terá outro poema nôvo.
faça da poesia uma companheira
de muitos e vários momentos.

minarciso
frustro
louca,o
nácar
lustro   lusco
(a)lousa   ôca,o   mimamãe
(pre)ciso,a (pré)tenso,a
(o) cisco   gasta,o   gosto,a
             cristo
incrusto,a   gasto,a
                      nau/ciso   (o)fusco
nuvem   ôca,o
(o)fusco   nana,o
causar   crosta
riso   cristo   no circo
cresta,o   crista   pesar
            cristo   ré-molusco.
lóquio
(p)ousar   nênia
lusco
mama,o

eliane zagury

Example 20*

ifestations of the period.[48] While this writer-critic cast a wide net, he did so from a fundamentally constructivist base. Leminski's vanguardism was well founded, as his inaugural poetic work originally appeared in *Invenção,* the organ of the latter phase of concretism in the 1960s. Beyond several extensions of the "inventive" (read: shaped, nondiscursive) approach, Leminski wrote verse which in its affability and breadth showed certain affinities with *poesia marginal.* In terms of publication status, Leminski's initial titles were, though never in mimeograph form, independent productions. After several contributions to organs of intersemiotic creation, his material was anthologized in a commercial edition.[49] The writer's seventies lyric ranged from minimalist to brief, was frequently light in tone or playful, and often seemed informal or colloquial. With this in mind, a contemporary of Leminski's observed that his early collected work could be seen to draw "a connecting arc between concrete poetry and the new nonspecialized sensibilities," but that despite Leminski's having often opted for "a language of more immediate communicative yield," the leitmotif was always language itself.[50] Indeed, some of his speech-related verse, though perhaps displaying a surface

* [heart / a lone word / as the best refrain]

similar to that of more commonplace *poesia marginal,* regularly had a distinguishing conceptual grain or formal feature (usually rhyme). In addition, in the semantic dimension of Leminski's poems, one might say, the "life" element was detached. A perceptive reader noted how, despite his practice of an all-embracing "good neighbor policy," Leminski's grace was lyrical renovation with containment: "As there is no emotive or referential anteriorness, everything being resolved graphically on the page, the poem closes upon itself without metaphors or symbolism" (Dantas 50). This affirmation should not be accepted as a rule, since figurative language was by no means absent in the repertory considered; it was simply associated with a telling self-awareness of fictiveness.

The following trio of examples will demonstrate the balance and suggestiveness of Leminski's poems. The epigrammatic — central to his output and to that of his generation — was best illustrated in an isolated portmanteau word (example 21). This one-word text appeared (125) in a section of nonverse, poster poems, visually oriented lines, advertising-related pieces, etc. While the use of English was in itself indicative of appeal to a noncolloquial level, the playful semantic combination — uncertainty and felicity — reinforced a level of indeterminacy uncharacteristic of any marginal endeavor. The language of another key untitled composition, in turn, is straightforward and personal but harbors a careful ambivalence: "lembrem de mim / como de um / que ouvia a chuva / como quem assiste missa / como quem hesita, mestiça / entre a pressa e a preguiça" (59) [remember me / as one / who heard the rain / as one attends mass / as one who hesitates, mestizo / between hurried and lazy]. The speaker here conceives a mixed self (mestizo) who could accept very traditional rites (mass) but would balk between hurried and lazy. The conventional semantic antithesis, extrapolated onto a historico-stylistic plane, suggests two positions that marked the discourse of *poesia marginal,* the implications of which Leminski's ideal speaker, here hesitating, could not accept. The simple poem is a projection of memory, lyrical but contemporarily rhymed. It is an uncommon rhyme that keys another, central, untitled text:

PERHAPPINESS

Example 21

apagar-me
diluir-me
desmanchar-me
até que depois
de mim
de nós
de tudo
não reste mais
que o charme*

These lines appear twice in the collection (66, 136), first in standard typeset, then in a boldface maxi-font. This is quite appropriate, for the poem is a declaration of purpose, and Leminski's aims are often two-edged. The articulation of objective condenses constructivist ideals: terse approach, verbal economy, subjective denial, filtering leading toward purification. The reflexive *desmanchar* connotes undoing, disjuncture, coming apart, becoming deranged or spoiling, with an additional potential etymological connotation of unstaining. All this is linked by rhyme to *charme,* whose most commonplace use simply involves alluring demeanor and social grace. One must also highlight the borrowed word's Latin to Old French origins: charm, enchantment, chant, lyric. In this way, and in the best tradition of modern poetry, Leminski's focus on self is a continual search for poetic essence. The seemingly casual manner of his verse-making is betrayed by larger artistic concerns, which, in keeping with contemporary conditions, may also incorporate an informed informality.

From a wider angle, the configuration of youth poetry in the 1970s is perhaps best encapsulated in the epigraph to *Caprichos e relaxos:*

Aqui, poemas para lerem, em silêncio,
o olho, o coração e a inteligência.
Poemas para dizer, em voz alta.
E poemas, letras, lyrics para cantar.
Quais, quais, é com você, parceiro.**

In five simple lines here Leminski affirms various contemporary means and functions of poetry. While conventional silent reading stands first,

---

*[erase myself / dilute myself / disarm myself / until after me / after us / after all / nothing is left / but charm]

**[Here poems to read in silence / the eye, the heart, and the intelligence / Poems to say out loud / and poems, song texts, lyrics to sing / Which is which is up to you, partner] poetry's oral operations, in recitation and song, come inexorably into play. The assignment of three orientations—visual (*eye*), emotive (*heart*), conceptual (*intelligence*)—pertinently recalls Pound's triaxial classification for lyric—melopeia (sound and melody), phanopeia (imagery for the eye), and logopeia (imagery for the intellect)—and is indicative of a constructivist consciousness. Leminski's open-ended final line most provocatively broaches issues of concern to intersemiotic creation: the contemporary questioning and testing of limits and distinctions between poetic categories, notably visuality and verbality. Leminski also participated in the poetry of song (at least one of the untitled items in *Caprichos e relaxos* was widely known as the lyric to a song recorded by Caetano Veloso as "Verdura" in 1979). The word with which Leminski closes the epigraph, *parceiro,* is commonly used to designate a cowriter or partner in songwriting. Here the partner is also the reader, viewer, listener, who, in the spirit of contemporary experimental literature, is encouraged to collaborate, to make judgments about the constitution of poetry, with its various interrelated elements.

Epilogue: Whither Marginalia?

The provocative epigraph further suggests the representativity of the material—by way of model or contrast—for an evaluation of trends in poetry of the 1970s, oriented by the basic dichotomy of informal marginality vs. informed constructivism. Leminski clearly understood the motivations for adopting elements of counterculture and informality in poetry, but in his own work he incorporated such impulses into a self-questioning literary project. The poet's subsequent collections— with their evident moves toward pointed formal control and relative de-emphasis of literal visual elements—support the idea that c. 1983 marked a transition out of the youthful period of the seventies. It must have been a very self-conscious writer who—with tendencies, labels, and implications in mind—later wrote:

> Marginal é quem escreve à margem,
> deixando branca a página
> para que a paisagem passe
> e deixe tudo claro à sua passagem.
>
> Marginal, escrever na entrelinha,
> sem nunca saber direito

quem veio primeiro,
o ovo ou a galinha.[51]*

The many notions of textuality and poetic making in these quatrains —
layout, visual imagery, paronomasia, subtlety, figuration, language-
generated mystery, etc. — all contribute to an ex post facto reaffirmation
of an important distinction between the "specialized" camp of Leminski
and informal alternative lyric.

   With the positionings of Leminski and others in mind, it can be said
that the significance of *poesia marginal,* while it is an obligatory reference
for seventies poetry, should be assigned carefully. The trend was, some-
what like that revolving around *Violão de rua* in the early sixties, indeed
healthy for self-expression and networking of politically disenfranchised
middle-class youth in the context of the authoritarian decade of the
seventies, thus meriting attention from the angles of urban sociology
and cultural history. There was a need to demonstrate creative vitality
during the dictatorship, as well as a critical desire, in some camps, to
verify the occurrence of something different from, or even in opposition
to, the continuity of vanguardism, which may explain a certain critical
reserve with respect to those young poets with concretist affiliations. Yet
little *poesia marginal* can stand up to standard literary exigencies, and the
enduring qualities of the most considered neocolloquial voices may have
been overshadowed by unfavorable generational traits. Whatever the
aesthetic limitations of the more public phenomenon, the effervescence
of casual options did represent an opening toward poetry in the midst of
Brazil's technological expansion of the 1970s. Constructivist poets, for
their parts, also showed youthful enthusiasm and confronted socio-
cultural perplexities of the decade, including those provoked by the
onset of media, in artistically responsive manners. The pole of inter-
semiotic creation, with its flexible range of individual interests, is more
difficult to classify but ultimately bears more aesthetic interest because of
its sources, goals, and idiosyncratic results.

---

*[Marginals are those who write on the margins / leaving the page blank / so that the
landscape may pass / and leave all clear upon its passage / Marginal, write between lines /
without ever really knowing / who came first / the chicken or the egg]

chapter six

Pagings and Postings: Historical Imperatives

of the Late Century

The 1980s were years of plurality, reexaminations, affirmations, perplex-
ities, and world awareness in Brazilian lyric. The decade was marked by
the political transition (from military rule to a civilian administration in
1985) and haunted by successive economic crises. In intellectual and
artistic circles, new developments included the appearance of the inter-
national specter of the "postmodern." Though most naturally associated
with the advanced industrialized world, the massive and multifaceted
matter of postmodernism inevitably provoked debate in the unevenly
developed nation of Brazil about its own conditions. With respect to the
rethinking of poetry in the 1980s, the Noigandres poets Haroldo de
Campos and Augusto de Campos made notable "post-" contributions,
and revealing exchanges sprung up around pertinent theoretical and
creative works of these leading voices of concretism. Their perceptions
of postmodernity in action, as well as reactions to and by them, keyed
aesthetically focused discussions. The topic of the postmodern figures
prominently in two compelling instances: a mid-decade polemic sur-
rounding "Pós-tudo," a particularly provocative poem by Augusto, and
the concurrent articulation of the notion of the "post-utopian poem" by
Haroldo. It should be useful to take a close look at these cases to see how
some general (theoretical, situational) questions and more specific (sty-
listic, textual) positions related to the postmodern unfolded in Brazil.
The contents and authorial contexts of these occurrences merit attention
both for their intrinsic interest and for their broader implications for an
understanding of contemporary Brazilian lyric. Directly or indirectly,
these events and circumstances activate forceful retrospection on mod-
ernist experimentalism and evaluation of its current validity. In the eight-
ies, the historical — encompassing the roles of the vanguards of the 1920s

and midcentury alike, as well as the historicity of text and text-makers in the present — comes into play with vigor. The Campos episodes invoke the principles of various poetries of intervening decades in Brazil, and, in wider scope, high points of the whole Western tradition that can inform poetry toward the end of the century. In creative texts, essays, and commentaries on the postmodern, Augusto and Haroldo adopt their own distinct perspectives. Both retain essential connections with the epoch of concrete poetry and maintain the centrality of invention, but their views on the present significance of the avant-garde, with its reliance on the impetus of change, prove to contrast. While their positions do have points of contact with international postmodernism, they evolve from national imperatives and debates, and what ultimately stands out, within the domain of lyric, are expressions of skepticism. In the late century, the Noigandres poets cannot but recognize a new present, and they are, necessarily, open to different senses of future.

As the end of the twentieth century approaches, defining and delimiting the "postmodern" or "postmodernism" is a daunting and unending task.[1] In the broadest sense, the terms refer to the latest stage of Western civilization and consciousness, as well as to the evolved cultural enterprises that characterize the epoch, including philosophy and the arts, both traditional and technologically influenced. One of the most common wide applications of the terms is to a style or mood deriving from the exhaustion of, or dissatisfaction with, modernism in art and literature, as José Guilherme Merquior noted.[2] Postmodernism also subsumes such other indicators of next-stage development as the post-industrial, poststructuralism, and postvanguard. Thus, for some, the umbrella term further covers directions of French philosophy since the 1960s (Foucault, Derrida, and deconstruction, especially Lyotard and the theory of simulacra in *The Postmodern Condition*) and concurrent cultural artifacts.

It is important to stress that postmodern phenomena are largely understood to be North American and European products or symptoms of (life in) the advanced capitalist world in the age of technology. In the Latin American domain, the acceptability and usefulness of postmodern models and theories have been challenged and debated for some time.[3] Even before the general challenges and objections to its conceptualization, the fundamental doubt about postmodernism in Latin America concerns the status of modernity — economic, political, large-scale cultural — in the region. How can one discuss *post*modernity in the face of the multiple paradoxes of modernism in dependent, peripheral nations of agrarian tradition and problematic illiteracy? In Brazil, in particular, there is a lasting incongruity of progress and backwardness, and irregular modernity is linked to the *pre*modern, the *sub*modern, the *pseudo*modern, the *anti*modern, and the *para*modern, as one Brazilian observer has put it.[4] It is the very unevenness of modernity in such nations as Brazil — whose cosmopolitan centers are hooked into international networks and inevitably feel, sometimes quite quickly, the impact of First World developments — that permits consideration of one's own postmodernism. Multiple surface manifestations and the variety of theoretical postulations of the postmodern allow for further speculation.

The very discussion of postmodern potential is a main aspect of Augusto de Campos's poem "Pós-tudo" (Post-everything, 1984) and of a contentious critique made by the prominent cultural critic Roberto Schwarz, which are scrutinized below. Critical treatment of the poem illustrates how details of immanence can fulfill significant functions in contextual criticism. "Pós-tudo" and related secondary texts further raise, or revive, questions about the vanguard of concretism, opposition to it, and the possibility of emancipation through cultural projects. To situate the particulars of that essential poem and to understand better the controversy it touched off, it will be advantageous to consider first the strategies of Augusto's production of the late seventies and early eighties and then how the poem represents and summarizes that output.

Postconcrete and the Relatives of "Pós-tudo"

The seventies are, for the Noigandres poets, a postconcrete phase with consistency and continuity but palpable change. Of the three principals, Augusto maintained the greatest fidelity to the foundational interdisciplinary aesthetic of condensation. In the early part of the decade, he produced some of his most minimalist work, including the exclamation that became the title of his collected poems, VIVA VAIA, and the poem-logo "Código." Augusto also took the idea of the poem as "useful object" a step further, releasing worded objects designed for actual handling (folding paper, cubes, etc.).[5] Since 1975, without sacrificing the visible synthesis achieved in concrete poetry, the poet's repertory shows a notable "recovery" of word and phrase. In this sort of intersemiotic return to lyricism, Augusto seeks materiality in both language itself and in its (ideally isomorphic) modes of presentation. Thus in different sets of poems he enriches phrase fields with graphic elements (typeface, color, layout) which reinforce effects and affects, which function as de facto structural constituents of tone, mood, and abstract "meaning," and which act as key factors in the making of poetic space. For the first time since the mid-fifties formalization of concrete poetry, the pronouns *eu* (I) and *você* (you) appear in the poet's creative texts.

In this "neo"-lyrical approach, pronouns and predicates may appear anew, but phrases and "verses" are submitted, in Augusto's own words, to "iconical bombardment through visual exploration of letters and their spatialization."[6] One best views such procedures in the series *stelegramas,* a heading that suggests the concision and communication technology of the telegram, as well as the celestial paradigm of two of the best known pieces. "Quasar" brings together an affective human dimension, urban imagery (implied neon) and an astronomical plane (quasar=quasi-stellar object) through placement of an enjoinder (think of the quasi-love of the quasi-human quasar) in a striking (starlike) baby-teeth font on a black background. The companion piece "Pulsar," with dots and stars for key recurring vowels, creates a sidereal space on a black page for a more developed expression of wonderment. The intersemiotic con-ception of this "stellar" poem is confirmed and amplified in Caetano Veloso's musical settings.[7] Another noteworthy item of this collection is "Memos," in which the physical structuring of numerous typefaces trans-forms discursive language and creates unexpected enigmas.[8]

Arrangement of lexical items in columns also keys "Todos os sons" (All the sounds), where multiple typographies suggest a kind of poly-vocalism and, to further the musical parallel, an affirmation of profanity in poetry akin to John Cage's position that all noise may constitute music. Augusto's poster-poem interrelation of sound and print figures in his fine-press portfolio *Expoemas.*[9] As a whole, this series seeks to project off or beyond the page with a sort of Gestaltist emphasis. In the concre-tist vein, verbal materiality — literal (type, texture) and linguistic (pho-nemic patterns, word fusion) — often configures a metalinguistic dimen-sion. The collection continues the pursuit of a visible "otherness" or "difference" in poetic space, where font or color, far from being inciden-tal or ornamental, aspire to integrality. Some of the poems may work in black and white but are fully realized in color "pertinent to the iconic context," which adds an appreciable plastic dimension, as in the bright red of "Viventes e vampiros" (Living and vampires). As for fonts, in many cases "the design is incorporated to such a degree in the compo-sition that without it the poem is destabilized."[10] Thus, in "Pessoa," homage to the Portuguese master poet, Augusto employs a "difficult," airy, ethereal lettering for the conceits and paradoxes expressed, and in "Afazer" (Task), where aphasia is an analogy for poetry, the gradual fading of a puffed-up lettering is absolutely essential. In the ingenious

"Anti-céu" (Anti-heaven), the poet uses fade-out in conjunction with Braille to obtain a unique true synesthesia of the visual and the tactile.

The linkage of shape and the metalinguistic takes different forms in *Expoemas*. In "Inestante" (Un+instant+bookstand), words are encased in rows of vertical strokes representing books in the shelves of a bookstand, apocopation of which broaches "writerly" time and mortality. In "2ª via" ("Second Squad") a pyramidal form is the vehicle to draw a curious analogy between poets and the "sandwich man," the individual walking around with two advertising boards, who is in the public eye, carries (others') succinct messages, and commands little respect.[11] On another plane, "Pó do cosmos" (Dust of the cosmos) establishes its poetic space on a dark blue background with words distributed as if in a vast astronomical ellipse. There is an existential dimension here; Augusto conceives of these works, beyond a certain "cosmic melancholy," as "macrometaphors of love, of solitude, of human incommunicability."[12]

This proposal is much more evident in "SOS," where first-person subject pronouns in many languages (*je, ich,* etc.) surround the rest of the poem. This textual labyrinth is "an ironic abyss printed on a black background and in infernal circles" in the words of a keen observer, who notes, on a larger scale, how "the old master key to 'I' poetry is lost before this skillfully laid trap."[13] With such formal diversification, this and other poems of *Expoemas* play to paradox, which is best understood against the historical denial of self in concrete poetry, as the texts question, elide, or limit the (poetic) self while reviving lyrical themes. Thus, perhaps the key item in the collection is "Dizer" (To say), which affirms in a trio of three-liners with three type sizes (example 22). The fragmentations allow for significant double readings and pairings, and the penultimate line comprises a self-allusion to the polychromatic *poetamenos,* the author's earliest concrete series.[14] In this "expoem," an aesthetic of interrelations remains clear, while vows of concision and self-contention are renewed. This stance and other related strategies — factitious, physical, thematic — link Augusto's poems of the early eighties.

"Pós-tudo": The Poem Itself

In one way or another, all of the conceptual dimensions and creative effects noted in *Expoemas* — the techno-communicational, polyvocalism, the cosmic, literary allusion, the metaphorical, the limitational, the display of urbanity, etc. — are implicit in the overarching scope of "Póstudo" (example 23), which can be considered as the culmination of the

Example 22*

*[to dis / appear (stop!) / (TO BE) / to create / WITHOUT / believing / howmuch-more / poetminus / SAYING].

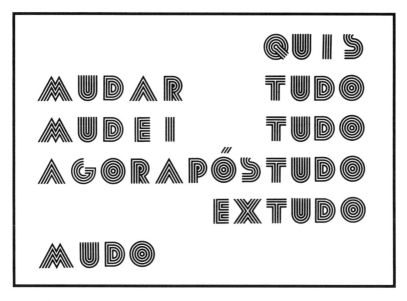

Example 23*

series to which it belongs. While some other individual poems, as witnessed above, have quite distinctive features, "Pós-tudo" has endured and proven to be the most stimulating. With an eye to uncovering its polyvalent logic, this section will offer an unhurried walk-through of the poem. The explication focuses on constructive elements and anticipates some of the debatable points Schwarz raises in his reading.

The construction of "Pós-tudo" revolves around a set of ironies, tensions, ambiguities, and paradoxes. While the title itself has a kind of sarcastic ring, reinforced in the combinations of the fourth line, the impact of that attitude is not fully appreciated until overtones and implications of the whole are considered. At the level of enunciation, the text has the makings of a lyrical or semilyrical "I" poem. While the subject pronoun *eu* is not enunciated, it is understood in the second preterit verb (*mudei*), which carries a first-person ending. This factor of person will be relevant when the identities (and values) of the "speaker" or "voice" come into play. Impersonal, third-person, feminine, or plural options would not work in this nuanced poem. The first-person condition — indeed the paronomasia of *mudo* (mute / I change) upon which

*[I wanted / to change / everything / I changed / everything / now-after-all-post-everything / ex-everything (I study) / I change- (I am) mute / mudaria = I would change; ria = laugh!]

all is premised — is determined by the power of the lexical coincidence of a conjugation (I change) and a masculine singular adjective (mute), not to mention the coagulating rhyme with *tudo*. The question of voice or lyrical self in "Pós-tudo" is also affected by the work's physicality and visual arrangement. The composition in large, nonstandard black-and-white capital letters in a Letraset font creates a media-age atmosphere. This styling serves as an attention-getting device — the poetic function of language is infused with a nonverbal phatic function — and makes for a very open poetic space of reception. It is as if the poem comprised the text of a poster, an advertisement, a declaration or notice. This public gesture is certainly as important as the private level of the poetic "I."

As far as lyrical self is concerned, "Pós-tudo" resists the narrow demarcation of a unified subject. Part of the poem's strength, in fact, resides in the slippery interface of different private and not-so-private poetic selves. On one level, the "I" here can simply be, in the tradition of modernist poetry, a fictional persona, an individual contemplating (and externalizing) desire, achievement, and a present aftermath. On another level, one can read a metaliterary and historical dimension into the poem, associate the artistic creation with the creator, and validate an auto- (or semi-auto) biographical element in the poem, a highly unusual fashion for a composition of Augusto's. Thus one can imagine a voice that is a historicized representative of modern art and evolution, a figure of radical change, such as, say, Pablo Picasso or John Cage. Closer to home, in Brazil, such a figure may be associated with Brazilian literature in general, with poetry specifically, and/or with an internationalist context. One can project a poetic self who encompasses the experiences of early and orthodox concrete poetry, its phase of invention, and later experiments of the 1970s and 1980s. Such a reading of "Pós-tudo" in context would necessarily include — against the strictures of impersonal criticism — Augusto's own trajectory as an interdisciplinary poet. But it cannot be limited to that. The breadth of the poem's fictive, or semifictive, voice, in any case, should be regarded as a virtue, in the productive sense of generating content, levels, and interest.

If this reading foregrounds the involvement of a persona in artistic spheres, the insistent "everything" of "Pós-tudo" can refer primarily to creative practices. In this instance, the subject's claiming to have "changed it all" would hardly come across as immodest. Yet that assumed claim is not so clearly self-assured; it becomes relativized in the course of the poem. "Everything," in turn, does not have to be interpreted literally, but rather, semantically, as a hyperbolic figure, and, technically, as a prime connector (*tudo* to *mudo*). In any case, when one infers reference to the concrete poets and considers their actual innovations, to affirm that they effected wide changes, if only within their own repertories, would not be outlandish. In conjunction, the present temporality of "Pós-tudo," its "now," is an "after-everything." In the context of Brazilian poetry, this would denote colonial heritage, the romantic tradition, *modernismo,* the neotraditionalist Generation of '45, the mid-century avant-garde, political poetry of the sixties, varied contemporary manifestations, and accompanying polemics. All of these form one backdrop against which to read "Pós-tudo." The prefix *pós-* itself, of course, targets postmodernism and its discussion.

Once the motif of all-encompassing change is established in "Pós-tudo," a counter-current begins to be generated. The primary meaning of the penultimate entry — "ex-everything" — works in tandem with the phrase of "after-all-post-everything" to fill out the quantitative sense of totality and the temporal senses of former and beyond. But phonetically *extudo* can be identical to *estudo* (I study). This latter activity would already begin to imply a dissatisfaction in the subject, as well as a need for further *in*vestigation and the *in*sufficiency of accumulated change. These "*in*-s" are a transition to the final *mudo,* which stands alone and whose semantic charge as verb immediately runs contrary to the sense of finality in the statement about having "changed everything." Implications surface quickly: the subject is still changing, himself and/or things; change cannot be complete; there is always room for additional transformations. The subject both represents a principle of perpetual modification and embodies the illusion of the possibility of absolute change. The poem's verbal paradigm (I wanted, I changed) makes "change" the first logical meaning of *mudo.* In no way, however, is this final word merely, or even primarily, an articulation of a desire for or implementation of change. The adjectival meanings — silent, mute, dumb, tongue-tied, taciturn — soon erupt. What most matters is the dialectical tension between the semanteme of change and the others.

At the end, notions of opening (*mudo* — I change) and closing (*mudo* — mute) play off against each other. What all can muted silence imply? At least two positions come to mind, and they themselves would be at odds. On the one hand, a (smug?) silence of contentedness and acceptance: all has been said, I have done it all, changes were definitive, I rest. On the other hand, doubt and lack of certainty: I am perplexed, I don't know what to say, there's a need for further contemplation. In any case, no unequivocal reading can emerge from this ending. Given the level of ambiguity, no unquestioning authority of an agent of transformation can stand clear. A continuity of change may be affirmed, but not without attendant inquiry. In terms of poetic realization and attitudinal play, the poem turns and depends on the key paronomasia. This ambiguous affirmation of "Pós-tudo" questions postmodernism as fashion and style, and opens the poem to diverse historical interpretations.

Given the visually aided and more-than-verbal rhetoric of "Pós-tudo," it is instructive to consider how nonhorizontal readings help balance the poem structurally and complement meanings. In a vertical direction, one perceives two basic columns of words. The left one is the syntagmatic synopsis of changing. The top three words (*mudar, mudei, agora*), each of five letters, form a block that, with the intervening blank space, highlights the shorter word *mudo* as foundation, with the crucial results elucidated above. On the right-hand side, the desire and ambition initiated in *quis* are fortified and amplified with the stacked repetitions of *tudo*. Where the more private aspect of the dialect of self is concerned, the two columns of letters farthest to the right subtly add to the sense of the poetic "I": the penultimate stack configures a hidden and instinctive *id*, while the right-hand border spells a drawn out *só* (sole, alone). The written accent may be missing, but it is recovered, as it were, in an inverted *só* contained in *pós* at the center of the poem. This detail of inner working and semantic attraction leads to the last piece of the construction: the temporally oriented prefixes *pós* and *ex* that connect the word-columns while breaking the illusory unity of "everything." Finally, one must look at the significant presence of two directional phrases in "Pós-tudo." Continuing vertically at the end of *mudar* one adds -*ia* and obtains the conjugation *mudaria* (I would change). This conditional utterance not only complements the preterit and present tenses, but further may imply resolution of a contrary-to-fact proposition — e.g., "if I had to decide," "if it were up to me" — that confirms, as it were, a quality of assertiveness in the poetic voice. In the broader context of the poem, this backing is more pointed if the reading of the line takes another turn and adds *póstudo*, to wit, "I would change post-everything," or even, allowing for a third-person subject, "post-everything would change." These added possibilities fuel the text's ambiguity and illustrate the perils of unilinear interpretation in this case. Still at the vertical center of "Pós-tudo," we also note *ria*, imperative of *rir*, to laugh. This is an invitation to ponder humor in this whole affair, and can be linked to the more particular irony of the title, as the command also connects at a right angle with *póstudo*.

The element of laughter contributes to a less-than-serious tone and suggests a measure of self-irony as well. Having postulated the validity of an autobiographical aspect in the discussion of "Pós-tudo," one can look to authorial comment to gain perspective on the scope of the poem.

Augusto has said: "It is a critical and self-critical poem that carries some of the perplexities of our time. There's a little bit of everything there. [Including] a summary-epitaph of my life."[15] The word *epitaph* here is not to be taken just in the standard sense of an inscription on a tomb, but also in a less usual Portuguese usage as a "kind of satirical poetry, usually in quatrain, about a living person, as if he were dead" (*Novo Aurélio*). From this angle, it is easier to understand the self-irony in conjunction with the historical dimension of the artistic poetic self.

The "Pós-tudo" Affair

"Radical Chic" is a Feiffer-like cartoon that appears in the Sunday magazine of a major Rio de Janeiro daily (example 24). In a most pertinent installment, the stylish young protagonist, in a succession of four frames and poses, muses: "When the Beatles broke up I was already post-hippie / Then I was post-romantic, post-tropicalist, post-chic, post-tacky, post-apocalyptic, post-political, post-Shiite, post-punk, post-everything . . . / Now I feel kind of pre-historical!" This send-up of trend-conscious cosmopolitan fashion and behavior followed the more restricted intellectual polemic that had been initiated by Augusto's "Pós-tudo." As stated above, among the poem's intents was to satirize the very stage-aware atmosphere of multiple "post-" labels, around the world and in Brazil. The cartoon's conclusion has, unwittingly, a further relevance to the positioning of lyric in the late century, when questions of historicity and reprise so concern poetics.

Augusto's compact poem sparked the greatest controversy in Brazilian poetry in recent years. Soon after the poem appeared in the press, Roberto Schwarz, the widely respected proponent of sociologically oriented criticism, published a most pointed critique; his very public approach was a vehicle for a more general discourse of anticoncretism. Journalistic exchanges ensued, touching off renewed debate about concrete poetry in advance of the commemoration of the movement's thirtieth anniversary, and spilling over into the matter of postmodernism. Critical mentions of the affair attest to the vitality of the poem-inspiration and to the symptomatic qualities of its debate.[16] Essayist Sérgio Paulo Rouanet has observed that what really mattered in the affair was the underlying *mood* of the poem, translated so well in the title, brought on by the proliferation of "post-" manifestations.[17] Far beyond just reflecting a mood, the poem — in its own fabric and in its argumentation — invites wonder about the postmodern, including via its (mis-) readings. While the affair does not center, despite the poem's title, on

Example 24

"post-" phenomena per se, discussion does pass through revealing post-modern terrain and set up related debate. As historicity of lyric permeates the poem and its responses, "Pós-tudo" inevitably provokes retrospection about lyric projects of preceding decades and contemplation of options in the 1980s and beyond.

Historical Landmark, Readings and Responses

To his critique of "Pós-tudo," Roberto Schwarz gives the title "Marco histórico" ("A Historic Landmark").[18] Through a close reading, the critic proposes to probe how the poem might represent "something in the air" (a new market-focused artistic era? postmodernism?). The article provides occasion to take the avant-garde to task and to combat Brazilian concrete poetry, objectives which interfere with the portrait of the poem. José Miguel Wisnik offers a good capsule account of what the critic wants to do and why he comes up short:

> Roberto [Schwarz] denounces the way the supposedly self-congratulatory avant-garde — disengaged from the virulence of its origins and willing to dissolve into the order of consumption, although emphatically affirming its critical nature — calmly accepts the lack of historical perspective of the postmodern world as a *positive* fact. . . . [He] relates the self-apology, generic character, and lack of historical concreteness of the text to an "atmosphere of softening," the historical landmark of which is that cultural logic of late capitalism that transforms international modernism into a pop element in the postmodern world.
>
> . . . Schwarz's analysis fails when he attempts to find internal formal elements on which to found his ideological criticism of concrete poetry, disdaining — with a very discursive reading — the analogical and polyvalent logic of Augusto de Campos's beautiful poem of ambiguous self-criticism.

In his explication of "Pós-tudo," Schwarz is preoccupied with ideological projections and historical evaluation. He poses a series of basic questions to probe the poem and speculate around it: When is "post-everything"? What is "everything"? What is "changing everything"? but most centrally "Who is its subject?" He argues that the text is founded upon a confrontation of self and "everything," of which he allows various interpretations. The first-level perceptions of the poetic construct — of linguistic fabric, lyric voices, differentiated levels, operative paradoxes, etc. — are on target, and Schwarz's analysis, to be sure, reveals much about the poem. Yet he betrays his arguments and the literary reading per se with the introduction of antipoetic principles and rhetorical demands that, ultimately, rather than elucidating the presumed object of analysis, simply underline the extratextual agenda of anticoncretism. In the interest of counterbalance, then, some points he raises merit direct cross-examination and rebuttal.

In his opening, Schwarz correctly notes that "Pós-tudo" intends to mark a historical inflection, that the title is ironic, and that the "deprivatized" design sets the poem in an exterior space. This and subsequent attention to the physicality of the text show no lack of understanding of a primary feature of Augusto's work. On the expository level, however, Schwarz lets inconsistencies get in his way. Following up the question of when, he begins "[r]ead as if it were prose" (188), hardly an auspiciously phrased starting point for the reading of a poem of a decidedly nonprose nature. Thus, it is hard to accept an ensuing parallel drawn between one of the main paradoxes of the poem — the nonachievability of an absolute "everything" — and, slightingly, late nineteenth-century verse that laments the unattainability of happiness. Linkage with old poetry, of course, is not in itself regressive, so one should consider, in contrast, how the expansive and universalizing "Pós-tudo" echoes eternal themes of Western civilization going back to classical Hellenic philosophy and, indirectly, to such surprising literary monuments as Edmund Spenser's "Mutabilitie Cantos," as well as such celebrated phrases of the heroic phase of *modernismo* as the early Carlos Drummond de Andrade's "e como ficou chato ser moderno, agora serei eterno" (and how boring it has become to be modern, now I will be eternal).[19]

Schwarz uses quite a different comparison to conclude his appraisal of "Pós-tudo": if "read discursively, and taking *extudo* as intercalated, the poem is extraordinarily natural and would be indistinguishable from the poetry which was born in determined opposition to the concretists, so-called marginal poetry, execrated by concretism" (196). Given the reservations many have with respect to "marginal poetry" (cf. chapter 5), the intent of this reference is to lessen the value of "Pós-tudo." But the premises for comparison are shaky: *extudo* is not intercalated but an integral part of a tight web of less than a dozen words (and combinations), and the "natural" whole is not meant to be read discursively. Whatever motives one ascribes to this line of inquiry, Schwarz himself would seem to debunk his own original comparison when he writes "However, it is not prose" (188). This self-admonition ought to have been taken more to heart. Lack of distinctions between symbolic and discursive tacks cloud the analysis, and in the course of the review one is struck with contentions that handle poetic language as if it constituted (or should) pragmatic prose. Thus, Schwarz faults Augusto's "trust" in verbal relations for "non-specificness" and "lack of intellectual precision" (189), as if the contrary were inherently necessary here or given as marks of a good poem, as opposed to an expository essay.

Schwarz treats the question of subject, appropriately, at much greater length, with varying results. To the veritable exclusion of the fictional option, he favors a specifically historicized version (i.e., the voice of the Brazilian concrete vanguard) to enable him to object to a perceived sense of self-propaganda on the part of the poet as cofounder of concrete poetry. In view of the critic's openly admitted bias here, one must separate the right to a (political) opinion from the exercise of textual criticism. And to counter one must (re-) affirm the poetic—as opposed to ideologically interpretive—weight of the ambiguous interplay of private and larger lyric selves in "Pós-tudo" and their attitudes. Moreover, Schwarz grounds his objection to a sense of self-aggrandizement (an inflated "I" transforming everything) in an overly literal reading of the subject(s), for whom the critic admits virtually no possibility of self-irony. Focused on ideology as he is, for instance, Schwarz simply overlooks the conditional *mudaria* and the tempering, and tempting, call to laugh of *ria*. In terms of breadth, he does suggest that if one takes the persona as a representative of the "international movement of Western art" then the "I changed everything" ought to be read with melancholy, and the concluding *mudo* takes on "something of futility and inconsequence . . . which registers (if the yardstick is the real necessities of humanity) the failure and the irrelevance of the cultural movements of the avant-garde in our century" (191). Here Schwarz appears to be blaming the poetic voice and the artistic vanguards for not having saved the world! That speaks for itself. Interestingly enough, he does posit other grander possible selves in the poem: the revolutionary after the revolution, or current humanity desirous of change.

Yet what Schwarz does with this multiplicity is again to punish plurisignification. Since none of the readings of "I" is privileged internally, he reasons, the poem remains open to interpretation and becomes an "empty allusion" and a "reiteration of commonplaces." One is left to wonder whether the only antidote to what is disputed would be a linear, realist, confessional approach, exactly what the poem aspires not to be. While recognizing the poem's many potential selves, Schwarz is fixed on his positional reading: "Pós-tudo" is a quintessential advocacy of the concretists' vision of their role in literary history; the poem "fuses together, for its own benefit, the authorities of the poet and the critic, of

poetic and theoretical discourse" (193). Context hardly impedes meta-
literary attributions here — to the contrary, as was suggested above — but
the breadth of allusion ought to preclude any such restricted or exclusiv-
ist conclusions. To single out the role of concretism for extratextual
attack is to abuse the poem by denying its paradoxes and ironies.

That is, again, precisely the problem with Schwarz's account of the
poem's end. He sees, rightly, that there is meaning in the fact that the
poem begins at the end of a line and ends at the beginning of a line
(implication: change will continue). For lack of parameters, however,
the end leaves only "abstract gesticulations of the desire to transform,"
which are applicable, in turn, to other contexts of poem. The "form of
transformative action . . . in the absence of an object is reduced to being
its own image, context and ideology" (196). This reference to "object"
carries an implicit demand for a type of exposition not to be expected in a
pointedly concise poem. But what is most problematic here is the ex-
treme focus on the desire to change, entirely to the detriment of the
fundamental paronomasia and the dialectical tension with the sense of
muted silence, itself diversifiable.

The issue of postmodernism comes up via the unsure question of
"changing everything." Schwarz is troubled that neither object nor
subject is specified in the poem. Nor is "the idea of change, which re-
mains neutralized, neither good nor bad" (194). This result captures
something of the mid-eighties climate, in concert with the title and its
ironic allusion to the debate about the postmodern. Here, a link with
Haroldo de Campos's article on the "post-utopian poem" is made ex-
plicit. Schwarz's summary historicization moves to an interesting anal-
ogy. The valid antagonist of "to change everything," he asserts, was im-
mobile bourgeois culture and property, which were penetrated both by
the Russian Revolution and by capitalism's own antitraditional de-
velopments (the avant-garde and other antiestablishment activity, one
assumes). Here Schwarz follows the sociologist Daniel Bell, who ex-
plains "the exhaustion of antibourgeois modernist culture . . . through
its wide acceptance and subsequent banalization."[20] The term *change,*
Schwarz continues, lost its primal sense, was co-opted by the system,
became conservative ideology, and now requires particularization to
have meaning. At this juncture, there follows a structural speculation
about "Pós-tudo": "between the body of the composition and the final
'*mudo,*' now taken as cynical and resigned, lies the distance between
those two moments, the modern and the postmodern: for the latter,
change is so to speak a law of adaptation (to the market?) and has no
connections with hope for revolution (expressed in the 'everything')"

(194). While raising an intriguing homological hypothesis, this reading provokes — quite apart from its reliance on other points of contention about the ideology in play — its own series of doubts. For instance, is not the supposed "post-" moment articulated in the poem from the fourth line on? And should that historical distance not be understood to *accumulate* to arrive at *mudo*? Equally important, what authorizes the qualification as "accommodated" and "resigned"? An automatic assumption of a postmodern cynicism? In any case, the desired picture depends somewhat on a minimizing of the oppositional — if not necessarily revolutionary — potential of contemporary art. In this epochal vein, Schwarz thinks that "Pós-tudo" marks the historical moment of the "transformation of modern art's agenda into the ideology of consumption and conduct" (196). Beyond the governing — and sometimes disorienting — concern with ideology in this analysis, the question remains whether one can understand this marking to operate, in the Brazilian context, in an implicitly "postmodern" way.

In a more general sociocultural account of contemporary Brazilian poetry, the British critic David Treece recognizes the significance of "Pós-tudo" and its commentaries in opening the discussion to "the refuge of postmodernism."[21] His speculations about the appeal of nontraditional poetics are instigating in their own right, notably where the relationship of Augusto's poem to an epochal aesthetic is concerned. Treece concurs with the premises and conclusions about "Pós-tudo" put forward by Schwarz, generously crediting him with no less than having "unmasked the vacuous pretensions of its subject's claim to the definitive act of transformation, to have had, literally, the 'last word' on an all-encompassing, monumentally abstract, and ultimately meaningless 'everything'" (309). Yet Treece is quick to note, within the established social perspective, a key limitation of Schwarz's analysis, to wit, that "it is one thing to deconstruct and expose" the project of vanguard formalism and quite another "to explain its longevity and continued acceptance among such a broad layer of the cultural community in Brazil" (309). Indeed, if concretism was supposedly so socially isolated, solely concerned with the manipulation of codes, and uninterested in probing the capitalist discourse of development, why has it exercised, throughout the dictatorship and beyond, such an influence on successive generations? Treece thinks there is a clue to the explanation in "Pós-tudo," which he takes as a manifestation of concretism. While he poses a good question, his application of the postmodern to Brazilian lyric is somewhat impaired by limited distinctions between the advanced industrialized domain and the periphery and by shaky assumptions about concretist positions. A discussion of Treece's commentary will further help bring into relief the place of concrete poetry and its successors from the 1960s to the 1980s.

The movement led by the Noigandres poets — Augusto, Haroldo, and Décio — clearly challenged, Treece asserts, the "discursive and figurative tradition" of *modernismo*. Furthermore, with the aggressive claim "to have superseded that tradition, it struck a local chord with the international mood of apocalyptic agnosticism and aestheticism which came to be known in the 1980s as Postmodernism. The key features typically attributed to the postmodern aesthetic *found an unmistakable echo in the theoretical language of Concretismo*" (309, emphasis added). While this assertion will require examination, one first needs to say what idea of postmodernism is intended. Treece highlights the following features:

> the idea, taken over from semiotics and poststructuralist philosophy, of simulation, our inability to talk of a world independent of our representations of it, to distinguish between some elusive and perhaps nonexistent 'basic reality' and its image; consequent upon this, the sensation of schizophrenia and the abolition of the coherent individual subject; the loss of interpretative depth, of reliable points of ideological reference; the collapse of the Grand Narratives of historical analysis, indeed, the "end of history" itself; the fondness instead for montage and collage, the assemblage of fragments from different discourses and media, for pastiche, and the endless recycling of infinite styles, and the self-reflexive, self-conscious nature of aesthetic activity, by which the form and process of artistic production become the subject of the work itself. (309)

Such postmodern traits do not constitute, many have argued, a fundamental interruption but are, rather, essentially consistent with the mainstream of Western Modernism. Those who defend a distinctive postmodernist aesthetic, Treece agrees, actually betray "continuity with Modernist tradition" (309–310). What is most pertinent here is the critic's desire to tie this irony to concretism, implying some sort of significant connection with postmodernism: "In a parallel and contradictory manner, the Concretists have repeatedly pointed to Modernist 'precursors' of their own project, such as Oswald de Andrade, while claiming to have broken with tradition and to have 'changed everything.'" Here there is a clear implication that the poem "Pós-tudo" is part of an ongoing concretist project with a false version of change.

Treece continues that the "cultural dominant" of the late capitalism of computer and media technology reminds one of concrete poetry's vision of a "post-utopian world of consumers and poem-commodities" (310).

To answer finally the well-placed question about the staying power of concretism, Treece outlines the conditions of disillusionment of younger generations (who may have been involved with political opposition in the sixties) during the repressive military dictatorship, officialized in 1968, and speculates that "the appeal of the formalist project during subsequent years is more comprehensible as a 'postmodernist' alternative to social and political marginalization from the new cultural environment of the Miracle" (312), the last word alluding to Brazil's economic boom of such high, if cruelly deceptive, growth rates in the 1970s.

This interpretation is in line with an idea of the prominent postmodern theorist, Fredric Jameson, who interrelates the current North American mind-set and the aftermath of the decade of radicalism: "Utopian representations had an extraordinary revival in the 1960s; if postmodernism is the substitute for the sixties and the compensation for their political failure, the question of Utopia would seem to be a crucial test of what is left of our capacity to imagine change at all."[22] While the general difference of condition between advanced/post-industrial (First World) and developing/industrializing (Third World) nations is crucial to any projection of postmodernism on the latter, it is safe to say that the Brazilian case in the sixties paralleled in some key ways North American and Western European experiences. The utopian factor, in particular, has a demonstrable transcontinental relevance. As seen in chapters 2 and 3, the developmentalism of the late fifties in Brazil gave way in the sixties to the socialist agendas that so affected poetry and the arts in general.

Returning to Treece's analysis, speculations about the specific case of "Pós-tudo," as well as about the broader issue of concretism's relationship to postmodernism, are problematic. It will be useful to contextualize some of the historical angles and to question some of the suppositions about the positions of others in Treece's sociocultural critique via poetry. For instance, the theoretical language of concretism was formulated in the 1950s and 1960s, and the major texts of postmodernism were published in the advanced industrialized nations in the 1970s and early 1980s. How is it that features of a postmodern aesthetic in the latter could "find an echo" in the former? In rereadings of the early concretist repertory twenty to thirty years after the fact? Concrete poetry belongs to post-*modernismo* in a chronological sense, of course, but it remains modernist-avant-garde in spirit, most notably in the work of Augusto, past the sixties. The concern of the Noigandres poets with the public sphere and their poetic media-mixing might suggest "postmodern" attitudes elsewhere, but if anything Brazilian concrete poetry—with its varied theoretical and creative instruments of presentation and justification — *anticipated* some of the perplexities of art in the media-dominated atomic age. Discussion of the postmodern in Brazil, which occasioned Augusto's poem, only really began in the 1980s.[23]

In the context of recent Brazilian cultural history, and the so-called "economic miracle" of the 1970s, the hypothesis of an assumed cynical postmodernism as an alternative to sixties political involvement would also have to take into account two pertinent factors: (1) the persistence and resurgence, if necessarily modified, of Left-oriented cultural discourse in many urban and university spheres, and (2) the historically continuous though "lagged" influence of Western cultural movements in nonhegemonic nations such as Brazil, in this case, for instance, the emergence of a local counterculture (hippie rebellion/rock), perhaps in part a reaction to political circumstances but certainly utopian in its own way.[24] The utopian is indeed a kind of fulcrum to balance judgments of the present and previous decades, so it is worthwhile to reiterate that concrete poetry — with its certain emancipatory element linked to arts, culture, and enlightenment — had been a collective movement of a utopian nature, if not in the usual socialistic sense. It is most curious, then, that Treece should cite the "poem-commodity," product of a midcentury artistic avant-garde, in a "post-utopian" vision. Concrete poetry's break with the discursive tradition of poetry was, again, in the spirit of the historical avant-gardes of modernism, and, getting back to the treatment of Augusto's poem, it makes more sense to read the historical element in "change everything" in the context of poetry, not society in general.

Treece seems to assume that concretism and "Pós-tudo" embodied the postmodern. Concrete poetry and some later production of the Noigandres group may indeed be suggestive of some postmodern traits — the cultural dominance of electronic media, the compression of high (literary) and low (nonliterary) culture, the radical questioning of the possibility of narrativity — but such links do not in and of themselves constitute a postmodern escape. There is some overlap between productions of concretism's phase of invention and other artistic manifestations in the West that have been labeled postmodern — montage and the self-reflexivity of art stand out as well — but an implication of a postmodern position in Noigandres poets in the 1980s should give pause. Neither the self-ironic poet of "Pós-tudo" nor the author of the "post-utopian poem" defends the postmodernism Treece has in mind. To the contrary, they too have skeptical views, or prefer to adopt distinct, though related, perspectives. Their positions and the foregoing, at the very least, complicate an explanation of the continuing appeal of concretism in Brazil via the postmodern as refuge.

Resisting the Postmodern, Embracing History

Linda Hutcheon writes that postmodernism produces "art marked paradoxically by both history and an internalized, self-reflexive investigation of the nature, the limits, and the possibilities of the discourse of art."[25] This characterization is quite applicable to "Pós-tudo," yet it proves to be insufficient. In the midst of the many different general versions and particular understandings of the postmodern, Augusto's changing poem also seeks to cast doubts on one aspect of the manipulation of postmodernism: the underscoring of the end of the avant-garde. Since the appearance of "Pós-tudo," moreover, citizen Augusto has raised numerous related objections to a certain ideology of the postmodern as poetic expression. He has resisted what he views as "the situation of rejection of the vanguard," the attempt of some (at home and abroad) "to file away everything experimental, everything that constituted modernity, for the sake of some alleged moderation or maturity."[26] He has reacted specifically to critical uses of the notion of postvanguard, especially in Brazil, that intend to close the book on research and experimentation in the arts, to put a hold on reflections about new language in lyric, and to justify a retreat, as it were, to well-worn languages.[27] With the poet-critic's rebuff of the premise of a wholesale surpassing of the avant-gardes comes a measured defense of a place for the vanguard. Banking on the centrality of assimilation, Augusto has asked how one can speak of the death of the vanguards if, understood as instruments of experimental language, they have simply *not* been assimilated beyond a tiny circle. In his assessment:

> discussions of the so-called post-modern tend to slip into . . . artificial and reproachable attempts to declare precociously the death of the vanguard, to bracket modernity, to put artistic practice back in the accommodating bed of a supposedly nonradical, limp eclecticism. Hiding behind this (im)posture, among other things, is a phobia for technology . . . That's the heart of the question of the "postmodern," an umbrella term with which attempts are made to plug the emptiness of this moment of transition, which I prefer to view from the perspective of the ultramodern.[28]

The positive potential of technology in art and poetry, for Augusto, means not only that the vanguard is not dead but that it is reborn as a "permanent disquiet" with respect to creative languages. In this discussion, it must be perfectly clear that the term *vanguard* now signifies inventive artistic experimentalism itself, not any collective movement built around it and oriented by future redemption. What Augusto aspires to keep alive may be thought of, to use a sixties frame, as art of transgression (nonlinear, non-oral, combinational, etc.), but its iconoclastic impulses target codes of lyric and modes of perception without the same antisystem ethos of the sixties. Again, emphasis must fall on the autonomously aesthetic, not on a project. There is still an undeniable future element in the poet's eighties work in the implications and reverberations of intermedia and, most especially, of the lyrico-electronic domain. While acknowledging the end of the *historical* cycle of the avant-gardes, Augusto continues to demonstrate faith in the artistic viability of new vehicles. He further relates a perception of what "postmodern" means for lyric, in this declaration on recent developments in the verbal arts:

> Without intending, in any way, to fetishize the new powers of technology, I believe that a great part of the future of poetry will be affected by them. Some current experiences that are now just incipient, such as computer graphics, videotext, holography, and recording techniques, demonstrate that concrete poetry is at the base of a viable language for these media. Having little in common with the traditional forms of discourse, they are going to require new forms of linguistic codification that imply a stricter involvement between the verbal and the nonverbal, which is exactly concrete poetry's field of action.
>
> It is perhaps there — in the exploration of new technological media, and in their interaction with the spectacular arts or multi-disciplinary events — that we will find "what remains to be done," probably not by us, but by still embryonic artists who will hold over us the advantage of having these new media at their disposal, and of having mastered them in their most complex and advanced forms.
>
> I myself already have had the opportunity to experiment with almost all the available vehicles in that area, from videotext to illuminated panels, from computer graphics to holography and lasers. . . . The virtual movement of the printed word, the typogram, is giving way to the real movement of the computerized word, the videogram, and to the typography of the electronic era. From static to cinematic poetry, which, combined with computerized sound resources, can raise the verbivocovisual structures preconceived by concrete poetry to their most complete materialization. In this moment of transition, marked by regressive indefinitions of the supposed "post-" (formerly, "retro" or "anti") modern, poetry

can leave saturation and impasse for unanticipated flights into the beyond-the-looking glass of video, and depart on a broad inter- or multimedia voyage.[29]

Where some see evidence of postmodernity in the emergence of technologically aided art, this media-age credo, curiously, is a statement against the "postmodern," precisely because the latter is sensed as regressive. The perceived danger in postmodern ideas of poetry is qualitative and stylistic. Given his heritage and openness to new channels, Augusto repudiates what others call a poetics of "nostalgia," i.e., contemporary practices that look back in order to sanction recourse to unchallenging free-verse and seemingly random pastiche.[30] This sentiment is given voice in the testimony of a next-generation poet who contemplates the late 1970s and 1980s and sees a different kind of refuge:

> Escaping the imprecision of the concept of art and poetry of *modernismo,* many take refuge in the still vague concept of "postmodernity" to justify a lack of poetic elaboration, a lack of criteria, be it in the creation or in the fruition of poetry, or even the unabashed retrogression, the return to what is most noxious in a certain romanticism or in a certain Parnassianism. Cheap sentimentalism and the adoption of rigid molds for the poetic. Poets commonly fall into two apparently opposed positions which in fact are complementary: that of a self-worshipping spontaneity of romantic character, often through an artificial and pseudo-erudite ornamentation of Parnassian character. . . . "The vanguards are dead" shouts the crowd of those who don't know how to outdo them and seek in the "postmodern" an excuse for shallow poetry.[31]

The less than sympathetic attitude toward those alluded to in this statement lurks, no doubt, in the shadows of the much discussed poem "Pós-tudo." On the crucial issue of attitude toward change, Augusto's poem and his subsequent commentaries about the postmodern are neither anachronistic reprises of *épater les bourgeois* nor outright or unmediated affirmations of the modernist-vanguard impulse of rupture. They indeed invoke, on the historico-literary plane, the radicalisms of high modernism, including those of Brazil, and of concretism itself. They also throw up a warning flag about the judgment in some postmodern thought that the capacity for transformation — in verbal page art at least — has simply dissolved. For his part, Benedito Nunes recognizes a pointed historicity in his presentation of "Pós-tudo" as a poem of the eighties:

the winds of the avant-garde spirit stopped blowing with the end of the combative *ethos* of the historical, to a certain degree prophetic, consciousness that filled its sails. The *new day* lost its mythical force. The future became simple expectation. Following the radical experience of change — and as radical change, definitive, turning a page of the history of poetry — comes the retrospective recapitulation . . .[32]

Indeed the poem considers what has transpired, recognizes a new present, and suggests a different sense of future. This sense, albeit without the same overall group thrust, may still involve change. Recapitulation is prominent, one could add to the long historical view, without precluding continuation. While Nunes's reading may seem to privilege one side of the equation of closure — the *mudo* as "mute" over that of "I change" — it should be kept in mind, as suggested above, that various motives for being "mute" may be posited. If not in fact linked to a larger project, "Pós-tudo" and its defense do maintain an essential part of the vanguard *esprit de corps,* the imperative of invention, without being dependent on integration into an articulated enterprise. The historical end of the Brazilian vanguards is not in question. What does carry over from the experience of concrete poetry to the aftermath, the post-something, is an abiding concern with creative focus. From his own vantage point, Haroldo de Campos will put forward a poetics imbued with consciousness of projects past.

The Post-Utopian Poem

The discussion provoked by "Pós-tudo" centered more on textuality and the roles of the (late modernist) vanguard of concrete poetry than on postmodernism per se. All three issues concern Haroldo de Campos in his relatively short but highly suggestive text on "the post-utopian poem," a position paper that offers a working concept for lyric in the 1980s. Haroldo first floated his alternative term in the afterword to a translation of Goethe's *Faust:* "we are in an epoch that some already call postmodern but which can better be defined as *post-utopian.* "[33] If parts of Haroldo's later work in lyric exhibit traits some would call "postmodern," he himself uses this term idiosyncratically as he bares a preference for "post-utopian" in the development of an overarching idea about making poetry in the 1980s.[34] While not an extended articulation of a theoretical framework, in the manner of the many essays prepared during the advocacy for concrete poetry, this article does give a useful general idea of Haroldo's perspective as poet-translator and has served as a critical point of reference for him and other interested critics. It is worth-while to note that this is the second part of an essay prepared on the theme of "the crisis of the vanguards."[35] The first part tackles the question of modernity in poetry and establishes Mallarmé's "Un coup de dés" as a historical fulcrum. With its explosion of space and syntactical operations, it is, in relation to the modern verse of Baudelaire, the first "post-modern" text, in a next-step sense quite different, clearly, from that advanced in the 1970s.

With respect to Brazil, Haroldo prefers the term "post-utopian" for the period after the heyday of concrete poetry and the last of the midcentury experimental groups. This view hinges on the idea that the avant-garde or vanguard can only exist as a collective project undergirded by a "hope-principle" (Bloch). Mallarmé's dream of a communitarian multi-book and Russian poet Mayakovsky's "ideal commune" both projected new languages of outreaching art with a transformed world on the horizon. With the foundation and diversification of concrete poetry, the Brazilian Noigandres group operated with the concept of a poetic project of ecumenical language, of national and international scope. As summarized here by Haroldo, the developmentalism of President Juscelino Kubitschek in the 1950s encouraged optimism and a future-oriented optic, in the arts as well as in the economic sphere. At the turn of the decade, the Cuban Revolution naturally fomented ideas of social transformation around Latin America. Concrete poetry engaged in socializing debate and studied the revolutionary role of Mayakovsky. These "hopeful" conditions collapse in Brazil with the military coup of 1964 and the frustrations of the dark years of the ensuing dictatorship.

On the international level, the dominant factors to be considered in this contemporary history are the acceleration of the crisis of ideologies and the off-setting of predatory imperial capitalism vs. the repressive and dogmatic bureaucratic state. Despite the potential that the new electronic media bring for a new "iconical universal writing" (foreseen by Mallarmé and Benjamin), Haroldo affirms, the utopian, redemptive, avant-garde function for poetry evaporates. What follows is a historically conscious opening: "the 'pluralization of possible poetics' succeeds the totalizing project of the vanguard, which can only be supported, at its limits, by a Utopia of redemption." In this transition, the future-oriented hope-principle is replaced by the reality-principle in the present. The new poetics of the here and now offers provisional syntheses. But what remains of the utopian—and it is a most significant residue—is the dialogical and critical dimension inherent in utopian projects.

Haroldo underlines that this *poesia da presentidade* (poetry of presentification) should not occasion a poetics of abdication nor serve as an excuse for the eclectic and the facile. The admission of a "plural history" calls, instead, for the critical appropriation of a "plurality of pasts" with no exclusive predetermination of the future. Concrete aspects of ancients and moderns alike can contribute to a new poetry that does not require a "dominant opposition," as the experience of concrete poetry did. Haroldo regards translation as essential as it allows for "recombining the plurality of possible pasts and for presentifying it as difference in the post-utopian poem" (5).

Since this invocation of "plurality" may suggest the kind of "natural," more speech-based verse the Noigandres poets do not promote, Haroldo has necessarily supplemented this position. What is stressed in subsequent comments in relation to making poetry in this present is the maintenance of rigor, both in the utilization of the past and in composition itself. What matters is: "the concretion of language, poetry that can ponder its own linguistic material," i.e., that stresses the Jakobsonian poetic function. New production should emerge "not from an eclectic starting point, but rather always maintaining that position of rigor, [which is] important because from that utopian proposal there remained a fundamental critical residue. The fact that we are in a post-utopian moment does not mean we abdicate the critical moment."[36]

Not given to assertions of a radical historical break from the modern age, of a major paradigm shift, or of a broad new cultural enterprise in the age of media, Haroldo avoids the international debate on the postmodern except to call the label "equivocal" and to explain the concepts behind his preference.[37] He invokes world history not so much in a broad civilizational sense but to generalize the atmosphere for creative production. The primary aim of his "post-utopian" stance is to focus on poetic enterprises. One advantage of this other term is its specificity as a qualified indicator of postvanguard. The "post-utopian" approach enables one to admit to a new phase of nonmovement-oriented production and diversification in the arts and, in wider angle, to an international climate of decadence, both of the (former) U.S.S.R. and of the "American dream." At the same time, using "post-utopian" eschews such other implications of the postmodern as reigning cynicism, the death of literature, or the primacy of simulacra. And, returning to the most fundamental doubt about postmodernism in Latin America, such an alternative term — though Haroldo does not make this claim — provides a way to speak of a changed contemporary consciousness without implying stages of capitalist development or wide access to technology that simply do not exist in Brazil. The "post-utopian" may share some of the common elements of the "postmodern condition" — lack of faith in master narratives, notably — but the concept is meant to resist, where lyric is concerned, such epiphenomenal textual conditions as contamination by "low" culture, unmediated collage, and random citation. The emphasis on rigor, after all, clearly owes to the modernist legacy of Valéry, Pound, and Eliot.

Haroldo's post-utopian perspective can be understood in light of Octavio Paz's grand view of contemporary poetry. Since *Los hijos del limo* (*Children of the Mire,* 1974), the Mexican thinker has spoken of "the twilight of the vanguards" and the emergence of a new age for poetry.[38] In late twentieth-century art, according to Paz, the centrality of rupture and the futuristic orientation have broken down. The power of negation that drove the avant-garde is gone, and transgression has become ceremony. Revolution and New Art, the art of change as redemption, are dying myths. The poetry of now, of the time that is emerging, is an "art of convergence" in contrast with the much-discussed "tradition of rupture." Fusion of temporal perspectives is central to a poetics of the present. Now there is a breakdown of two concepts that constituted modernity: time as linear progression toward something better, and change as the best form of succession. For Paz, a new (or emerging) epoch exists or has existed, but it ought not to be conceived as "postmodernism." He objects to the term on various, universal, and hemispheric grounds: the label is as ambivalent and contradictory as modernism itself; it is prisoner to successive, linear, progressive time, meaning only what succeeds modernism; and it shows "cultural arrogance, ethnocentrism, and historical insensitivity" when used by shortsighted Anglo-American critics.[39] Paz's idea of "convergence" without "postmodernism" finds a parallel in Haroldo's "plurality" as manifested in the "post-utopian" poem.

The Education of the Five Senses and the Final Voyage

There is no question that a "plurality of pasts" informs Haroldo's creative output of the 1980s, which ranges from final fruition of the vast prose-poetry project *Galáxias* to translation (transcreation) of the Old Testament from the original Hebrew, as well as varied forms of lyric expression, inspired by, on one extreme, Homer and Dante, and on the other, contemporary urban existence. In this repertory, the plural post-utopian mode is first avowed in *A educação dos cinco sentidos* (The education of the five senses).[40] While the collection's five sections contain pieces written in the 1970s (and homages from as early as 1962 and 1967), eighties material comprises the bulk. Without a restricted stylistic unity and with a willingness to admit different registers, the collection gives evidence of an operational plurality in which "presentified" poems are made from varied literary and, to a much lesser degree, experiential sources. The overall dominant note is given through an engagement with universal literary heritage, be it in the set of *transluminuras* (original re-creations of texts from Western and Oriental languages), compositions inspired in literary styles or moments from the age of the troubadors to high modernism, or in contemplations on lyric. Hence such indicative titles as "provença: motz e.l som" and "tenzone," or "opúsculo goetheano" and "portrait of the artist as an old man," with clear historical tones or allusions to individual authors (Goethe, Joyce), in addition to the metaliterary function in "le don du poème," the citational "ode (explícita) em defesa da poesia no dia de são lukács" ([explicit] ode in defense of poetry on st. lukacs day), and "ex/planation," written in English:

> there is no
> plain meaning
> in a
> poem
>
> when one
> begins to ex-
> plain it
> and reaches the
> end
> only the ex
> remains:
>
> dead end
>
> (no exit:
> try it
> again)
> (42)

This wry poem opens the section "Austineia desvairada" — an allusion to Mário de Andrade's noted *Pauliceia desvairada* (*Hallucinated City,* 1922) — which includes surprising ironic and short lyrics on quotidian events. It is one such poem of "tones and semi-tones" that motivates Nunes's historical placement of the poet and the sense of tradition in the decade of the eighties:

Among the front-line vanguard poets, unidirectionality in poetic creation, practiced in the service of the "progress of forms," gives way to an attitude of reevaluation of heritages and of poetic compatibilities. . . . It might be understood as tradition as recuperation of various styles or nuances of style of Western and Oriental poetry, practiced by Haroldo de Campos, as if to deliver the message that poetry is ludic before being revolutionary. (177)

The collection in question, concluding within literary circumscriptions with texts about the experience of translation (of Paz, Vallejo), has one of its most intense moments in the minimalist outburst "Minima Moralia" (1982):

já fiz de tudo com as palavras

agora eu quero fazer de nada*
(25)

This distich yields an antithetical contrast of plenitude and rest, and more. With its title the poem cites Adorno's eponymous book, and in its brevity recalls Oswald's versions of the joke-poem. In addition, there are historical resonances of aphorism and of haiku, a very popular practice in Brazil in the 1980s, with concretist connections.[41] The poem, furthermore, in the manner of Augusto's "Pós-tudo," invites a sort of "personal" reading as a condensed literary biography. As Horácio Costa has noted, Haroldo's two-liner embodies below the surface the poet's "transit from the vanguard to the postvanguard, from the utopia of self-nurturing projects to the post-utopia that feeds on the experience of what is to come: humor, irony, the clarity of one who managed to be his own heir and observes himself through the prism of (re)conciliation."[42] With these self-conscious, metalinguistic, citational, and declarative elements, the poem is ballast in the collection that encompasses it and a premonition of the post-utopian position to be outlined.

The most emphatic implementation of Haroldo's post-utopian poetics is *Finismundo- a última viagem* (The last voyage).[43] The relatively extended text — half a dozen pages, over one hundred twenty lines — is accompanied by an explanatory afterword, a necessary paratext, that clarifies the sources and the two-part design of this very literary piece. The author's point of departure is one of the longest standing and most compelling *topoi* in the Western literary tradition: the last voyage of

---

*[I've already done everything with words / now I want to do nothing]

Odysseus-Ulysses. Noting Homer's silence regarding the great hero's ultimate fate and Dante's celebrated speculation about him in *The Inferno,* Haroldo imagines a "free retake" in two movements: the opening in "epic cadence" via the theme of shipwreck in Mallarmé and the closing, in an "ironic paraphrase," a projection onto the contemporary world. The more elaborate first part is quintessentially intertextual and celebrates artistic audacity. The shorter second part is a condensed satire of the world where ideologies are in crisis and poetry has been abandoned.

What unifies the vision of Odysseus in *Finismundo* is the paradigm of opposition, nonacceptance, daring. The hero's destiny is to resist counsel that advises against further travel, to test the unknown, to seek the unmapped:

Ultimo
Odisseu multi-
ardiloso   — no extremo
Avernotenso limite   — re-
propõe a viagem.

. . . .
. . .   — onde passar avante quer
dizer trans-
gredir a medida   as si-
gilosas siglas do Não.
                                        Onde
a desmesura   húbris-propensa   ad-
verte não
ao nauta . . .

. . . . . .
Ousar o mais:
o além-retorno   o apōs im-
previsto filame na teia de Penélope.

. . . .
            Assim:
partir o lacre ao proibido.   des-
virginar o véu . . .*

---

*[The last / Odysseus of multiple / crafts in the extreme / Avernotenso limit pro- / poses anew the voyage / where to go forward / means to trans- / gress the measure the sigillate siglas of No. / Where impropriety hubris-favorable does / warn the sailor / against / To dare more: / the beyond-return the post-un / foreseen filament in Penelope's web / Thus: to break the seal of the forbidden. de / virginize the veil . . .]

The admiring re-creation via Dante's influential portrait is significant because "in its mythology and in its moral implications this is a revolutionary version of the final voyage of Ulysses," in which the hero becomes a "symbol of sinful desire for forbidden knowledge."[44] Though shipwreck awaits the hero, Haroldo's use of Dante's episode of *il folle volo* (the foolish flight) is a celebration of the ceaseless adventure of knowing and creating; in a literary parallel, the revisitation here lends generalized support to a transgressive mode of discovery.

Stylistically, this first part of *Finismundo* is marked by a historical spectrum. Given the theme, the classical airs seem natural. Other epochal echoes — Renaissance, baroque, romantic, modernist — are achieved through various means: allusions, syntactical inversions, lexical levels, fragmentations, line breaks, etc. The question of lexicon has a particular scholarly interest in the history of Brazilian literature. Numerous items may seem arcane, unnecessarily refined, even contrived. In fact several words are neologisms, as the contemporary poet coins words in homage to the inventive Brazilian translator Odorico Mendes (1799–1864), who reformulated Portuguese words and invented analogous ones in his translations of Virgil and Homer the better to approximate some of the features of the original. Whatever the motivations, it is safe to say that the first and major part of *Finismundo* (requiring a knowledge of classics uncommon in the late twentieth century) is unusually challenging in its pointed erudition.

The tension that the "classical" part of the poem may cause is resolved in the contrast of the second section, in which eloquence is overshadowed by a mode of degradation. The hero, now an urban Ulysses, appears in an ultramodern context of "computerized chance" with airs of death:

. . . .
                                 Teu

epitáfio?   Margem de erro.   traço
mínimo digitado
e à pressa cancelado
no líquido cristal verdefluente.*

. . . .

In this wholly unheroic atmosphere, there is no *periplus,* i.e., narration of voyage, or poetry; a term used by Pound to describe the technique of *The*

---

*[Your / epitaph? margin of error: minimal / trace digitalized / and quickly canceled / in the greenflowing liquid crystal]

Cantos, which are invoked here. Traffic signals keep track of the hero, whose Promethean fire is reduced to the head of a match, and noisy sirens (*sirenes*) replace the mermaids (*sereias*) or mythological sirens. The epic space of discovery gives way to a trivialized world. This state of affairs, in a way, embodies a post-utopian poetic space where an ideal literary adventuresomeness has become lost.

Finismundo exhibits some traits that have been associated with the aesthetics of postmodernism, notably the compression of distinctions between artist and critic. Also potentially relevant to Haroldo's case are those most "frequent poetic means" to achieve a characteristic "multiple coding" which Calinescu (285) records: "allusion and allusive commentary, citation, playfully distorted or invented reference, recasting, transposition, deliberate anachronism, the mixing of two or more historical stylistic modes." Given the very dialogical nature of Haroldo's poem and its "classical" tones, these means might suggest a postmodern mode. But again, this Brazilian author is more concerned with other negative aspects. Haroldo uses the opportunity of commentary on his poem to imply vice in the non-oppositional mixes of contemporary verse and to reinforce a position of distance from the postmodern, explaining that "instead of eclecticism and conformist acceptance of the past, as a nostalgically innocuous ornament, the factor that presides over the selection of topoi and the stylemes of tradition is a critical spirit (inalienable residue of utopia in crisis)."[45] The attitude toward the construction of the poem summarizes the objective of the post-utopian lyric: presentification with invention and rigor.

Postscripts

Despite authorial protestations, the juxtaposition of an ancient classical hero and an entirely up-to-date image of a computer screen in the second part of *Finismundo* might well come off, like other examples above, as a typically "postmodern" mix. Having a digital-age element, the image also can be suggestive of late-century intermedia poetics, and one could further wonder whether the ultramodern lyricism of Augusto de Campos is not reflected in the glare and sharp irony of Haroldo's "antipoetic" scene. In this regard, the crucial phrase therein is "computerized chance." This phrase in the sketch of the plight of the urbanized Ulysses does not support a parallel with Augusto's "computerized" items, because their poetic space is so deliberate and meticulous, anything but chance. Yet *Finismundo* and its "post-utopian" framework do invite comparison with "Pós-tudo," its own relatives in *Expoemas,* and their authors' locations in the "post-" environment. *Finismundo* is epico-lyrical and, in its intensely literary composition, projects a historicity favoring heritage and origins. "Pós-tudo" is techno-lyrical, embodies cross-disciplinary shifts, and may be seen to emanate light forward as well.

Compared to Augusto, for whom acknowledging the passing of the avant-garde phase does not preclude continued employment of the term *vanguarda* as experiment, Haroldo's postconcrete position is more openly accepting of the end of the avant-garde, whose collective principles he stresses. And if one can detect a certain nostalgia for the combative years of concretism in "Pós-tudo" and its defense, a core element of challenge can also be felt in the post-utopian "critical residue" of the utopian concrete venture. Both Noigandres poets want to resist any sense that a "post-" climate should be able to justify nihilistic posturing or free use of lyric repertories. Sharing an insistence on verbal agility and textual control, their desire for continuity of inventiveness means aggressive attention to the substance of language, as well as an emphasis on poetic function—through paronomasia, interrelations, abstraction, etc. Where disagreement between Augusto and Haroldo does exist—on the manner in which the notion of "vanguard" remains useful—there is an opportunity to demonstrate to those who would still critique concretism as a monolith that the later production of the Noigandres poets simply does not warrant such a narrow approach. More than thirty years after the formation of a team, the original project keeps its status in history, but individual trajectories have outdistanced the group ideals.

Counteracting a counterproductive "post-" situation has been one of the aims of the Noigandres poets in the final decades of the twentieth century. In the long run, concern with lyric circumscribes the relevancy of the postmodern, not vice versa. While Augusto, in the very ambiguity of "Pós-tudo" or in point-blank expressions of preference, defends a vanguardlike end-of-the-century creativity, Haroldo seeks to affirm, defining the post-utopian poem and steering the last voyage of the model hero of *Finismundo* into pedestrian circumstances, a synchronic constant of exploration. In these positionings, whether via poem or prose disclosure, the importance of historicized perception is paramount. Augusto and Haroldo are unaccepting of a certain postmodernism because it is perceived as inimical to poetic principles of critical command, linguistic vitality, and experimentation. Therein lies an essential backlink with the historical vanguards, including those of *modernismo,* as well as with concrete poetry. Maintenance of a concrete rigor in "post-" times translates not only into a textually and materially sensitive employment of language, but also into a historically aware vigilance. Historicity wholly invades post-utopia, the confrontation of the postmodern, and post-everything. What prevails in these episodes of contemporary Brazilian poetry is, beyond an epochal situating, a concern for an integrated poeticity.

Coverage and Countenance

The final decades of the twentieth century in Brazilian lyric are marked by plurality and retrospection, as evidenced by the shaping of the post-utopian poem and by the poetics and polemics of "Pós-tudo." These developments, joining and reflecting a multiplicity of events, brought with them inescapable senses of contention, transition, and transformation. Around these moments there coalesced natural considerations of epoch and an unprecedented awareness of historicity in lyric, with a questioning of the making of poetry from ancient times to an artistic present energized by electronic technology. The "everything" of Augusto de Campos's poem and the ultimate focus of Haroldo de Campos's post-utopian approach return to, clarify, and resituate the imperative of invention that has always driven the poetics of the Noigandres group, previous to and since the inception of concrete poetry. At the same time, their problematizing interventions make certainties and consensus about the sphere of lyric in the eighties and nineties all the more difficult, which ought to encourage an open and wide-angle view of contemporary production. Haroldo's essay carries the weight of history and, crossing Octavio Paz's path of convergence, concedes a present-future of plurality, while the unique *Finismundo,* even with its classical charge, connects with other key texts and processes of the literarily un-unified eighties and early nineties, when all (everything) may contribute to complicate the separation of strains and stains in the fabric of poetry.

Alfredo Bosi elucidates divergences and differences in recent lyric with a comparison to the situation of Brazilian narrative:

> Parallel to what occurred with prose fiction, which moved from engagement and testimonial to extreme individualism, the poetry of

this end of the millennium seems to have cut the binds that tie it to any ideal of unity, whether ethical, political, or aesthetic, in the modern sense of constructive of an artistic object. Many of its texts stage the theatre of postmodern dispersion and its centrifugal tendencies: motifs are atomized, styles are mixed, and the sharpest sensibilities bare, for the reader, the consciousness of disintegration itself.[1]

On the point of historically conscious diversification, another interested observer of lyric in Brazil remarked that "poets of the eighties move at will through all spaces, styles, forms and rhythms, going from the *redondilha* to cubist clippings, from the sonnet to the joke-poem, from the prose poem to the false ode. Collage, internal rhyme, sound play, ruptures, extensions, none of this is strange or casual; it even gives the impression that [poets] have in mind, with multiplicity, not only the synthesis of various epochs but also a balance of previous aesthetic experiences."[2] Since the early eighties, such amalgamation and evaluation have meant, in different circumstances, more careful manipulation of oral language, outright de-informalization, and relatively overt confrontations of poetic legacies. In the late century, a competition of practices naturally continues, though without the levels of intensity and dedication characteristic of previous decades. The primacy of individual making has clearly surpassed participation-in-project as the motivation of contemporary lyric. Variance and motion occur in the field as a whole and within individual repertories, both current and historical. The latest publications of Ferreira Gullar, for instance, show renewed interest in the celebrated decompositions of his early career and in the vanguard experiments he came to denounce in favor of "directed" verse, as well as the internalizing of what Benedito Nunes calls poetry's "collective political sensibility."[3]

To sound the hybrid poetry of the eighties, it is beneficial to return to Nunes's reading of the domain, in which he had posited four "compositional constants" (179): (1) metapoetic, reflexive themes; (2) the technique of the fragment; (3) epigrammatic configuration; and (4) the neo-rhetorical. Keeping in mind the always necessarily arbitrary division of symbolic production into even chronological units, this profile may be profitably traced back into the seventies and forward into the nineties. The scheme provides, moreover, an opportunity to review the significance of major facets of twentieth-century lyric production in Brazil. Self-conscious reflection on writing and genre is, of course, an essential characteristic of modern verse. Late-century tunings to such frequencies in Brazil have their precedents in *modernismo* but are a more direct effect of the inquisitive provocations of concretism and subsequent conflagrations of semiotics. The nationalist needling of *modernismo,* the theoretical impact of concrete poetry, the success of song as a poetic vehicle in the sixties and seventies, and the protests of political-existential verse, all contribute to an abiding presence of constitutional questions in lyric. Fragmentation—especially in more visually oriented poetry—harks back to the ever-present Oswald de Andrade and evolves most obviously from the vanguard experiences of the 1950s and 1960s. There is a closely related parallel in verse in the epigram, what one might call a discursive relative of fracture and partializing. Such contemporary practices are linked wholly to Oswald, to certain efforts of Manuel Bandeira, to the Carlos Drummond de Andrade of "In the Middle of the Road" and "Seven-Sided Poem," to the impulse of condensation in João Cabral de Melo Neto, and to the deep cleansing of concrete poetry.[4] The counterpart to points two and three in Nunes's account, the neo-rhetorical, refers to an expansive, oratorical model of discursive, neo-epical, or narrative verse. Nunes places within the purview of this eighties constant, in turn, a Northeastern example of a chain-of-texts that forms an extensive parody of styles and forms.[5] This item circles back to the reflexive opening of the profile that the critic draws, and reaffirms the surge toward retrospection in lyric.

As far as the neo-rhetorical in late-century Brazilian lyric is concerned, prominent examples in the late 1970s had been Gullar's *Dirty Poem* and Sant'Anna's "indigenous" cantos. Two long poems by authors of the next generation that embrace and incorporate twentieth-century traditions and renewals quite vividly are *Táxi ou Poema de amor passageiro* (*Taxi or Poem of Love in Transit*) by Adriano Espínola (b. 1951) and *O livro dos fracta* by Horácio Costa (b. 1954). In contrasting ways, these works put into play the *periplus* which in *Finismundo* was cited as lacking. A wandering and wondering love poem, *Taxi* traverses the Western hemisphere and multifarious linguistic terrain to end in the "delirium of the present." With intuitive intention, and often assuming informal roles, *Taxi* maintains high levels of textual intensity. It involves calculated invocations of a factitious paradigm—from Mallarmé to futurism and concrete poetry—and of the discourses of modernism (Eliot and others) and homespun *modernismo.*[6] For its part, *O livro dos fracta* stands out as an updated lyrical epic and as a poem of pointed historical amplitude.[7] The work comprises arousing paratextual front matter and fifty-four compositions of three-lines, using intertwined motifs. It operates on multiple levels of cultural reference, ranging from ancient history (e.g., Pontus

Euxinus, the Ottoman Empire) to modern astronomy (e.g., blue shift, black hole), from neoclassical poetics (e.g., Boileau) to the streets of Brazilian *carnaval* and "fractal" theory. Costa uses multilingual phrases and allusions to set up an extensive dialogue with world literature and the history of Brazilian civilization, notably with Oswald and the travel paradigms of his prose fiction. While the striking formula of *O livro dos fracta* is original, Costa's texts are comparable to those of the Brazilian modernist master in their acute national-cosmopolitan awareness, sequentiality, and ambiguity of genre. *O livro dos fracta* is — in self-reflexive, fragmentary, and epigrammatic forms — a self-proclaimed "novel," neo-rhetorical, and exemplary of its own time and place in lyric.

The cosmopolitan elements and travel motifs of these two instances of the neo-rhetorical lead to the matter of the international projection of Brazilian lyric, which has persisted since Oswald's modernist assertion of a "poetry for export." The Noigandres poets founded the movement of concrete poetry in league with a European ally in a consciously transnational move, and there is little question that this uniquely theorized experimental poetry has gained more exposure for Brazil — mostly in the late 1960s and early 1970s, but continuing until the present day — than any other proposal in poetry. In terms of attention abroad, Brazilian popular music as a whole — including the Tropicalist movement that adopted Oswaldian ideas of appropriation — has, not surprisingly, outshined concretism and all aspects of literature, but not with specific reference to the lyrical artistry of the songwriting. The poetry of MPB remains, above all, an outstanding feature of contemporary national culture. On other fronts, while foreign analysts have not focused much on Brazil's manifestations of political and youth lyric, these represent interesting national case studies for comparative approaches to *engagé* and underground verse.

In the Brazilian context itself, contemporary poetry can be said to have pervasive social interests if the range includes activity and idealizations in the public sphere in addition to more obvious counterdiscourse. Social data in the sphere of lyric are constant, differing in accordance with group organizing principles. In contrast with the contemporaneous Generation of '45, João Cabral de Melo Neto reconciled real-life portraits with his severe discipline of textual architecture. Concrete poetry in the 1950s may have seemed wholly esoteric, but one of the aims of the project was to institute an ad-like immediacy of communication, and certain compositions (e.g., "terra") had perfectly relevant thematic dimensions. The changes, formulations, and inventions of concretism in the sixties, in turn, formed an indispensable part of concerned artistic debate of the period. The populist approach typified in *Violão de rua* involved, beyond the overt messages of the writing, an activism that linked verse, personal participation, and historical events concretely. Other vanguard ventures of the decade—*poesia praxis, poema processo*—merited attention for having entangled theory and political discourse and provoked further questions of evaluation. Protest and social commentary formed a key aspect of the poetry of song, most notably in the work of Chico Buarque. Some marginal poetry addressed head-on the conjuncture of the dictatorship, but the social side of that manifestation is best sought in its attempts to create audiences and in the symbolic "resistance" to industrial models implicit in the making of alternative circuits. In postconcretist youth poetry, attempts to subvert language and to incorporate surrounding realia (physical images) into verbal art may reflect discontent with the difficulty and available means of saying, and can also be interpreted as acts in the public sphere. And to the extent that the "tale of the tribe" subsists in neo-epical texts, the element of collectivity inevitably comes into play. In the efforts of all those involved with poetry in the late century to make something more of poetry in the age of media dominance, there must be an element of community and a consideration of public air space.

The constant of experimentalism in contemporary Brazilian lyric involves various responses to nonliterary media and relationships with technology. While a young Cabral had broached the issue of intelligent use of communication media in a view of the modern functions of poetry, the concrete poets were true pioneers in the incorporation of technological factors into poetics and textual undertakings. They responded to the provocation of media, in the retrospective words of one founder, as if media connections with poetry were intentional. The concrete movement having opened the way, subsequent players—other neovanguards, poet-musicians, "marginal," and postconcrete colleagues—experimented lyrically and reacted visibly to the influence of nonliterary media. In the vanguard schisms and offshoots of concrete poetry, mass-media techniques of containment and material focus persisted. In early sixties projects of political poetry, the very attempts to achieve a new orality and to emphasize rural (folk) sentiment in urban settings served to sharpen contrasts with competing discourses that valued urban charges. The ability of the poet-composers of MPB, in turn, to maintain an artistically focused endeavor within the context of the commercial recording industry was remarkable. Marginal poets wanted to bypass the publishing industry and take advantage of amateur technology, while those involved in intersemiotic creation often desired to embody the best suggestions of their forerunners and to use technology to confront the facts of literature's diminishing status and of poetry's changing roles. Could such continued (or even earlier) experimentalism represent some sort of compensation for the condition of "underdevelopment"? An artistic way to be equal with the advanced industrial world? To accept outright a positive response to such queries would be to deny local creativity and vision, and to undervalue the circumstances that may distinguish modern Brazilian production. Laser poems and multimedia-video texts are high-intensity solutions to the "problem" of poetry in the digital age, even in a less than developed nation such as Brazil. Whether in neotechnological modes or on historically conscious pages, much contemporary Brazilian poetry has shown a telling fascination with vehicle: the poster, portfolio, poem-object, chapbook, sound recording, *samizdat,* glossy, plastic sack, serigraph, etc. This proliferation of vehicles — for experimental and more standard texts alike — cannot but suggest a fundamental disquiet and is hard evidence of transition in course. These social and aesthetic tensions, with or without resolution or necessity thereof, run through the repertories that have comprised the subjects of this book.

The proposals and practices of contemporary Brazilian poetry present, sometimes disconcertingly, a diversity that is central to any assessment of the genre. As has been seen in the course of these deliberations, organized efforts and identifiable tendencies since the mid-1950s are quite varied in approach, objectives, reach, and frameworks of operation. Yet all challenge in some way convention, long-held assumptions about poetry and its dissemination, or empowered notions of the genre of lyric. Alterity surfaces in different guises and at various levels of oppositional intent. There is "otherness" of act or behavior — be it political, existential, or professional, in the realm of the arts — and of text, whereby poets may explore new interrelations of literature, write the extraverbal, or venture beyond the typescripted page. In a loose historical metaphor of specific Brazilian resonance, poetic options from organic concrete poetry to lyrical neo-rhetoric may represent different ways, recalling Drummond's foundational iconoclasm, to "be *gauche* in life." And these faces of contemporary poetry must articulate or imply rationales to countenance their own kind of newness or deviance.

Following what is generally conceded to have been a reactionary posture on the part of the neo-Parnassians of the Generation of '45, the Noigandres poets began to question the concept of poetry as expressive of an emotive self. Ensuing vanguard projects performed a radical rejection of the very notion of verse-making. Declaring the death of verse, the inventors of *poesia concreta* introduced non-affectivity, antidiscursivity, and graphico-spatial paradigms of representation. This positioning went beyond the historical evolution of styles and normal opposition to the fashion of the previous generation. The concrete poets sought to shake the very foundations of poetry, and they succeeded in creating a new category. Taking the limits of "poetry" to nonverbal levels — *poema semiótico, poema processo,* visual poetry — the most radical neo-avant-garde extremes, in Brazil as elsewhere, required expanded definitions and additional articles in the constitution of poetry to remain within the circumference of the genre of lyric. Much postconcretist production (after 1965) has continued to undermine customary senses of poetry as a literary item. Since the 1970s, intersemiotic creation has further complicated senses of textuality in the age of technology. With the emergence of notable poet-composers, the songwriting of *música popular brasileira* (MPB) came to be recognized as a channel of poetry in the late 1960s, raising a series of issues concerning the nature and media of (nonpopular) poetry, long held to be a literary (writerly) manifestation. Earlier in the 1960s, *poesia praxis* followed a definition of poetry as form while pursuing the engagement characteristic of the protest movement of *Violão de rua.* This attitudinally defined practice with openly political aims combated all that ran counter to its social mission: the individualism of traditional lyric poetry, formalism of any stripe, and, in principle at least, the literary system that valued aesthetics over intention. The "underground" traits of that experience foreshadowed so-called marginal poetry, whose practitioners, also largely suspect in quality from establishment points of view, were indifferent or defiant. Marginal poetry formed a network of production and distribution whose significance may be understood in terms of its peripheral status, its very functioning outside standard circuits. Informal free-verse-making may have been quite uneven and not particularly innovative, and the surface discourse of contemporaneous constructivist lyric may have been less than critical from a sociohistorical vantage point. Yet both manifestations of youth poetry found and constituted the need, ways, and means to ponder the predicaments of growth in a dictatorial and technologically developing nation. In that context, there emerged a specifically feminine discourse in lyric — ironically conscious of expressive parameters from Drummond's "faces" to the *mise-en-page* of postconcretism — that should merit a separate study. For their part, the Noigandres poets, boisterous lyrical scientists of the 1950s, recognized a fundamental cycle of change in the eighties, still resisting — in defense of their imperative of invention — international versions of the postmodern in lyric. The trends of contemporary Brazilian poetry are manifestly diverse in conceptual underpinnings, ideological reflections, aesthetic contributions, and historical impacts. The contrasts and interfaces of the field over the decades of the second half of the century are what prove to be most revealing.

1 Leaders and Legacies: From *Modernismo* to Reactions and the Contemporary

1 For the sake of clarity and distinction, the Portuguese term *modernismo* will be used throughout to refer to the Brazilian movement. The more general term "modernism" will be employed to refer to the early-century renewal of the arts in the Western world, especially in Europe. It should be kept in mind that the Spanish usage of *modernismo* refers to the late nineteenth-century aestheticism (influenced by Parnassianism and symbolism) in Spanish America and Spain that preceded the experimentation of the *vanguardia*, or avant-garde, which would be the nearest equivalent to Brazilian *moderismo*. Epigraph from *Toda a América* (1926).

2 For extensive bibliography on the key avant-garde phase, see Merlin H. Forster and K. David Jackson, *Vanguardism in Latin American Literature: An Annotated Bibliographical Guide* (Westport, Conn.: Greenwood Press, 1990). The Brazil section of this most useful source (pp. 62–91) focuses on studies published since 1970. Some notable English-language studies will be highlighted here.

3 David William Foster, "Spanish American and Brazilian Literature: A History of Disconsonance," *Hispania* 75, no. 4 (October 1992): 969.

4 The only book-length English-language study of the movement focused on poetry is John Nist, *The Modernist Movement in Brazil* (Austin: University of Texas Press, 1967). Nist also edited, with Yolanda Leite, *Modern Brazilian Poetry: An Anthology* (Bloomington: Indiana University Press, 1962). In the former, Nist narrates circumstances leading up to and involving the Modern Art Week. See also the introduction to Giovanni Pontiero, ed., *An Anthology of Brazilian Modernist Poetry* (Oxford: Pergamon Press, 1969), pp. 1–17, which is derived from an essay by Mário da Silva Brito, the leading historian of the movement. For a broader view of *modernismo* in an English-language source, see Wilson Martins, *The Modernist Idea: A Critical Survey of Brazilian Writing in the 20th Century,* trans. Jack E. Tomlins (New York: New York University Press, 1970; reprint, Westport, Conn.: Greenwood Press, 1979), and Afrânio Coutinho, *An Introduction to Literature in Brazil,* trans. Gregory Rabassa (New York:

Columbia University Press, 1970), pp. 210–97. For a summary account and additional bibliography on *modernismo,* as well as individual author entries, see Irwin Stern, ed., *Dictionary of Brazilian Literature* (Westport, Conn.: Greenwood Press, 1988).

5 Benedito Nunes, "O pensamento estético no Brasil," in Adolpho Crippa, ed., *As idéias filosóficas no Brasil* (São Paulo: Convívio, 1978), p. 100; cited in text by author and article title. For the historical framework of these affairs, see Jeffrey D. Needell, *A Tropical Belle-Époque: Elite Culture and Society in Turn-of-the-Century Rio de Janeiro* (New York: Cambridge University Press, 1987), esp. pp. 10–22.

6 Trans. Frederick G. Williams, *Brazil's Finest Poets: A Bilingual Selection* (Santa Barbara, California: Jorge de Sena Center for Portuguese Studies, 1989), p. 34; cited below by author.

7 Alfredo Bosi, *História concisa da literatura brasileira,* rev. and exp. ed. (São Paulo: Cultrix, 1994), p. 234; cited below by author.

8 From a lecture by Benedito Nunes at the University of Texas, Austin, November 18, 1980.

9 Peregrino Júnior, *O movimento modernista* (Rio de Janeiro: MEC, 1954). Cited in text by author.

10 For translations of various authors, see Elizabeth Bishop and Emanuel Brasil, eds., *An Anthology of Twentieth-Century Brazilian Poetry* (Middletown, Conn.: Wesleyan University Press, 1972), cited below by editors, and such other sources as Charles Richard Carlisle, *Tesserae: A Mosaic of Twentieth-Century Brazilian Poetry* (Fort Worth, Tex.: Latitudes, 1983), cited below by title, and *Modern Poetry in Translation* (King's College, University of London), New Series, no. 6 (Winter 1994–95).

11 To avoid confusion with Oswald de Andrade, no relation, first names will be used in the text. Mário's foundational work of fiction appeared as *Macunaíma,* trans. E. A. Goodland (New York: Random House, 1984), in a version that hardly reflects key linguistic dimensions. The novel and its critical reception are further exposed in the film version; see Randal Johnson, *Cinema Novo x 5: Masters of Contemporary Brazilian Film* (Austin: University of Texas Press, 1984), pp. 25–34, and Robert Stam, *Subversive Pleasures: Bakhtin, Cultural Criticism and Film* (Baltimore: Johns Hopkins University Press, 1989), pp. 133–37 and 146–50.

12 Mário de Andrade, *Hallucinated City,* trans. Jack E. Tomlins (Nashville: Vanderbilt University Press, 1969), cited in text by title. See the commentary of Iumna Maria Simon, "Poetic Evolution in the Industrial Era: The Brazilian Modernists," in John D. Wirth and Robert L. Jones, eds., *Manchester and São Paulo* (Stanford: Stanford University Press, 1978), pp. 35–50, as well as the general comments on modernism by Richard Morse in "Manchester Economies and Paulista Sociology," pp. 19ff. in the same volume. On the outstanding long poem "Enfibraturas do Ipiranga," the final oratorical experiment of Mário's book, see the analysis as performance manifesto by Vicky Unruh, *Latin American Vanguards: The Art of Contentious Encounter* (Berkeley: University of California Press, 1995), pp. 42–50, cited below by author. Mário was also interpreted in English by Gordon Brotherson, *Latin American Poetry: Origins and Presence* (London and New York: Cambridge University Press, 1975), pp. 77ff.; cited below by author.

13   In this regard, see Randal Johnson, "Art and Intention in Mário de Andrade," in Margo Milleret and Marshall C. Eakin, eds., *Homenagem a Alexandrino Severino: Essays on the Portuguese-Speaking World* (Austin: Host, 1993), pp. 167–79.

14   In translation, see, of *Memórias sentimentais de João Miramar* (1924), "Sentimental Memoirs of John Seaborne," trans. Ralph Niebuhr and Albert Bork, in *The Texas Quarterly* 15, no. 4 (1972): 112–60, and, of *Serafim ponte grande* (1933), *Seraphim Grosse Pointe*, trans. Kenneth D. Jackson and Albert Bork (Austin: Nefertiti Press, 1979), with an afterword by Haroldo de Campos. These works are further interpreted as vanguard texts by Unruh, pp. 114–22.

15   See the pertinent study by K. David Jackson, "Three Glad Races: Primitivism and Ethnicity in Brazilian Modernist Literature," *Modernism/Modernity* 1, no. 2 (1994): 89–112.

16   Jean Longland, trans., in Bishop and Brasil, p. 11.

17   Cf. Cassiano Ricardo, "O humor na poesia," *Revista do livro*, vol. 36 (1969).

18   The best study of these procedures in Oswald's poetry remains Haroldo de Campos, "Uma poética da radicalidade," preface to Oswald de Andrade, *Poesias reunidas* (Rio de Janeiro: Civilização Brasileira, 1974), pp. 9–62.

19   "Manifesto da poesia Pau-Brasil" (1924), Stella de Sá Rego, trans., "Manifesto of Pau-Brasil Poetry," *Latin American Literary Review* 14, no. 27 (1986): 184–87.

20   For an annotated version in the original, see Jorge Schwartz, *Vanguardas latino-americanas: polêmicas, manifestos e textos críticos* (São Paulo: EDUSP-Iluminuras-FAPESP, 1995), pp. 142–47. In English, see the annotated translation and bibliographical references of Leslie Bary, *Latin American Literary Review* 19, no. 38 (1991): 35–47, as well as her provocative "The Tropical Modernist as Literary Cannibal: Cultural Identity in Oswald de Andrade," *Chasqui* 20, no. 2 (1991): 10–19. See also the neo-Adornian analysis of Roberto Schwarz, "The Cart, the Tram, and the Modernist Poet," in *Misplaced Ideas: Essays on Brazilian Culture*, trans. John Gledson (New York: Verso, 1992), pp. 108–25, as well as relevant references to Oswald's "triumphalist" vision of Brazilian underdevelopment in "Brazilian Culture: Nationalism by Elimination," pp. 7ff.

21   Raul Bopp, *Movimentos modernistas no Brasil 1922–1928* (Rio de Janeiro: Livraria São José, 1966), p. 63. Oswald published the manifesto in the first issue of his lively arts journal *Revista de antropofagia* (1928). For a descriptive analysis, see K. David Jackson, "A View on Brazilian Literature: Eating the *Revista de Antropofagia*," *Latin American Literary Review* 7, no. 13 (1979): 1–9.

22   For a clear capsule contextualization of this dispute, see Randal Johnson, "Tupy or Not Tupy: Cannibalism and Nationalism in Contemporary Brazilian Literature and Culture," in John King, ed., *On Modern Latin American Fiction* (New York: Noonday, 1989), pp. 41–59, volume cited below by editor. Additional perspective on this relatively neglected topic of the nationalist alternative is given by Randal Johnson, "Notes on a Conservative Vanguard: The Case of Verde-Amarelo/Anta," *Hispanic Studies*, vol. 4 (1989), *Literatura de vanguarda luso-brasileira*: 31–42. Johnson disputes the idea that Oswald's opponents developed their version of cultural nationalism in response to him or Pau-Brasil. See also Randal Johnson, *Rereading Brazilian Modernism*,

Texas Papers on Latin America no. 89–04. An earlier related study was Ilan Rachum, *"Antropofagia* against *Verdeamarelo,*" *Latin American Literary Review* 8 (1976): 67–81. For details of the Oswald-Anta confrontation from a local point of view, see Maria Luisa Fernandes Guelfi, *Novissima: estética e ideologia na década de 20* (São Paulo: USP/Instituto de Estudos Brasileiros, 1987), pp. 135ff.

23　Alceu Amoroso Lima, interview, "Modernismo: 50 anos depois," *Revista de cultura Vozes* 66, no. 1 *50 anos de modernismo brasileiro* (January 1972): 15.

24　Cited items from Manuel Bandeira, *This Earth That Sky,* trans. and intro. Candace Slater (Berkeley: University of California Press, 1989), which has an extensive bibliography on the poet. A notable recent addition to Bandeira criticism is Davi Arrigucci Jr., *Humildade, paixão e morte: a poesia de Manuel Bandeira* (São Paulo: Editora das Letras, 1991).

25　In addition to Slater's translation, see the commentary and contextualizations of Brotherson, pp. 89ff.

26　Drummond is widely available in English. In addition to numerous appearances in periodicals, see John Nist, trans., *In the Middle of the Road* (Tucson: University of Arizona Press, 1965), volume cited below; Virginia Peckham de Araújo, trans., *The Minus Sign* (Manchester, N.H.: Carcanet Press, 1981); and Thomas Colchie and Mark Strand, eds., *Traveling in the Family* (New York: Random House, 1986). A synopsis and assessment of the literary career is given in Charles A. Perrone, "Carlos Drummond de Andrade," in *Critical Survey of Poetry* (Pasadena: Salem Press, 1987), pp. 93–102.

27　Carlos Drummond de Andrade, ed., *Uma pedra no meio do caminho: biografia de um poema* (Rio de Janeiro: Editora do Autor, 1967).

28　Bishop, trans., in Bishop and Brasil, p. 63. This translation has been chosen from a pool of several for its overall quality, but the problem of the key penultimate stanza should be raised. With its interrelation of technique, rhyme, poetic space, experience, and purpose, this strophe has been the most revealing, and the most difficult to render in translation. In "Poem of Seven Faces," Nist is literal and direct: "World, world, vast world, / if my name was Twirled / it'd be a rhyme, it wouldn't be a solution. / World, world, vast world, / even vaster is my heart" (*In the Middle of the Road,* p. 17). This option results in a phony name and lost final rhyme. Williams (p. 69), in his "Poem of Seven Faces," is more clearly concerned with reproduction of effects: "World world wide wide world, / if I had been christened McCurld / it would be a rhyme, it wouldn't be a solution though. / World world wide wide world, my heart is much wider I know." Yet the name here is still awkward. Other drawbacks are found in the rendering of "Heptagonal Poem": "World world wide world / if my name were Harold / 'twould be a kind of rhyme, but no solution. / World world wide world / wider still my heart" (Jack Tomlins, trans., in *Literary Review* 21, no. 2 [Winter 1978]: 167, cited below by journal title). A more obscure version is D. Ackerson and R. Sternberg, "Poem of Seven Facets," in *Dragonfly* (Pocatello, Idaho) 3, no. 1 (Spring 1972): 4.

29　Emanuel de Moraes, "As várias faces de uma poesia," in *Carlos Drummond de Andrade,* ed. Sonia Brayner (Rio de Janeiro: Civilização Brasileira, 1978), p. 102. Among the other segments in this collection, it is interesting to note that Mário de Andrade wrote on Drummond's first book, *Alguma poesia,* in "A Poesia em 1930."

30 This is the contention of Affonso Romano de Sant'Anna, *Drummond, o gauche no tempo* (Rio de Janeiro: Lia Editora, 1972).

31 Ricardo da Silveira Lobo Sternberg, *The Unquiet Self: Self and Society in the Poetry of Carlos Drummond de Andrade* (Valencia: Albatros Hispanofila, 1986), p. 25. The observation that follows is from pp. 29–30.

32 Massaud Moisés, *História da literatura brasileira,* vol. 5, *O modernismo* (São Paulo: Cultrix-USP, 1989), p. 38.

33 For an enumeration of a series of perceived excesses and of points of what is seen as "false Modernism and its disfigurements," see the brief study of Murilo Araújo, *Quadrantes do modernismo* (Rio de Janeiro: MEC, 1958), pp. 24–28. The author was one of the Festa poets. See also for the conservative view of a poet who would be at the center of the Generation of '45: Ledo Ivo, *Modernismo e modernidade* (Rio de Janeiro: Livraria São José, 1972). An interesting early source of select Brazilian modernist and '45 poems in translation is Leonard Downes, *An Introduction to Modern Brazilian Poetry* (São Paulo: Clube de Poesia, 1954), sponsored by the "poetry club" of '45 poets themselves.

34 Sérgio Buarque de Hollanda, *Diário carioca,* September 9, 1951, no pagination (files of the Oficina Literária Afrânio Coutinho, Rio de Janeiro).

35 Sílvio Castro, *A revolução da palavra: origens e estrutura da literatura brasileira moderna* (Petrópolis: Vozes, 1976), p. 272.

36 Affonso Ávila, "Aspectos da poesia pós-modernista," *Correio da manhã,* January 12, 1957, p. 10.

37 José Guilherme Merquior, "Falência da poesia ou uma geração enganada e enganosa: os poetas de 45," in *Razão do poema: ensaios de crítica e de estética* (Rio de Janeiro: Civilização Brasileira, 1965), pp. 34–35.

38 The most complete apology is Gilberto Mendonça Telles, "Para o estudo da Geração de 45," *Revista de poesia e crítica* 12 (December 1986): 14–46. With a recapitulation of the group's emergence and a critical synopsis of reception, the critic argues that the Generation of '45 can be understood as part of the "sense of transformation of *modernismo*" (21).

39 Eduardo Portella, quoted by Emilia Silveira, "Geração 45: o re-encontro com a forma," *Jornal do Brasil,* June 21, 1975, caderno B, no pagination (files of the Oficina Literária Afrânio Coutinho, Rio de Janeiro).

40 For further elaboration on this difference, see Haroldo de Campos, "The Geometry of Commitment," in *World Literature Today* 66, no. 4 (Fall 1992): 617–21. This special issue in honor of the 1992 Neustadt Prize Laureate contains a dozen additional studies of Cabral's work, with appropriate corresponding bibliographies. Lyrical examples in the articles are translated too. A synopsis of the poet's work is given in Charles A. Perrone, "João Cabral de Melo Neto," *Encyclopedia of Literature in the Twentieth Century* (New York: Crossroads, 1993), pp. 1634–35.

41 Richard Zenith, trans., *Latin American Literary Review* 14, no. 27 (1986): 101. The symptomatic text "A lição de poesia" ("A Lesson of Poetry") and other titles from the

original book are included in the bilingual volume edited by Djelal Kadir, *João Cabral de Melo Neto, Selected Poetry 1937–1990* (Middletown, Conn.: Wesleyan University Press, 1994), cited below by editor.

42   Versions of the dramatic verse by Elizabeth Bishop first appeared in *Poetry* (Chicago) (October–November 1963); reprinted in Kadir, pp. 84–97. See meta- aspects in the small-press translation of Kerry S. Keys, *A Knife All Blade* (Camp Hill, Pa.: Pine Press, 1980), and in Kadir, pp. 78–81.

43   James Wright, trans., in Bishop and Brasil, pp. 148–149, reprinted in Kadir, pp. 130–31.

44   *The Devil to Pay in the Backlands* (New York: Knopf, 1963) is the translation of *Grande sertão: veredas* (Rio de Janeiro: José Olympio, 1956). The translation of Rosa's major work, and of most others, hardly reflects the poetic character of the prose. On this and other critical issues, see Jon Vincent, *João Guimarães Rosa* (Boston: Twayne, 1978) and Charles A. Perrone, "An Endless Passage: João Guimarães Rosa," in King, pp. 117–35.

45   In Emanuel Brasil and William Jay Smith, eds., *Brazilian Poetry 1950–1980* (Middletown, Conn.: Wesleyan University Press, 1983), pp. 14–15, cited below by editors.

46   Ferreira Gullar, *A luta corporal,* 4th ed. (Rio de Janeiro: José Olympio, 1994), p. 62.

47   Richard Zenith, trans. in Brasil and Smith, pp. 90–91. Faustino published but one book in his short life. His poems and translations are collected in Benedito Nunes, ed., *Poesia completa e traduzida* (São Paulo: Max Limonad, 1985). Faustino's studies of poets and poetry are collected in *Poesia experiência* (São Paulo: Perspectiva, 1977).

48   Some writers in the "tradition of the image," including some of the Generation of '45, are in translation in *Tesserae*. Representative anthologies of more "standard" Brazilian poetry include Carlos Néjar, ed., *Antologia da poesia brasileira contemporânea* (Lisbon: Imprensa Nacional-Casa da Moeda, 1986), which covers poets born since 1920.

2   The Imperative of Invention:
Concrete Poetry and the Poetic Vanguards

1   The primary reference for international history, documentation, and anthology is Mary Ellen Solt, ed., *Concrete Poetry: A World View* (Bloomington: Indiana University Press, 1970). Examples cited from Solt in this chapter have lexical keys or are translated; many have additional annotations. Another fundamental source is Emmett Williams, *An Anthology of Concrete Poetry* (New York: Something Else Press, 1967), no pagination; while the introduction is sparse, there are more numerous examples of Brazilian production, and each example has a brief critical commentary alongside the lexical key. The Solt and Williams volumes will be indicated by editor's name below whenever specific Brazilian texts can be seen there. Some pertinent examples also appear in Emanuel Brasil and William Jay Smith, eds., *Brazilian Poetry 1950–1980* (Middletown, Conn.: Wesleyan University Press, 1983), also cited below by editors' names. With respect to other representations of this output, see the section on international reception of Brazilian concrete poetry later in this chapter.

Two recent exhibitions with accompanying publications demonstrate the continuity of international interest in the Brazilian concrete movement: a special show at Archivio di Nuova Scritura, Milano, Italy, March–June 1991, documented in Lenora de Barros, ed., *Poesia Concreta in Brasile,* and "Material Poetry of the Renaissance/ Renaissance of Material Poetry," Widener Library, Harvard University, May–June 1992, with essential Brazilian participation. See Roland Greene, ed., *Harvard Library Bulletin,* New Series, vol. 3, no. 2 (1992), cited below by editor. As for recent academic events, witness "A Symphosophia on The End of Language: Experimental, Visual and Concrete Poetry since 1960, in Honor of Brazilian and Portuguese Experimental Poets," April 7–8, 1995, at Yale University.

2   A rather detailed synopsis of the movement (1950–1965) is appended, along with a chronological list of publications of the authors, to Augusto de Campos, Décio Pignatari, and Haroldo de Campos, *Teoria da poesia concreta,* 2d. ed. (São Paulo: Duas Cidades, 1975), cited in the text and notes as *Teoria.* To avoid awkward repetitions of the family name of the Campos brothers, they will be referred to in the text by their first names throughout.

The first edition of *Teoria* was in 1965, and the third (by Brasiliense) in 1987. Only four of the thirty essays have appeared in their entirety in English; see citations below of translations in *Poetics Today* by Jon Tolman. His complete version of *Teoria* was excerpted in *Studies in the Twentieth Century* 7 (1971): 31–49. The present chapter will cite additional English-language sources wherever possible. The most complete bibliography on Brazilian concrete poetry appears in *Código* (Salvador, Bahia), no. 11 (1986).

3   In anticipation of such questions, an analyst of the development of the theory of Brazilian concrete poetry specifically notes that his focus is "not the vanguard but rather concrete poetry and its meaning in Brazilian literature" (Paulo Franchetti, *Alguns aspectos da teoria da poesia concreta* [Campinas: Editora da UNICAMP, 1989], p. 12); cited below by author. In addition to many parts of *Teoria* itself, numerous bibliographical items concern the avant-garde in Brazil; see issues dedicated to vanguard poetics of *Revista de cultura brasileña,* vol. 11 (December 1964); *Tempo brasileiro,* vol. 26–27 (January–March 1971) (*Vanguarda e modernidade*); *Revista de cultura Vozes,* vol. 67, no. 10 (December 1973) (*Vanguarda e comunicação*); and others cited below. See also Eduardo Portella, *Vanguarda e cultura de massa* (Rio de Janeiro: Tempo Brasileiro, 1978); Margarida de Aguiar Patriota, *Vanguarda, do conceito ao texto* (Belo Horizonte: Itatiaia-INL, 1985); and Álvaro de Sá, *Vanguarda produto de comunicação* (Petrópolis: Vozes, 1977), which is mostly concerned with the graphic experimentation of *poema processo;* see notes 82–85. With more specific reference to social involvement, see Iumna Maria Simon, "Esteticismo e participação: as vanguardas poéticas no contexto brasileiro (1954–1969)," *Novos estudos CEBRAP* 26 (March 1990): 120–40; subsequently cited as "Esteticismo."

4   On these terms and background in the arts, see the thorough coverage of Caroline Bayard, *The New Poetics in Canada and Quebec: From Concretism to Post-Modernism* (Toronto: University of Toronto Press, 1989), pp. 16ff., cited below by author, as well as Felipe Boso, "Concretism," in César Espinosa, ed., *Corrosive Signs: Essays on Experimental Poetry (Visual, Concrete, Alternative)* (Washington, D.C.: Maisonneuve Press,

1990), pp. 45–50, subsequently cited by title. On specific uses in Brazil, see also Gilberto Mendonça Telles, "O nome poesia concreta," *Revista de cultura Vozes* 71, no. 1 (January 1977): 19–22; reprinted in *Retórica do silêncio I,* 2d ed. (Rio de Janeiro: José Olympio, 1989), pp. 205–10, cited below; and Augusto de Campos, "Concreto e ismo," *Convivium* 7, no. 5–6 (July–September 1965): 34–36, special issue on contemporary poetry, especially vanguard.

5   In addition to those cited below in the development of concrete theory, the Noigandres poets' extensive translations included Arnaut Daniel and other troubadours, John Donne, Dante, Göethe, and Mayakovsky. Renderings of numerous other North American, European (especially French), and Asian authors have appeared from the 1970s to the 1990s.

6   The thorny problem of defining or delimiting "concrete poetry" is universal. Solt opens her introduction with attempts to come to terms with diversification. Twenty-one kinds of related practices are listed by Aaron Marcus in "An Introduction to the Visual Syntax of Concrete Poetry," *Visible Language* 8, no. 4 (Autumn 1974): 333–60; this study cites numerous Brazilian examples. See the section on international reception below and note 61 on the transition from "clean" to "dirty" concrete.

7   T. S. Eliot, ed., *The Literary Essays of Ezra Pound* (1954; reprint London: Faber and Faber, 1985), p. 23.

8   The Noigandres poets broke with the Clube de Poesia de São Paulo, the unofficial organization of the Generation of '45, in 1950 and sought alternate outlets. On these early years, see Antônio Risério, "Formação do grupo Noigandres," in *Cores vivas* (Salvador, Bahia: Fundação Casa de Jorge Amado, 1989), pp. 67–96. Their respective collected poems include work from that initial period through the mid- to late 1970s: Haroldo de Campos, *Xadrez de estrelas* (São Paulo: Perspectiva, 1975); Décio Pignatari, *Poesia pois é poesia* (São Paulo: Duas Cidades, 1976); and Augusto de Campos, *VIVA VAIA Poesia 1949–1979* (São Paulo: Duas Cidades, 1979); no paginations. Both the latter appeared in second edition by Brasiliense, 1986. The three collections are cited below as *Xadrez, Poesia,* and *VIVA VAIA.*

9   The most recent suggestion is that the word actually means "to scare off boredom." The most complete study of speculation about the meaning(s) of this word is Alfred Hower, "O mistério da palavra *noigandres:* finalmente resolvido?" *Discurso crítico* (Universidade de São Paulo) 8 (1978): 160–68. Background historical information in this paragraph is taken from Augusto and Haroldo de Campos, "O grupo concretista," in Leodegário A. de Azevedo Filho, ed., *Poetas do modernismo,* vol. 6 (Brasília: Instituto Nacional do Livro, 1972), pp. 127–38; volume cited below by title.

10   According to Augusto, quoted by Lúcia Santaella, *Convergências: poesia concreta e tropicalismo* (São Paulo: Noble, 1988), pp. 53–54.

11   These sources are discussed in numerous places. Douglas Thompson, "Pound and Brazilian Concretism," *Paideuma* 6, no. 3 (Winter 1977): 279–94, scans the strategic use of the "predecessors." A complete study is Fredrick G. Rodgers, "The Literary Background of Brazilian Concrete Poetry: The Impact of Pound, Mallarmé and Other Major Writers on the Noigandres Group" (Ph.D. diss., Indiana University, 1974). For specific details from an inside point of view, see also Augusto de Campos,

"Points-Periphery-Concrete Poetry" (1956); trans. Jon Tolman, in Richard Kostela-
netz, *The Avant-Garde Tradition in Literature* (Buffalo, N.Y.: Prometheus Books,
1982), pp. 259–66, cited below by title.

12 Claus Clüver, "Klangfarbenmelodie in Polychromatic Poems: A. von Webern and A.
de Campos," *Comparative Literature Studies* 18, no. 3 (September 1981): 386–98. The
example of these early color poems in Solt is "eis os amantes" (here are the lovers),
previously in Williams without color. In the early 1950s, the Noigandres poets associ-
ated with the new music group Ars Nova, one of whose guest artists was French
composer Pierre Boulez. The group would later perform multiple-voice arrangements
for concrete poems.

13 Additional examples of early concrete output in Solt and in Williams. Haroldo's "o
âmago" and "ovo novelo" appear (with translations) in Décio Pignatari, "Concrete
Poetry: A Brief Structural-Historical Guideline," *Poetics Today* 3, no. 3 (Summer
1982): 189–95, originally in *Teoria*, pp. 62–69 (1957). Cited below as "Guideline." See
also Claus Clüver, "Augusto de Campos' 'terremoto': Cosmology as Ideogram," *Con-
temporary Poetry* 3, no. 1 (Winter 1978): 39–56. On "ovo novelo," see Antônio Sérgio
Mendonça and Alvaro de Sá, *Poesia de vanguarda no Brasil: de Oswald de Andrade ao
poema visual* (Rio de Janeiro: Antares, 1983), pp. 162–65; cited below by authors.

14 Gomringer was then secretary to concrete sculptor Max Bill, who visited Brazil in the
early 1950s. The first German anthology appeared in 1957, and the first international
exhibition with Brazilian participation was in 1959 in Stuttgart. On the major German
movement, see Liselotte Gumpel, *"Concrete" Poetry from East and West Germany: The
Language of Exemplarism and Experimentalism* (New Haven: Yale University Press,
1976). There are surprisingly few mentions of the Brazilian connection in this study.
In 1959, Haroldo had traveled abroad widely, and his extensive network of correspon-
dence with avant-garde artists around Europe was important in the growth of the
international movement. In 1964, Haroldo de Campos was a guest lecturer at a
technical institute in Stuttgart at the invitation of poet-critic Max Bense.

15 See Claus Clüver, "Brazilian Concrete: Painting, Poetry, Time, Space" in S. Scher et
al., eds., *Proceedings of the IXth Congress of the International Comparative Literature
Association,* vol. 3, *Literature and the Other Arts* (Innsbruck: AMQ, 1981), pp. 207–17.
On the sociocultural context of concretism and early 1950s' artistic events in Brazil, see
Mendonça and Sá, pp. 93–98.

16 See Mendonça and Sá, pp. 101–109, for details of the first exhibitions of concrete
poetry, as well as the "photographic documentary" in "Concretismo," a special issue of
Revista de cultura Vozes 71, no. 1 (January 1977): 65–70. Gullar's *o formigueiro* (the
anthill), a sixty-page experiment in syntagmatic verbal dissolution, was not published
until the early nineties, when, despite the author's having disavowed all association
with concretism, the poem appeared in a limited (1500 copies) luxury edition (Rio de
Janeiro: Europa, 1991). Dias-Pino's piece subsequently appeared in several different
formats and venues, including in Williams.

17 At the exhibition, poems appeared without actual titles. "Terra" appears in Solt and in
Williams. For a detailed litero-scientific discussion of the poem, see Haroldo de
Campos, "Poesia Concreta — Linguagem — Comunicação" in *Teoria*, pp. 70–85.

18   Pignatari, "Guideline," p. 192, with an approximate English version. The poem fig-
     ured in the original article and in Williams.

19   Moacy Cirne, *Vanguarda: um projeto semiológico* (Petrópolis: Vozes, 1975), p. 48; cited
     below by author. For a minutely detailed analysis of the poem, see Pedro Xisto, *Poesia
     em situação* (Fortaleza, Ceará: Imprensa Oficial, 1960; reprint of Rio press articles,
     1957).

20   Olegário Martins, quoted in "Arte concreta questão aberta," *Jornal de letras,* March
     1957. Lins do Rego in *O jornal,* February 28, 1957, and *Diario da noite,* February 15,
     1957. Augusto de Campos compiled a series of like headlines and citations for a
     collage to commemorate the twentieth anniversary of the launching of concrete po-
     etry. The piece, called "The Gentle Art of Making Enemies," appeared in *Corpo es-
     tranho* 2 (1976); reprinted in Augusto de Campos, *A margem da margem* (São Paulo:
     Companhia das Letras, 1989), pp. 181–84.

21   See Faustino's article "A poesia concreta e o momento poético brasileiro" in *Poesia e
     experiência* (São Paulo: Perspectiva, 1976), pp. 209–18. The Noigandres poets collab-
     orated on the literary page of the *Suplemento dominical do Jornal do Brasil* from late
     1956 to mid-1958; most contributions dealt with foreign authors or issues of poetry in
     general rather than concrete poetry.

22   Pignatari's February 10, 1957, lecture was later condensed into "Guideline." Houaiss
     complements his summary of the public address with information taken from articles
     published in the Rio press. His critical essay appeared in the press and later in *Seis
     poetas e um problema* (1960), which was incorporated into *Drummond mais seis poetas e
     um problema* (Rio: Imago, 1976), pp. 229–54, from which in-text citations are taken.
     In the North American sphere, John Nist, *The Modernist Movement in Brazil* (Austin:
     University of Texas Press, 1969), based his early — and clearly frightened — account of
     concretism on Houaiss.

23   Jon Tolman, "The Context of a Vanguard: Toward a Definition of Concrete Poetry,"
     Poetics Today 3, no. 3 (1982): 159; cited below by author.

24   Haroldo de Campos, "The Informational Temperature of the Text" (1960), *Poetics
     Today* 3, no. 3 (Summer 1982): 177–87. The words "voluntary castration" are specifi-
     cally mentioned at the outset.

25   Max Bense, quoted by Hansjörg Schmitthenner, "konkrete poesie," introduction to
     exhibition catalog *Konkrete Poesie Deutschsprachiger Autoren* (Munich: Goethe In-
     stitute, 1973), p. 8.

26   All of Pignatari's relevant poems appear in Williams. "Beba Coca Cola" also appears in
     Solt and in Brasil and Smith; it was interpreted usefully by Rosemarie Waldrop, "A
     Basis for Concrete Poetry," *Bucknell Review* 22, no. 2 (1976): 145–46 (volume pub-
     lished as *Twentieth Century Poetry, Fiction, Theory,* ed. Harry R. Garvin [Lewisburg:
     Bucknell University Press, 1977]), cited below as Waldrop, and by Marjorie Perloff,
     Radical Artifice: Writing Poetry in the Age of Media (Chicago: University of Chicago
     Press, 1991), pp. 115–18, cited below as Perloff. "LIFE" appears again in Brasil and
     Smith; see the comments of Abbie Beiman, "Concrete Poetry: A Study in Metaphor,"
     Visible Language 8, no. 3 (1974): 197–223. On other portfolio items: Williams has
     Augusto's poems "uma vez" (once) and "eixo" (axis), which appears also in Brasil and

Smith. Augusto's "sem um número" (numberless) is in Solt; Bayard (p. 25) makes an interesting interpretation of the poem vis-à-vis iconic fallacy. Haroldo's "branco" (blank) appears in Williams, and his "fala prata" (silverspeech) is in Solt. Azeredo's "ruasol" (streetsun) and "velocidade" (velocity) are both in Williams. For readings of such "orthodox" examples (e.g., "beba coca cola" and "branco"), see Claus Clüver, "Reflections on Verbivocovisual Ideograms," *Poetics Today* 3, no. 3 (1982): 137–48, which also has a synthetic account of later Noigandres output; cited below by title.

27 Clüver discusses "ruasol" (streetsun) in "Reflections." Williams reproduces "vai-e-vem" (comes-and-goes). Grünewald (b. 1931) collected his lyric and concrete poems in *Escreviver* (Rio de Janeiro: Nova Fronteira, 1987), with a brief historical afterword about the movement. His socially aware "petróleo" (petroleum) is in Williams.

28 (Putting on the mask), both examples in Williams. Pignatari's "hambre-hembra-hombre" (hunger-female-man) is discussed in Augusto de Campos, "The Concrete Coin of Speech" (1956) *Poetics Today* 3, no. 3 (Summer 1982): 167–76; cited below by title.

29 The starting point for the third example is the idiom "ficar a ver navios," meaning, literally, "to stay watching ships," and figuratively, to be left behind, holding the bag. All examples in *Xadrez*. While various "more/less" phrases are in the scope of the second poem, the ideogram "mais menos" was actually written as a homage to Dutch painter Piet Mondrian (1872–1944) and his painting *Plus and Minus* (1917).

30 This approach is developed in *The Semiotics of Poetry* (Bloomington: Indiana University Press, 1978). For a summary account, see Jonathan Culler, *The Pursuit of Signs* (Ithaca, N.Y.: Cornell University Press, 1981), pp. 80–99.

31 See on "branco," "Concrete Coin," p. 174; "fome de forma" ("famished for form") is in Williams and in Solt.

32 In the presentation of the poem in Williams, Haroldo briefly comments on its "pre-sentification" of the artistic treatment of the life-death cycle by the Russian poet-painter Wassily Kandinsky (1866–1944), as compared to the poetic angle of Göethe. The lexical key there is adequate but incomplete; the translation in Solt is also shallow. For a detailed structural analysis, see Mendonça and Sá, pp. 154–59. As a complement to the "spiritual" aspect of the reading that follows here, it is curious to consider the occult claims of John McAuley, "Concrete Poetry: The Story of a Further Journey," in Ken Norris and Peter Van Toorn, eds., *The Insecurity of Art: Essays on Poetics* (Montreal: Vehicle Press, 1982), pp. 89–90.

33 This commentary is based on standard Brazilian pronunciation. In very formal Brazilian speech, the syllable "se," whether in word-initial or word-final position, could be pronounced /se/ and thus rhyme with an equally formal word-final "-re" or word-initial "re-" pronounced /Re/. The phoneme /R/ in the text can be either a multiple flap *r* (trill) or a velar fricative /x/, in either case identical in the word "morre" and the prefix "re-". That the prefix "des-" has several different acceptable pronunciations is immaterial to the present account.

34 Sílvio Castro, *A revolução da palavra: origens e estrutura da literatura brasileira moderna* (Petrópolis: Vozes, 1976), p. 274.

35 The pilot plan of *Noigandres* 4 was reprinted in *Invenção*, no. 1 (1962): 66–67; *Teoria*, pp. 156–58; and Solt, pp. 70–72 (both versions); it was appended by Mike Weaver, "Concrete Poetry," *The Journal of Typographic Research* 1, no. 3 (1967): 324–25, and reproduced in *The Avant-Garde Tradition*, pp. 257–58.

36 Haroldo de Campos, "Evolução de formas: poesia concreta" (1957), *Teoria*, p. 52.

37 Franchetti, p. 57. It is in this area that the analyst perceives "weak links" in the series of theoretical articles about multifaceted orthodox concrete poems. For an insightful treatment of this difficulty, see Simon, "Esteticismo, pp. 126ff.

38 In a sequence of the short film *Poema Cidade* by Tata Amaral and Francisco César Filho (1986), shown at "Brazilian Concrete and Visual Poetry from the Ruth and Marvin Sackner Archive," University of Florida, Gainesville, March 2–April 6, 1989, cited below by film title.

   In a sense, the concrete poets were responding to a point raised by João Cabral de Melo Neto in a paper presented at the São Paulo Writers Congress in 1954 ("Da função moderna da poesia," reprinted in Benedito Nunes, *João Cabral de Melo Neto: poetas modernos do Brasil* [Petrópolis: Vozes, 1971], pp. 196–201), to wit, that poets had not yet discovered poetic forms that corresponded to the demands of modern life, which included intelligent use of communication media. While Cabral was thinking in terms of objectifying metric verse and of actually writing, for example, with radio broadcast in mind (instead of merely reading on the air), it is not difficult to see how his observations may have encouraged the technological ponderings of the Noigandres group.

39 The first edition of *Teoria* contained pieces written 1950–1960. The only post-pilot-plan title that presented any fresh perspectives was "Contexto de uma vanguarda" by Haroldo, which confronted social issues integrated into a subsequent argument (see notes 52 and 54). The second edition of *Teoria* (1975) further added Pignatari's presentation of his so-called "semiotic poems" (1964) from the last phase of the movement (see note 59).

40 *Teoria*, p. 8. If one were to follow the complete bibliography in the press, different angles would be more evident, as the group would include four or five names at any given time, with the participation of Gullar, Grünewald, and others in the public debate. Franchetti is clear in his statement that concrete theory developed with "contradictions, hesitations, tactical advances, and strategic retreats" (p. 73).

41 On the point of "product of evolution," Clüver also makes the useful reminder that: "It is in the nature of manifestos to raise the preoccupation of the moment to the status of a norm or inevitable law" ("Reflections," p. 147). The phrase "historical illusion" is Benedito Nunes's.

42 Iumna Maria Simon and Vinícius Dantas, eds., *Poesia concreta* (São Paulo: Abril Educação, 1982), p. 103.

43 Quoted by Cremilda Medina, "Haroldo de Campos, perseguidor da poética universal," *Estado de São Paulo suplemento literário* 938 (September 22, 1984): 9. This is also the source of the next quote in the text.

44 Roland Greene, "From Dante to the Post-Concrete: An Interview with Augusto de Campos," in Greene, p. 32. With respect to the criticism of concretism noted here, an

observer writes that the Kubitschek links "detonate a strong reaction that tends to grow progressively throughout the decades of the 70s and the 80s." Heloísa Buarque de Holanda, "Will the Third World overcome the modernist syndrome? Sugestões para uma releitura das vanguardas brasileiras," *Hispanic Studies* 4, *Literatura de vanguarda luso-brasileira* (1989): 6. Of note here is the lack of exemplification of the reaction.

45 Interview with Albenísio Fonseca, *A tarde* (Salvador, Bahia), December 17, 1986, p. 62.

46 Pignatari announced the "leap" in the conclusion to "A situação atual da poesia brasileira," presented at a national literary congress in late 1961. The paper was published in the inaugural issue (1962) of *Invenção,* alongside the paper of Cassiano Ricardo, "'22 e a poesia hoje," a lengthy consideration of concretism vis-à-vis the poetry of *modernismo,* which later appeared as a monograph, with small anthology (Rio de Janeiro: MEC, n.d.). Pignatari's paper was included in *Contracomunicação,* 2d ed. (São Paulo: Perspectiva, 1973), pp. 91–112. See chapter 3 on the meaning of the verb *participar.*

47 Fábio Lucas, "Em busca de uma expressão poética nacional," *Estado de São Paulo,* December 23, 1961. See next paragraph on subsequent rapprochement.

48 Adolfo Casais Monteiro, "Situação da poesia," *Estado de São Paulo,* October 21, 1961, and "Avanço ou recuo concretista," *Estado de São Paulo,* November 11, 1961.

49 Alfredo Bosi, *História concisa da literatura brasileira,* rev. and exp. ed. (São Paulo: Cultrix, 1994), p. 482.

50 Reprinted in Affonso Ávila, *O poeta e a consciência crítica* (Petrópolis: Vozes, 1969), pp. 99–100, and in 2d exp. ed. (São Paulo: Summus, 1978), pp. 137–38. See related articles in both editions. In 1993, a multimedia event was held to reconsider issues of avant-garde poetry and to commemorate the thirtieth anniversary of the original seminar; see Eleonora Santa Rosa, ed., *30 anos Semana Nacional de Poesia de Vanguarda 1963/93* (Belo Horizonte: Prefeitura/Secretaria Municipal de Cultura, 1993).

On sixties' poetics and social stances of concretism, Tendência, and others, see Iumna Maria Simon, "Esteticismo" and "Projetos alternativos / confronto de poéticas," *Revista iberoamericana* 43, no. 98 & 99 (January–June 1977): 169–80. It is essential to consider in this regard the anti-vanguard essays of Ferreira Gullar cited in chapter 3.

51 Haroldo de Campos (next note) quoting [Alberto] Guerreiro Ramos, *A redução sociológica: introdução ao estudo da razão sociológica* (Rio de Janeiro: MEC/ISEB, 1958). See pp. 19–26 on "critical consciousness" and pp. 44–47 for a definition and description of sociological reduction. In the second edition (Rio: Tempo Brasileiro, 1965), the author cites, pp. 19–20, an interview with Haroldo de Campos where he again suggests the aesthetic parallel.

52 Haroldo de Campos, "A poesia concreta e a realidade nacional," *Tendência* 4 (1962): 86–87.

53 Antônio Risério, "Poesia concreta: por dentro e por fora," *Revista de cultura Vozes* 71, no. 1 (1977): 60. Other observers point to contemporaneous developments such as Brazil's assuming world leadership in soccer, with the performances of Pelé, and the emergence of Bossa Nova as a planetary music.

54 Haroldo de Campos, "The Rule of Anthropophagy: Europe under the Sign of De-voration," trans. Maria Tai Wolff, *Latin American Literary Review* 14, no. 27 (1986): 42–60. Originally in the Portuguese journal *Colóquio Letras,* vol. 62 (1981), with subsequent versions in French and Spanish.

55 See the first examples in Williams, in Solt, and in Brasil and Smith. A cumulative version of *Galáxias* (43 fragments) appeared in *Xadrez.* The complete cycle (50 fragments, plus commentaries) was published in a large fine-press edition (São Paulo: Ex Libris, 1983). Examples in translation by Christopher Middleton and Norman Potter appear in *via* 1 (Berkeley, Calif.) (1976): 55–57, and by Suzanne Jill Levine in *The Plaza of Encounters* (Austin: Latitudes, 1981), pp. 36–37.

56 "Greve" and "cubagrama" appeared in *Invenção,* no. 2 (1962). Other political poems, on Hiroshima and surplus value, appeared in *Invenção,* no. 3 (1963). One of the poet's best-known texts, "cidade-cité-city" (1963), appeared with two original English texts, the formalist "Black and White" and the social satire "brazilian football," in "The Changing Guard II," *Times Literary Supplement,* September 3, 1964. This issue of *TLS* features international experimental poetry and avant-garde movements. The first part of the series, August 6, 1964, focused on British material. "LUXO-LIXO" is a fold-out in Solt.

57 On the left: "Do Not Enter," in the middle: "Thru Traffic," on the right: "Right Turn Only," and on top: "Danger!" as explained by Augusto de Campos, "Sem palavras," in *Poesia antipoesia antropofagia* (São Paulo: Cortez, 1978) pp. 86–87; cited below by article title. The popular piece was noted in a review by John Russel, "Between Poetry and Painting," *Art in America,* vol. 54, no. 1 (January 1966). It appears in Williams, in Solt, and in Brasil and Smith. It is also shown by Wendy Steiner, *The Colors of Rhetoric* (Chicago: University of Chicago Press, 1982), p. 205, cited below by author. This section of Steiner (pp. 197–219) is a moderately expanded and better illustrated version of the essential essay "Res Poética: The Problematic of Concrete Poetry," *New Literary History* 12, no. 3 (1981): 529–45.

58 "Stèle" appears in *Invenção,* no. 2. "Disenfórmio" was in *Invenção,* no. 5 (1967) and was reproduced with a brief discussion in Tolman, "Context." "Christ" is in *Invenção,* no. 5, and Brasil and Smith.

59 Examples in Williams and in Solt. For a brief English presentation, see Décio Pignatari, "Concrete Poetry," *Times Literary Supplement,* September 3, 1964, p. 791. The theoretical explanation of this experiment first appeared in *Invenção,* no. 4 (1964) and was included in *Teoria,* pp. 159–69.

60 The later poetry and concrete-related graphics of Edgard Braga were assembled in Régis Bonvicino, ed., *Desbragadas* (São Paulo: Max Limonad, 1984). See the concrete repertory of Pedro Xisto in *Caminho* (Rio de Janeiro: Berlendis and Vertecchia, 1979); English material previously in *toronto pomes* (Toronto: Ganglia Press, 1972). Illustrating the idea that spatialized words can "communicate," Xisto's "espaço" is used by Roland Grass, "Concrete Treatment of Space," in Richard Konstalanetz, ed., *Visual Literature Criticism* (Carbondale: Southern Illinois University Press, 1979), pp. 135–39.

61 On the transition from concrete to more "permissive" experimentation, see César Espinosa, "Corrosive Signs: For a Liberating Writing," intro. to *Corrosive Signs,* pp. 5–

22. The question of "clean" vs. "dirty" concrete is acknowledged by Perloff, pp. 114ff. As noted in note 6, problems of definitions, distinctions, and boundaries between different kinds of concrete poetry are constant. Already in 1960, reacting to typographical experiments, Gomringer feels the need to declare that in principle he "finds it wisest to stay with the word" (Solt, pp. 69–70). Further implications are taken up in the section on international reception below.

62 Alberto da Costa Marques, "Concretismo," in Afrânio Coutinho, ed., *A literatura no Brasil*, vol. 5 (Rio de Janeiro: José Olympio, 1986), p. 235; volume cited below.

63 Gerald Thomas, "Theater and Film," in *Brazil Designs*, special issue of *Print* 61, no. 6 (November–December 1987): 101, 104.

64 Rudolf Arnheim, "Visual Aspects of Concrete Poetry," *Yearbook of Comparative Criticism*, vol. 7, *Literary Criticism and Psychology*, ed. Joseph P. Strelka (University Park, Pa.: Pennsylvania State University Press, 1976), p. 102. This critic does not himself take note of Brazilian implementations.

65 This quote, the display of "cidade," and the commercial appropriation of the design of "LUXO-LIXO" are witnessed in sequences of the film *Poema Cidade*. "VIVA VAIA" (hurray for hissing!/long live the boos!), in red and white in the original, was inspired by the boldness of the noted singer-songwriter Caetano Veloso when he confronted a boisterous negative response at a festival of popular music in 1968. See chapter 4 on Augusto's relationship with popular music.

Also of note in the relationship of poetry to the urban landscape is the making of "cidade" into a huge metal sculpture of meter-high letters to encircle the Museum of Modern Art (1986) and the appearance of other slogans of Augusto's, such as "REVƎЯ," as graffiti on São Paulo walls. In late 1991, a São Paulo newspaper, reporting on a celebration of the centenary of the famed Paulista Avenue, highlighted a special event: street readings and laser-cannon projections of poems by the Noigandres group and others. December 11, 1991, *Folha de São Paulo;* this cosmopolitan daily was also celebrating its own seventieth birthday.

66 See Haroldo de Campos, "Structuralism and Semiotics in Brazil: Retrospect/Prospect," *Dispositio* 3, no. 7 & 8 (Spring–Summer 1978): 175–87.

67 Affonso Romano de Sant'Anna, "Perspectivas da poesia brasileira moderna," *Estado de São Paulo*, July 8, 1967; the conclusion and notes appeared in part 2, July 15, 1967.

68 Simon and Dantas, eds., *Poesia concreta* (1982) appeared in the series of illustrated fascicules *Literatura comentada,* which was sold at newsstands.

69 Carlos Nejar, ed., *Antologia da poesia brasileira contemporânea* (Lisbon: Imprensa Nacional-Casa da Moeda, 1986), p. 9, and Eduardo Portella, preface, p. 8. The other collection mentioned is Henrique Alves, ed., *Poetas contemporâneos* (São Paulo: Roswitha Kempf, 1985).

70 Stephen Bann, ed. and intro., *Concrete Poetry: An Anthology* (London: London Magazine Editions, 1967). Eugene Wildman, ed. and intro., *An Anthology of Concretism* (Chicago: University of Chicago Press, 1968). In a suggestively titled review of available collections, North American reviewer Richard Konstalanetz noted both the confusing uses of the term "concrete" and how much less distinguished some material may be, which can affect overall reception. Some contributions, he discouragingly

wrote, "can be summarily dismissed as abstract arrangements of letters that are neither particularly distinguished as design nor communicative as language" ("Sabotaging the New Poetry," in *The Old Poetries and the New* [Ann Arbor: University of Michigan Press, 1981], p. 155). The reviewer also noted that Wildman's first edition had even erroneously cited Pignatari's "LIFE" as anonymous.

71 R. P. Draper, "Concrete Poetry," *New Literary History* 2, no. 2 (Winter 1971): 329–40.

72 Claus Clüver, "From Imagism to Concrete Poetry: Breakthrough or Blind Alley?" in *Rudolf Haas, ed., Amerikanische Lyrik* (Berlin: Erich Schmidt Verlag, 1987), p. 125.

73 Perloff's discussion, pp. 114–20, concerns Augusto de Campos's concentrically constructed "código" (1973), which was given a close reading by Claus Clüver, "Languages of the Concrete Poem," in K. David Jackson, ed., *Transformations of Literary Language in Latin American Literature: From Machado de Assis to the Vanguards* (Austin: Abaporu Press, 1987), pp. 32–42.

74 Veronica Forrest-Thomson, *Poetic Artifice: A Theory of Twentieth-Century Poetry* (New York: St. Martin's Press, 1978), pp. 44–48. Her one example ("ik/ok" by Robert Lax) is taken from Bann. It is worthwhile to note two other instances of selective focus here. A prime international source for twentieth-century experimental literature is Guillermo de Torre, *Historia de las literaturas de vanguardia* (Madrid: Guadarrama, 1965), cited below by author. In his review of concretism (pp. 754–60), he documents European manifestations, mentions an Iberoamerican "version," and concludes that concrete poetry is simply words in phonoplastic dimensions with no or almost no meaning. The basic nondistinction between levels of production naturally results in short shrift for concrete poetry that seeks to integrate its elements. For her part, Carole Anne Taylor, in *A Poetics of Seeing: The Implications of Visual Form in Modern Poetry* (New York: Garland Publishing, 1985), pp. 221–50, is aware of various kinds of concrete poetry but stresses those poets "seeking nothing beyond visual form as image [who] often rely on trivial or insignificant word play, or simply invoke no referent beyond the page's imaged words" (p. 226). The critic finds justifiable limitations in worldwide concretism, but does not look in depth at such proposals as the "verbivocovisual ideogram" to get beyond single-effect word games or the perceived simplicity of examples.

75 Gullar and others signed a statement of position called "Poesia concreta: experiência intuitiva" in *Suplemento dominical Jornal do Brasil* on June 23, 1957. The actual neoconcretist manifesto appeared in the same publication on March 22, 1959, and was followed by "Da arte concreta à arte neo-concreta" on July 18, 1959. The coverage of Costa Marques (*A literatura no Brasil*, pp. 236–44), who cites Gullar extensively, focuses on common theory, sculpture, and painting rather than poetry. Oiticica would become one of Brazil's leading internationally recognized artists and was featured in *Art in America* 54, no. 1 (January 1986): 110–20, 163–65.

76 Ferreira Gullar, *Toda poesia 1950/1980* (Rio de Janeiro: Civilização Brasileira, 1981), pp. 161–75. Other neoconcretists were Oliveira Bastos, Reynaldo Jardim, and Theon Spanudis.

77 The document was an afterword to *Lavra lavra* (São Paulo: Massao Ohno, 1962). All

of the author's supporting work is contained in Mário Chamie, *Instauração práxis,* vol. 1, *manifestos, plataformas, textos e documentos críticos, 1959–1972,* and vol. 2, *textos e documentos críticos, 1959–1972* (São Paulo: Quirón, 1974). His poems, including all those of the *praxis* phase, were collected in *Objeto selvagem* (São Paulo: Quirón, 1978).

78   Quoted by Telles, *Retórica do silêncio,* p. 190, who notes the assimilation of ideas that Paul Valéry began to expound in his 1937 poetics course.

79   The comparison with concrete was made in *TLS,* "Changing of the Guard II." On *linossigno,* see Cassiano Ricardo, *Algumas reflexões sobre poesia de vanguarda* (Rio de Janeiro: José Olympio, 1964), pp. 39–40. On the *praxis* association, see his *A poesia praxis e '22* (Rio de Janeiro: José Olympio, 1967). Ricardo's own long experimental poem of the sixties, *Jeremias sem chorar* (Rio de Janeiro: José Olympio, 1964), was not composed in the *praxis* mode.

80   Examples of *poesia praxis* by diverse poets are discussed in Assis Brasil, *A nova literatura II A poesia* (Rio de Janeiro: Americana-INL, 1975), pp. 101–18; and Mário Chamie, "A poesia praxis," in *Poetas do modernismo,* vol. 6, pp. 205–80.

81   Torre, p. 740. *Lettrisme* was the 1945–48 French avant-garde that made nonsense "verse" of invented sound-effect words.

82   By Anchieta Fernandes (1967), in *Poetas do modernismo,* vol. 6, p. 348. Numerous other examples with commentary, pp. 325–53; see further sources in next notes.

83   *Diário de notícias* (Salvador, Bahia), April 19, 1968, no pagination (files on the Oficina Literária Afrânio Coutinho, Rio de Janeiro).

84   Manifesto issued at 4th National Exhibition of Process-Poem (April 1968, Salvador, Bahia) and reprinted in Wlademir Dias-Pino, *Processo: linguagem e comunicação,* 2d ed. (Petropolis: Vozes, 1973), no pagination, in which a later manifesto and multiple examples of this output appear. Rare later manifestos of avant-garde / visual material in Brazil were individual statements, not documents of associated movements; see, for example, Márcio Almeida, "The DEYEdeitic: A Post-Reading of Visual Poetry" (1985), in *Corrosive Signs,* pp. 101–107, which can be read in the context of events discussed in the second part of chapter 5.

85   See especially Sebastião Nunes, *Antologia mamaluca e poesia inédita,* vol. 1 (Sabará, MG: Edições duBolso, 1987). "Comeback" editions appearing in the early nineties include Álvaro de Sá, *poemics 12×9+n* (Rio de Janeiro: Reprodata, 1991), with reprints of numerous *processo* items, the loose-leaf Moacy Cirne, *Balaio incomun: uma folha porreta* (Rio de Janeiro: Leviatã, 1992), as well as his rather verbal *Qualquer tudo* (Rio de Janeiro: Leviatã, 1993).

3   The Social Imperative: *Violão de rua* and the Politics of Poetry in the 1960s

1   Jean-Paul Sartre, *Qu'est-ce que la littérature?* (Paris: Gallimard, 1948); trans. Bernard Frechtman, *What Is Literature?* (New York: Harper & Row, 1965). On Plato, Sartre, and the functions of literature, see Vitor Manuel de Aguiar e Silva, *Teoria da literatura* (Coimbra: Livraria Almedina, 1973), pp. 117–40, and Terry Eagleton, *Marxism and*

Literature (Berkeley: University of California Press, 1976), ch. 3, "The Writer and Commitment," pp. 37–58, for a discussion of historical origins and related issues, mostly with reference to the Russian Revolution.

2   Hans Magnus Enzenberger, "Poetry and Politics" (1962), in *The Consciousness Industry: On Literature, Politics and the Media,* trans. M. Roloff (New York: Seabury Press, 1974), p. 75. Cited later in text.

3   Michael André Bernstein, "O Totiens Servus: Saturnalia and Servitude in Augustan Rome," in Robert von Hallberg, ed., *Poetry and Poetic Value* (Chicago: University of Chicago Press, 1987), p. 38; the following quote in the text from p. 39. Subsequent citations from this volume as von Hallberg. For a useful bibliography of literary value as related to a case of politically charged poetry, see von Hallberg, p. 250.

In *The Tale of the Tribe: Ezra Pound and the Modern Verse Epic* (Princeton: Princeton University Press, 1980), Bernstein confronts notions of "pure" poetry and those of poetry committed to sociopolitical efficacy. Another analyst, in a case study of a noted Latin American poet, elaborates on the question of evaluation as relative to the application of value systems; he notes that in judgments of technique, "stance toward life," or belief, "our response is diagnostic not only of the nature of the poem but also of the nature of our assumptions about art and politics" (Reginald Gibbons, "Political Poetry and the Example of Ernesto Cardenal," in von Hallberg, p. 300).

4   Fernando Py, *Chão de crítica* (Rio de Janeiro: Francisco Alves, 1984), p. 186.

5   *Violão de rua: poemas para a liberdade,* 3 vols. (Rio de Janeiro: Civilização Brasileira-CPC, 1962–1963); citations in the text by volume number. Epigraph from vol. 1, p. 39. With respect to the classification of contemporary lyric, one typical account divides post-1956 production into two stylistic currents — the vanguard and epic-existentialism (i.e., lyrical continuity) — and a third line defined by ideological purpose, the *participante* (*cunho socio-político*); see Nelly Novaes Coelho, "A renovação poética da Geração de 60," *Cultura* 1, no. 4 (1971): 95.

6   By way of illustration of the title's imprecise use, one editor notes that critic Affonso Romano Sant'Anna (note 23) (himself a contributor to the original anthology) uses the term "somewhat improperly and restrictively"; see Guido Bilharinho, "Poesia brasileira século XX: breve notícia documentada," *Dimensão* 4, no. 7 (1983): 26; cited in text by author. Another involved poet-historian characterizes *Violão de rua* in appropriate sociohistorical terms but inexplicably headlines it as an outgrowth of the splinter vanguard of *neo-concretismo,* apparently because the well-known Ferreira Gullar was prominent in both; see Gilberto Mendonça Telles, *Retórica do silêncio I Teoria e prática do texto literário* (Rio de Janeiro: José Olympio, 1989), p. 189.

7   Antônio Carlos Secchin, "Caminhos recentes da poesia brasileira," *Iberoromania* 34 (1991): 60.

8   Manoel Sarmiento Barata, *Canto melhor: uma perspectiva da poesia brasileira* (Rio de Janeiro: Paz e Terra, 1969); the title translates as "better song." Later citation by author.

9   On these works in historical context, see Mike Gonzalez and David Treece, *The Gathering of the Voices: The Twentieth-Century Poetry of Latin America* (New York: Verso, 1992), pp. 159ff. and 175ff.

10   Sebastião Uchoa Leite, *Participação da palavra poética* (Petrópolis: Vozes, 1966). Other studies of the period that provide trajectories of social discourse are Ferreira Gullar, "Situação da poesia brasileira," in *Cultura posta em questão* (Rio de Janeiro: Civilização Brasileira, 1965), pp. 72–92, cited below by book title, and Roberto Pontual, "Poesia hoje: tarefa revolucionária," *Tempo brasileiro* 2 (1962): 55–80, cited in text by author.

11   A full discusssion of the tensions of vanguardism and (vs.) social orientation in the 1960s comprises a topic unto itself. The following bibliographical sequence gives some basic facts. Following the "leap" announced by Pignatari, Pontual took the occasion to publish a rare defense of concrete poetry as evidence of passage from a "progressive" to a "revolutionary cycle" in poetry. A quick response gives a better idea of commonly held opinions against concretism, from both political and literary vantage points: Luiz Paiva de Castro, "Concretismo e participação," *Tempo brasileiro* 3 (1963): 230–49; subsequent citation in text by author. On the conflict of concrete and other social poetics, see Iumna Maria Simon, "Esteticismo e participação: as vanguardas poéticas no contexto brasileiro (1954–1969)," *Novos estudos CEBRAP* 26 (March 1990): 120–40, and "Projetos alternativos / confronto de poéticas," *Revista iberoamericana* 43, no. 98 & 99 (January–June 1977): 169–80.

12   Benedito Nunes, "Trinta anos depois," in *30 anos Semana Nacional de Poesia de Vanguarda 1963/93* (Belo Horizonte: Prefeitura Municipal/Secretaria Municipal de Cultura, 1993), p. 28; cited in next note.

13   Nunes, pp. 28ff. and Hamilton Trevisan, "Que é participar?" *Revista praxis* 1, no. 1 (1962): 99.

14   Eduardo Portella, *Literatura e realidade nacional* (Rio de Janeiro: Tempo Brasileiro, 1963), p. 77. Cited below by author.

15   Félix de Atahyde, review of *Violão de rua*, in *Tempo brasileiro* 2 (1962): 249–50. See a representative sample of this writer's situated verse below.

16   This partnership is described by Enio Silveira, preface to Jalusa Barcelos, *CPC da UNE: uma história de paixão e consciência* (Rio de Janeiro: Nova Fronteira, 1994), a collection of interviews with those who organized and operated the CPC. The statement of editor Moacyr Félix, pp. 349–70, has details of the linkage of CPC and *Violão de rua*. On CPC's major thrust, theater, see Margo Milleret, "Pedagogy and Popular Art for the Masses from the CPC," *Brasil Brazil* 3, no. 3 (1990): 19–31. For a full list of CPC publications, see Manoel Berlinck, *CPC: o Centro Popular de Cultura da UNE* (São Paulo: Papyrus, 1984), pp. 36–38. For a contemporaneous description of the local and national structures of CPC, as well as of its internal organization and committees, such as Direction and Coordination of the Movement for Mass Consciousness-Raising, see Marcos Konder Reis, "Centro Popular de Cultura," *Cadernos brasileiros* 5, no. 1 (1963): 78–82; cited in text by author.

17   Carlos Estevam Martins, "Anteprojeto do manifesto do CPC," in *A questão da cultura popular* (Rio de Janeiro: Tempo Brasileiro, 1963), pp. 79–109; reprinted in *Arte em revista* 1 (1980): 67–79. Martins' document was first distributed in mimeograph form; it was soon criticized by the leading poet-critic of the Tendência group, who cited the danger in endorsing, or even admitting, a return to popular (folk) forms in

order to mold consciousness of national reality; see Affonso Ávila, *O poeta e a consciência crítica* (Petrópolis: Vozes, 1969), pp. 72–76. For a partial English translation of Martins with a brief commentary in relation to film, see Randal Johnson and Robert Stam, eds., *Brazilian Cinema*, 2d ed. (Austin: University of Texas Press, 1988), pp. 55–67.

18   See *Cultura posta em questão*, pp. 1–5. For critical summaries of the approaches of this emblematic set of essays, as well as of the later and related *Vanguarda e subdesenvolvimento* (Rio de Janeiro: Civilização Brasileira, 1969), see Jõao Luis Lafetá, "Traduzirse (ensaio sobre a poesia de Ferreira Gullar)," *O nacional e o popular na cultura brasileira: artes plásticas, literatura* (São Paulo: Brasiliense, 1983), pp. 97–108; subsequent citations in text. Much skepticism was aroused by the concept of "popular culture" as something "new" in Brazilian life, with only a political function; see, for example, Clarival Valladares, "Uma questão de cultura," *Cadernos brasileiros* 7, no. 30 (1965): 83–88.

19   Quoted by Heloísa Buarque de Hollanda, *Impressões de viagem: CPC, vanguarda e desbunde: 1960/1970*, 2d ed. (São Paulo: Brasiliense, 1981), p. 28; subsequently cited by author in text.

20   Maria Zaira Turchi, *Ferreira Gullar: a busca da poesia* (Rio de Janeiro: Presença, 1985), p. 90; additional citations in text by author.

21   Compare the argument that concrete poetry "participates" by deconditioning perception and by questioning habits of reception, as formulated by José Lino Grünewald, "Alienação e participação," *Correio da manhã*, February 12, 1967.

22   On this still surprisingly active folk literature, see Candace Slater, *Stories on a String: Brazil's Literatura de Cordel* (Berkeley: University of California Press, 1982).

23   So designated by Affonso Romano de Sant'Anna, *Música popular e moderna poesia brasileira* (Petrópolis: Vozes, 1978), p. 152, who cites other examples; subsequent citations by author. See Hollanda (pp. 20–25) for commentary of poems exemplary of being "people," of the future transformed, and of the division of wealth.

24   Janel Mueller, "The Mastery of Decorum: Politics as Poetry in Milton's Sonnets," in von Hallberg, p. 76.

25   Portella, p. 83. In this regard, it is interesting to note that some of the most exclamatory subpoetry is by Ferreira Gullar himself. The unforgiving reactions of a conventional critic are illustrated in this comment: "The two *Violão de rua*, for example, are false and awful popular poetry . . . certain works are so primary that they glow with grotesqueness" (Fausto Cunha, *A luta literária* [Rio de Janeiro: Lidador, 1964], p. 20).

26   Augusto de Campos, *Verso reverso controverso* (São Paulo: Perspectiva, 1978), p. 257.

27   For Moacyr Félix, problems arise when form is prioritized over content in any verse, or when semantics are not clarified, "which also frequently happens in so-called participatory poetry, when such words as 'worker,' 'woman,' 'people,' 'peasant,' float loose, for example, in a worldview that is 100% bourgeois, with Jesuit traits, stale, yet serving to give us the illusory appearance that its authors are revolutionaries." Quoted by Olga Werneck, ed., "Poetas falam de poesia," *Revista civilização brasileira* 1, no. 4 (September 1965): 205.

28 The most complete source on this topic is Régine Robin, *Socialist Realism: An Impossible Aesthetic,* trans. Catherine Porter (Stanford: Stanford University Press, 1992). See especially pp. 20–25 on "The Debate Over Poetry."

29 Stephen Spender, "Notes on Revolutionaries and Reactionaries," in Richard Jones, ed., *Poetry and Politics* (New York: William Morrow & Co., 1985), p. 59; volume cited by editor below.

30 Jorge Wanderley, "Anotações em torno da intenção de vanguarda e a série *Violão de rua,*'" *Ideologies and Literatures* 2, no. 1 (1987): 117.

31 Denise Levertov, "On the Edge of Darkness: What Is Political Poetry?" in Jones, p. 171.

32 A survey of renewed political criticism of artists in the late 1970s during redemocratization shows how the underlying attitudes of the early 1960s died very hard; see Heloísa Buarque de Holanda and Carlos Alberto Messeder Pereira, eds., *Patrulhas ideológicas, marca reg.: arte e engajamento em debate* (São Paulo: Brasiliense, 1980). Turchi (p. 97), among others, also notes this persistence.

33 An example of this position is Anazildo Vasconcelos da Silva, *Lírica modernista e percurso literário brasileiro* (Rio de Janeiro: Editora Rio, 1978), p. 88.

34 Quoted by Cremilda Medina, "Mário Chamie entre a ação da poética e a poética da ação," *Estado de São Paulo suplemento literário,* no. 962, March 9, 1985, p. 9.

35 Hollanda (pp. 43–48) seeks out the factor of engagement in *praxis* and looks (pp. 49–50) at the additional choice for affiliation via an interview with a leading poet, who gives a personal outlook on *engagé* poetry and social vanguard in the early 1960s in writing; see Armando Freitas Filho, "Poesia vírgula viva," in *Anos 70 II- Literatura* (Rio de Janeiro: Europa, 1980), pp. 83–88.

36 M. Cavalcanti Proença, "Poesia brasileira, 1964," *Revista civilização brasileira* 1, no. 1 (1965): 164–65.

37 Quoted by Olga Werneck, ed., "Poetas falam de poesia," *Revista civilização brasileira* 1, no. 3 (July 1965): 138.

38 See Fernando Mendes Vianna et al., *Poesia viva 2* (1979), which followed the historical *Poesia viva 1* (Rio de Janeiro: Civilização Brasileira, 1968).

39 Turchi, pp. 98–113, looks closely at post-CPC social poemas. See also Lafetá.

40 Alfredo Bosi, *História concisa da literatura brasileira,* rev. and exp. ed. (São Paulo: Cultrix, 1994), p. 473.

41 José Guilherme Merquior, "Capinan e a nova lírica," preface to José Carlos Capinan, *Inquisitorial,* 2d ed. (Rio de Janeiro: Civilização Brasileira, 1995; originally Salvador, Bahia: n.p., 1966), excerpts from which appeared in numerous anthologies, collections, and studies. The critical study first appeared in the press and in *A astúcia da mimese* (Rio de Janeiro: José Olympio/CEC-SP, 1972), pp. 173–92.

4   The Orphic Imperative: Lyric, Lyrics, and the Poetry of Song

1 On popular music in general, see the intelligent trade book by Chris McGowan and Ricardo Pessanha, *The Brazilian Sound: Samba, Bossa Nova, and the Popular Music of*

Brazil (New York: Billboard Books, 1991). On the current of contemporary popular music known as MPB (*música popular brasileira*) (Brazilian popular music) and its most renowned singer-songwriters, see Charles A. Perrone, *Masters of Contemporary Brazilian Song: MPB 1965–1985* (Austin: University of Texas Press, 1989). Song texts therein are rendered in English, most often with poetic qualities in mind. Subsequent reference to this source will be made throughout this chapter, in notes and text, via the abbreviation *MCBS*.

2   Epigraph above from *Nova história da música popular* (São Paulo: Abril Cultural, 1978), fascicule no. 10 (Caetano Veloso), no pagination. Historical interpretations of cutting-edge late sixties popular music were made in articles collected in Augusto de Campos et al., *Balanço da bossa* (São Paulo: Perspectiva, 1968), 2d. exp. ed., *Balanço da bossa e outras bossas* (1974); cited as *Balanço* in the course of the chapter.

3   From the literary perspective, a frequently cited work is Affonso Romano de Sant'Anna, *Música popular e moderna poesia brasileira* (Petrópolis: Vozes, 1978); subsequently cited by author. The poet-chronicler assigns an "interregnum" of popular music in poetry 1967–1973.

4   Significant recent examples of traditional scholarship include David Michael Hertz, *The Tuning of the Word: The Musico-Literary Poetics of the Symbolist Movement* (Carbondale: Southern Illinois University Press, 1987); Jean-Pierre Barricelli, *Melopoiesis: Approaches to the Study of Literature and Music* (New York: New York University Press, 1986); and Lawrence Kramer, *Music and Poetry: The Nineteenth Century and After* (Berkeley: University of California Press, 1984).

5   Steven Paul Scher, "Music and Literature," in Jean-Pierre Barricelli and Joseph Gibaldi, eds., *Interrelations of Literature* (New York: Modern Language Association, 1982), pp. 225–50.

6   "Rock Lyric," in Alex Preminger, ed., *Princeton Encyclopedia of Poetry and Poetics,* enl. ed. (Princeton: Princeton University Press, 1974), pp. 979–80, with a list of fundamental bibliographical references. The 3rd ed. (1993) dispenses with the "rock lyric" entry, demonstrating the relatively ephemeral character of the phenomenon in English.
    In a response to Allan Bloom's attack on rock in *The Closing of the American Mind: How Higher Education Has Failed Democracy and Impoverished the Souls of Today's Students,* María Rose Menocal discusses the relationship of rock text to the "great tradition" and to the continuity of Western lyric. Most of her examples are drawn from the sixties. See her "We Can't Dance Together," *Profession* (MLA) (1988): 53–58.

7   Monroe C. Beardsley, *Aesthetics: Problems in the Philosophy of Criticism* (New York: Harcourt Brace and Co., 1958), p. 345.

8   Northrop Frye, ed., intro. to *Sound and Poetry* (New York: Columbia University Press, 1957), p. xxv. Cf. Susanne K. Langer, *Feeling and Form* (New York: Charles Scribner's Sons, 1953), chapter 10, "The Principle of Assimilation," and her account of why music "swallows" words.

9   See discussions of textual difficulty vs. musical form in Andrew Welsh, *Roots of Lyric* (Princeton: Princeton University Press, 1981), especially pp. 236–38.

10 Betsy Bowden, *Performed Literature: Words and Music by Bob Dylan* (Bloomington:

Indiana University Press, 1982). Emphasizing such features as phrasing, vocal inflection, voice-forced rhyme, oral onomatopeia, sliding pitch, and pause, she posits an ideal situation of live performance, including audience reaction. See especially chapter 7 on aesthetics and methodology.

11   Mark W. Booth, *The Experience of Songs* (New Haven: Yale University Press, 1981), p. 35.

12   Bertrand H. Bronson, "Literature and Music," in James Thorpe, ed., *Relations of Literary Study* (New York: Modern Language Association, 1967), p. 137.

13   David Pichaske, *A Generation in Motion — Popular Music and Culture in the Sixties* (New York: Schirmer Books, 1979), ch. 6. For an example of the incorporation of lyrics into the study of poetry, see David R. Pichaske, ed., *Beowulf to Beatles: Approaches to Poetry* (New York: The Free Press, 1972).

14   For a more in-depth treatment, see Charles A. Perrone, "Pagings and Stagings: Musical Echoes of Literary Heritage," *Latin American Literary Review* 14, no. 27 (1986): 78–91.

15   The poem is from Giovanni Pontiero, *An Anthology of Brazilian Modernist Poetry* (Oxford: Pergamon Press, 1969), p. 65. The song "Cobra Criada" (João Bosco-Paulo Emílio) is on João Bosco, *Linha de Passe*, RCA 103 0294, 1979.

16   For salient examples and further elaboration, see Charles A. Perrone, "From Noigandres to 'Milagre da Alegria': The Concrete Poets and Contemporary Brazilian Popular Music," *Latin American Music Review* 6, no. 1 (1985): 58–79. Cited below as "From Noigandres."

17   Afrânio Coutinho, *An Introduction to Literature in Brazil*, trans. Gregory Rabassa (New York: Columbia University Press, 1969), p. 46. On the evolution of music and poetry in Europe, a useful recent in-depth study is James Anderson Winn, *Unsuspected Eloquence: A History of the Relations Between Poetry and Music* (New Haven: Yale University Press, 1981).

18   Araripe Júnior (1848–1911), quoted by José Ramos Tinhorão, *Pequena história da música popular* (Petrópolis: Vozes, 1974), p. 6.

19   James Amado, "A foto proibida há 300 anos," intro. to Gregório de Matos, *Obras completas,* vol. 1 (Salvador: Januária, 1969), pp. xxvi–xxvii.

20   Barbosa's lyrics circulated in Portugal as early as the 1790s in rudimentary songbooks/chapbooks called *jornais de modinhas*. On this author, see David Brookshaw, *Race and Color in Brazilian Literature* (Metuchen, N.J.: Scarecrow Press, 1986).

21   José Ramos Tinhorão, "Da valsa, da polca, do tango — a história do samba," *Cultura* 8, no. 28 (January 1978): 44–54.

22   Alfredo Bosi, *História concisa da literatura brasileira,* rev. and exp. (São Paulo: Cultrix, 1994), p. 115.

23   Noel Rosa, *Literatura comentada,* ed. João Antonio (São Paulo: Abril Educação, 1982), a pedagogical series that include Buarque, Veloso, and Gilberto Gil.

24   The complete lyrics are now available in Vinícius de Moraes, *Livro de letras* (São Paulo: Companhia das Letras, 1991). Moraes (old spelling) had already included lyrics in his collected poems, *Obra poética* (Rio de Janeiro: José Aguilar, 1968). English renderings of his poems are in *The Girl from Ipanema* (Merrick, N.Y.: Cross

Cultural Communications, 1982), a title from his most revered song with Jobim, "A garota de Ipanema" (1962).

25 *Estorvo* (São Paulo: Companhia das Letras, 1991); English trans. Peter Bush, *Turbulence* (New York: Pantheon, 1993). For an English-language critique, see Roberto Schwarz, "Chico Buarque's New Novel," in John Gledson, trans., *Misplaced Ideas* (London and New York: Verso, 1992), pp. 197–201. On the dramatic works, see Charles A. Perrone, "Dissonance and Dissent: The Musical Dramatics of Chico Buarque," *Latin American Theater Review* 22, no. 2 (1989): 81–94.

26 Adélia Bezerra de Meneses, *Desenho mágico: poesia e política em Chico Buarque* (São Paulo: HUCITEC, 1982), p. 17.

27 Jacket of *Chico Buarque de Holanda,* vol. 3, RGE XRLP 5320, 1968, verified in Chico Buarque, *Letra e música,* vol. 1 (São Paulo: Companhia das Letras, 1989), p. 57. Further references by title. Volume 2 of this biographical collection of Buarque's complete songs has fifty lead sheets. In 1972, following the suggestion of this song, Buarque wrote "Soneto," a true sonnet-song; see *Letra e música I*, p. 102. The most compelling recording of "Retrato em branco e preto" was by vocalist Elis Regina (1945–1982), on *Elis and Tom,* Verve 824 418, 1974. A new CD release of this title comes with literal translations of lyrics. The song has been recorded as an instrumental as "Zingaro."

28 Chico Buarque, *A banda: manuscritos de Chico Buarque de Hollanda* (Rio de Janeiro: Editora Paulo de Azevedo, 1966), p. 2.

29 *Letra e música I*, p. 247. *Chico Buarque*, RCA BMG Ariola 150 0008, 1989.

30 Among other places, Veloso expressed his poetic intentions in an interview with Décio Bar, "Acontece que ele é baiano," *Realidade* 3, no. 33 (1968): 193. For text in translation and discussion of "Coração vagabundo" and other exemplary titles cited in this section, see *MCBS*, chapter 2. This song is included on the acoustic U.S. release *Caetano Veloso,* Nonesuch 79127, 1986, with bilingual lyric sheet.

31 The first example is noted in *Balanço,* p. 292; it appears on the self-titled Philips R 765 086L, 1969. The other is the title track of *Outras palavras,* Philips 6328 303, 1981.

32 Philips R 765 040L, 1968, rereleased on CD. See *MCBS*, pp. 57ff. and 98ff. After their fiftieth birthdays, the leaders of the movement collaborated on a twenty-five-year "retrospective"; see Veloso and Gil, *Tropicália 2,* Polygram 518178, 1993, cited in the next subheading. While not a calculated effort of reprise, this album has numerous implicit references to the late-sixties affair. In terms of literary links, it is curious that this release has been interpreted in the structural terms of *Mensagem,* Fernando Pessoa's national epic of 1934; see Ivo Lucchesi and Gilda Korff Diegeuz, *Caetano, por que não?: Uma viagem entre a aurora e a sombra* (Rio de Janeiro: Leviatã, 1993), pp. 222ff. Cited below by authors. This volume comprises readings of the poetic subject in Caetano's complete works, as well as a selection of his most revealing statements in the press.

33 The collection in question is *Araçá Azul,* Philips 6349 054, 1972, which set an industry record for most customer returns. This and all other Veloso albums have been rereleased in CD format, making his œuvre eminently accessible for study. On "Acrilírico" and other examples, see "From Noigandres."

34 "DE TENTATIVA DE SIMULAÇÃO DE SALADA DE TREINO DE," in Waly Salomão and Torquato Neto, eds., *Navilouca* (Rio de Janeiro, 1974), no pagination. Also in Waly Salomão, ed., Caetano Veloso, *Alegria Alegria* (Rio de Janeiro: Pedra Q Ronca, n.d. [1977]), pp. 147ff. Cited in next note. The next selection is from p. 153, originally in the arts journal *Polem* (1974): 67.

35 Respectively, Philips 6349 132 and 6349 142, 1975. The texts, which appeared in numerous periodicals, are reproduced in *Alegria Alegria,* pp. 163–66.

36 José Miguel Wisnik, "O minuto e o milênio, ou por favor professor uma década de cada vez," in *Anos 70 música popular* (Rio de Janeiro: Europa, 1979), p. 23.

37 *Estrangeiro,* Polygram 838 297, 1989; the U.S. release of this recording contains a bilingual lyric sheet. The album's front-jacket art keys the cover story of Christopher Dunn, "It's Forbidden to Forbid," *Americas* 45, no. 5 (September–October 1993): 14–21, a fresh look at Tropicalism.

38 First recorded on Milton Nascimento, *Txai,* CBS Brazil, 1989; U.S. Columbia 46871, 1990; later by Veloso, *Circuladô,* Polygram 510639, 1991, from whose inner sleeve the song lyric is transcribed.

39 João Guimarães Rosa, *The Third Bank of the River and Other Stories,* trans. Barbara Shelby (New York: Knopf, 1968). These renderings, unfortunately, emphasize story line over linguistic flavor, consciously avoiding the very "literary" quality of Rosa's often exploratory prose.

40 Carlos Ávila, "Tom Zé: Poemúsica," *Minas Gerais suplemento literário* 8, no. 361 (July 20, 1973): 4–5.

41 The influential rock star David Byrne produced two collections of the Brazilian's songs, an anthology of his seventies material—*The Best of Tom Zé,* Warner-Sire Luaka Bop 9 26396, 1990—and a wholly new project, *The Return of Tom Zé: The Hips of Tradition,* Warner-Sire Luaka Bop 9 45118, 1992. Both have bilingual lyric sheets that facilitate appreciation of word craft. The former collection includes a collaboration with Augusto de Campos, who, on original Tom Zé releases, contributed a declamation ("cidade") and a visual poem ("olho por olho" as cover art).

42 Interview with the author, July 12, 1983; positions confirmed in numerous periodical sources.

43 The most notable of these was *Boca do inferno* (Rio de Janeiro: MEC-FUNARTE-SNT, 1980), about Bahia's famed colonial poet Gregório de Matos.

44 Jacket of *Trem dos condenados,* Marcus Pereira 9351, 1976. The following brief examples are from the jacket of *Dedalus,* Marcus Pereira 9408, 1980 (reprint) and the title track.

45 Walter Franco, "No pátio dos loucos," *Ou não,* Continental 1-01-404-027, 1973.

46 The best examples are on *Revolver,* Continental 1-01-404-118, 1975. An example of a triangular text is in "From Noigandres."

47 The cooperative ventures of this celebrated team, which lasted into the 1980s, are studied in *MCBS,* ch. 5. Blanc has since worked with several other songwriters.

48 See *MCBS,* ch. 6; numerous U.S. releases of Milton Nascimento with bilingual lyric sheets; and insightful pieces on his music in the popular press. The cited song is from *Sentinela,* Ariola 201 610, 1980.

49 This variant appears in the lyrics section of Torquato Neto, *Os últimos dias da paupéria*, 2d ed. (São Paulo: Max Limonad, 1982), no pagination. The first version, with some additional adjectives, appeared in Neto's newspaper column and was reproduced in the journalism section of the book, p. 246. The lyric sheet and the actual recording — on *Jards Macalé*, Philips 6349 045, 1972 — also differ slightly.

50 Portions of this section of *O guesa errante* (1877) appear in *Latin American Literary Review* 14, no. 27 (1986): 92–99, trans., Robert E. Brown. For a critical reading see Frederick Williams, "'The Wall Street Inferno:' A Poetic Reading of the Gilded Age," *Chásqui* (February 1976): 15–32.

51 Arnaldo Antunes, *Psia* (São Paulo: Expressão, 1986) and *Tudos* (São Paulo: Iluminuras, 1990). Both these titles show the author's propensity for antinormative behavior. The former, he indicated, is the (invented) feminine form of *psiu*, the vocable Brazilians use to call someone's attention or to request quiet. The second title is the equivalent of *alls*, i.e., the (nonexistent) plural of the noun for "everything." Antunes further invested in and coedited the special issue *Atlas (Almanak 88)* (São Paulo: n.p., 1988), a 12″ × 18″ fine-press album of all kinds of postconcretist word designs and page art.

52 Antunes et al., three-item package: (1) *Nome*, BMG Ariola home video 3-01500, 1993; (2) M30.072 CD (with booklet of mini-stills and basic texts, cover seen in example 14), and (3) book of texts and video stills. The principal collaborators were Celia Catunda, Kiko Mistrorigo, and Zaba Moreau. This last colleague performed some of these pieces with Antunes at the September 8, 1995, Long Beach Museum of Art opening of Dentro Brasil, an exhibition featuring single-channel video works and a video installation by Antunes.

5   Margins and Marginals: New Brazilian Poetry of the 1970s

1 Franklin Jorge, "Quase prefácio," quoted by Heloísa Buarque de Hollanda and Carlos Alberto Messeder Pereira, eds., *Poesia jovem anos 70* (São Paulo: Brasiliense, 1982), p. 85.

2 Some of Drummond's later work — *Impurezas do branco* (1973), *Boitempo*, I-II-III (1968, 1973, 1979) — can be found in translation in Thomas Colchie and Mark Strand, eds., *Traveling in the Family* (New York: Random House, 1986).

3 While one of the key studies of recent Brazilian poetry — Benedito Nunes, "A recente poesia brasileira: expressão e forma," *Novos estudos CEBRAP* 31 (October 1991): 171–83 — focuses on the 1980s, the critic exemplifies nonexperimental "reflexive poetry" with writers of several different generations, most of whom produced in the 1970s. Nunes will be cited by name below. For summary background leading up to the seventies, and the decade itself, see Antônio Carlos Secchin, "Caminhos recentes da poesia brasileira," *Iberoromania* 34 (1991): 55–69. On continuing lyrical currents in the 1970s, see also José Guilherme Merquior, "Musa morena moça: notas sobre a nova poesia brasileira," *Tempo brasileiro* 42–43 (1975): 7–19.

4 Antiregime material of Gullar's is in *Dentro da noite veloz* (1975). The epical long poem is the somewhat autobiographical *Poema sujo* (1976), which appeared in English as *Dirty Poem*, trans. and intro. Leland Guyer (Lanham, Md.: University Press of America, 1991). See the study by Ricardo Sternberg, "Memory and History in Ferreira Gullar's *Poema Sujo*," *Revista canadiense de estudios hispánicos* 14, no. 1 (Fall 1989): 131–44. Sant'Anna, who also made the transition from vanguard interests to experientially based lyric, contributed to the neo-epical paradigm with *A grande fala do índio guarany perdido na história e outras derrotas (Moderno Popul Vuh)* (São Paulo: Summus, 1978), trans. of canto 11 by Fred Ellison, "The Great Speech of the Guarani Indian: Lost to History and Other Defeats," *Dactylus* 8 (Fall 1987): 31–36. The ever present Sant'Anna published his collected poems as *A poesia possível* (Rio de Janeiro: Rocco, 1987).

5 Heloísa Buarque de Hollanda, ed. and intro., *26 poetas hoje* (Rio de Janeiro: Labor, 1976), p. 7; subsequently referred to as *26 poetas*.

6 José Guilherme Merquior, "Comportamento da musa: a poética desde 22," in *O elixir do apocalipse* (Rio de Janeiro: Nova Fronteira, 1983), p. 176.

7 Nunes (p. 173), with specific reference to the opinion of noted literary historian Alfredo Bosi. Both participated in a roundtable discussion recorded by Berta Waldman and Iumna Maria Simon, eds., *Rebate de pares (Remate de males)* no. 2 (Campinas: UNICAMP), 1981, special issue on recent poetry.

8 Affonso Romano de Sant'Anna, *Música popular e moderna poesia brasileira* (Petropolis: Vozes, 1978), p. 165; subsequent reference by title.

9 José Guilherme Merquior, "Com a imaginação da liberdade," in *As idéias e as formas* (Rio de Janeiro: Nova Fronteira, 1981), p. 334.

10 Heloísa Buarque de Hollanda, *Impressões de viagem: CPC, vanguarda e desbunde: 1960/1970* (São Paulo: Brasiliense, 1981), p. 101; subsequently cited as *Impressões*. Armando Freitas Filho ("Poesia vírgula viva," in *Anos 70: literatura* [Rio de Janeiro: Europa, 1979], p. 106), even noted that Chacal, a key figure of *poesia marginal*, had supported the idea of concrete poetry and had published a veritable concrete poem in an original appearance in *Navilouca*, a postconcretist edition of intersemiotic character, as seen below. This young poet's early roles are an example of overlap between camps and mindsets. Freitas is cited in the text by name below.

11 See examples in addendum to Hollanda, *Impressões*, and in *Arte em revista*, no. 8 (*Independentes*) (São Paulo: Kairós, 1984).

12 Iumna Maria Simon and Vinícius Dantas, "Poesia ruim sociedade pior," *Novos estudos CEBRAP* 12 (June 1985): 55. I use my own translations here, and in citations below, but there is an abridged English version with lyrical examples, "Bad Poetry, Worse Society," trans. Holly Staver, in George Yúdice, Jean Franco, and Juan Flores, eds., *On Edge: The Crisis of Contemporary Latin American Culture* (Minneapolis: University of Minnesota Press, 1992), pp. 141–60.

13 Carlos Alberto Messeder Pereira, *Retrato de época: poesia marginal anos 70* (Rio de Janeiro: FUNARTE, 1981), p. 92.

14 Antônio Carlos de Brito, "Tudo da minha terra, bate-papo sobre poesia marginal," *Almanaque* 6 (1978): 42.

15   Afonso (Guimarães de) Henriques Neto, "Poesia, anos 70: contra que cultura?" *Módulo* 56 (November–December 1979): 42. Cited below by author.

16   Chacal (pen name of Ricardo de Carvalho Duarte), "Meu nome é Ricardo," *Verve* 4, no. 37 (July 1990): 5–6. Quotations of poems in the text from Chacal, *Drops de abril* (São Paulo: Brasiliense, 1983).

17   Silviano Santiago, "O assassinato de Mallarmé," in *Uma literatura nos trópicos* (São Paulo: Perspectiva, 1978), p. 180.

18   Antônio Carlos de Brito and Heloísa Buarque de Hollanda, "Nosso verso de pé quebrado," *Argumento* (January 1974): 82–83; reprinted in *Arte em revista* 8, 70–72.

19   In the collective dimension, the seventies also saw the emergence of identity politics in poetry, most notably of African-Brazilian groups, which can be related to *poesia marginal* but must be understood in contexts of their own, especially as practices develop in the next decade. See pertinent sections of the unique study by Luiza Lobo, "Literatura negra brasileira contemporânea," *Estudos afro-asiáticos* 14 (1987): 109–39; reprinted in *Crítica sem juízo* (Rio de Janeiro: Francisco Alves, 1993), pp. 161–204, cited below by book title. For creative texts, see the collection *Axé: antologia da poesia negra* (São Paulo: Global, 1986), as well as the special bilingual issue on African Brazilian literature of *Callaloo* 18, no. 4 (1995).

20   Vinícius Dantas, "A nova poesia brasileira & a poesia," *Novos estudos CEBRAP* 16 (December 1986): 47; later citations by author in the text.

21   Ronaldo Santos, interview with Charles [Peixoto], "Café com letras," Radio MEC, n.d. [c. 1976], archives of the Centro Interdisciplinar de Estudos Contemporâneos, School of Communication, Federal University of Rio de Janeiro.

22   "Nova poética," from *Belo belo* (1948), quoted by Sant'Anna, *Música popular* (p. 252), who first cited the poem in relation to youth poetry in a review in the news weekly *Veja*.

23   Sebastião Uchoa Leite et al. (roundtable debate), "Poesia hoje," *José* 2 (August 1976): 5.

24   Nunes, p. 179. On glosses and intertextuality in Ana Cristina César, see Ivan Junqueira, "In memoriam," in *O encantador de serpentes* (Rio de Janeiro: Alhambra, 1987), pp. 199–210, and Luiza Lobo, "A (der) rota na metáfora da navegação," in *Crítica sem juízo,* pp. 74–83. On César, Uchoa Leite, and other late seventies poets in social context, see Mike Gonzalez and David Treece, *The Gathering of the Voices: The Twentieth-Century Poetry of Latin America* (London: Verso, 1992), pp. 328ff.

25   Ellen Watson, trans., *Alphabet in the Park* (Middletown, Conn.: Wesleyan University Press, 1990), p. 6; originally in *Bagagem* (Rio de Janeiro: Imago, 1976). Sant'Anna (*Música popular,* p. 171) places a poem of Prado's under the rubric "Pós-vanguardas e marginália," illustrating how the latter category is not perfectly useful.

26   José Guilherme Merquior, "Sobre o verso de Francisco Alvim," *Tempo brasileiro* 26–27 (March 1971): 77.

27   Geraldo Carneiro, *Pandemônio* (São Paulo: Art Editora, 1993), p. 43, originally in *Verão vagabundo* (Rio de Janeiro: Achiamé, n.d. [c. 1977]). This author was hailed as an exceptional young voice by Jorge Wanderley, Luiz Costa Lima, and Silviano Santiago, in "Um poeta novo: Geraldo Carneiro," *José* 10 (July 1978): 30–35.

28 The graphic assemblages of self-styled *poesia intersignos,* for instance, which emerged from *poema processo* and later semiotically tinged concretism, began to appear after the turn of the decade. For an early formulation of this term, see Philadelpho Menezes, "Guide for Reading Intersign Poems," in César Espinosa, ed., *Corrosive Signs: Essays on Experimental Poetry (Visual, Concrete, Alternative)* (Washington, D.C.: Maisonneuve Press, 1990), pp. 40–43; book cited below by title. For a semiotic reading of visual poetry by this poet-critic, see: Philadelpho Menezes, *Poetics and Visuality: A Trajectory of Contemporary Brazilian Poetry* (San Diego, California: SDSU University Press, 1995).

29 Massaud Moisés, *História da literatura brasileira,* vol. 5, *Modernismo* (São Paulo: Cultrix-USP, 1989), p. 529.

30 Insert to his own *Regis hotel* (São Paulo: Edições Groovie, 1978) and quoted by Dantas, p. 43.

31 Nelson Ascher, "Marginália marginal," *Corpo estranho* 3 (1981): 165.

32 Carlos Ávila, "Linguagem construtiva," *Folhetim (Folha de São Paulo),* June 29, 1986, pp. 10–11. Trans. as "Constructive Language: The Generation of the 1970s in Brazil," in *Corrosive Signs,* pp. 109–113.

33 Carlos Ávila, *Aqui e agora* (Cataguases, MG: Edições Dubolso, 1981), no pagination, cited below.

34 Nelson Ascher, *O sonho da razão* (Rio de Janeiro: Editora 34, 1993), p. 55; originally in *Ponta da língua* (São Paulo: n.p., 1983), p. 15, with slightly different punctuation.

35 Duda Machado, *Zil* (Rio de Janeiro: Grupo de Planejamento Gráfico, 1977), no pagination. Reprinted in *Crescente* (São Paulo: Duas Cidades, 1990). This line, with its central portmanteau word, can be approximated as: "morning blue-com-pl-mane-ing the sky of my senses" (*azul*=blue, *crina*=mane, *azucrinar*=to annoy).

36 On the development of related criticism, see Haroldo de Campos, "Structuralism and Semiotics in Brazil: Retrospect/Prospect," *Dispositio* 3, no. 7–8 (Summer 1978): 175–87. A curious reflection of the poetic use of theory occurs more recently in a "joke poem" by one of the most acclaimed new poets of the 1990s, Carlito Azevedo (b. 1961), who pens "GRAFITO SEMIÓTICO OU LENNON REVISITED": "give peirce a chance." *Collapsus Linguae* (Rio de Janeiro: Lynx, 1991), p. 25; the allusions are to Charles Sanders Peirce, the North American philosopher of signs, and John Lennon, one of whose last songs was built on the refrain: "all we are saying is give peace a chance."

37 Ávila, *Aqui e agora,* no pagination.

38 Ávila, "Linguagem construtiva," is one who voices this position.

39 *Polem* (1974): 92.

40 Régis Bonvicino, "A marginalidade circunstancial," *Folhetim,* no. 267 (February 28, 1982): 5; reprinted in *Arte em Revista,* no. 8: 78. From a different, nonsectarian position, there is a later and more historically nuanced instance of critical irony based on terminology associated with Oswald. A contemporaneous poet-critic notes that parody may actually affirm its object and that antinormative poetry may backfire or stall, as with the "mimeograph generation," whose efforts at Oswaldian *poesia-minuto* became unreflexive *poesia-segundo,* figuratively gone in a second; see Antônio Carlos Secchin, "João Cabral: Marcas," *Range rede* 1, no. 0 (1995): 6.

41 This and the previous example from Régis Bonvicino, *Sósia da cópia* (São Paulo: n.p., 1983). In a new edition of his early poems, the author does not include "vingança de português." It remains, nevertheless, representative of an attitude of the early 1980s. See *Primeiro tempo* (São Paulo: Perspectiva, 1995).

42 Alice Ruiz, *navalhanaliga* (Curitiba: ZAP, 1980), no pagination. In a later version, the graphic scheme intensifies the themes of motherhood and the body as object of gaze, as the text+design is superimposed, in a fold-out, on a black-and-white photo of the poet, pregnant and nude. See *Alice Ruiz* (Curitiba: Scientia e Labor, 1988).

The montage depends largely on lexical similarities and contrasts, many of which are self-evident. The phrases read counterclockwise: "used and abused / palpable but empty / diminished to be a mother / accused and refused / quiet and badly spoken of / alienated and forgotten / solicitous and solicited / embroideress and approached / kept away and always at hand / moderate and well decorated / gives birth and lives hidden / transcendent in descent / badly informed she teaches people / she was taught to have no vocation / no necessities only caprices / a natural instinct to be at home / criticized and fated at a critical age / economical but understanding nothing about economics / Sunday, Lord's day, she does not rest / what is style in a man in her is laxity / she doesn't set the tone and dances whatever they play / she cries when she has nothing else to say / voracious consumer and voraciously consumed / it's the most obvious and the least noticed / in the dictionary she is the female of the man / to understand she doesn't have much to learn / the best view through the keyhole / she reproduces little because she reproduces and that is enough for her / she doesn't need to be brought up to date but she better follow fashion / the strength she uses to be fragile is still hidden / her attempts at participating are taken as intruding / since she has no responsibility she can't be in a bad mood / she has to be a work of art that does not remain for posterity / she loses so much blood that she gets what they call 'cockroach blood' (to be meek) / docile, soft, subtle and submissive, leave the corresponding defects to men / Wanted: mechanical lathe operator, accountant, systems analyst, engineers, etc., with proven ability and a (female) receptionist with optimum appearance / she may choose between heaven and hell but not earth, that belongs to the opposite sex / a shackle for masculine liberty through the beams of obedience / the more spirit the better but the future ends along with beauty / if she is great it is because she is behind a great man / always waiting and being known for making others wait / her enthusiasm is called anger / born inside there she will remain until the earth eats the remains the sons and men leave / she makes a pair but down below."

43 In the arts journal *Muda* (1975): 19–21.

44 The source in question appears to be Manoel de Andrade de Figueiredo, *Nova escola para aprender a ler, escrever, e contar* (Lisbon: Oficina de Bernardo da Costa de Carvalho, 1722). The author created a style of calligraphy in Portugal that was widely used until French and English models gained preference in the second half of the eighteenth century.

45 See a full-page reproduction of this piece, as well as other examples, in Charles A. Perrone, "The Imperative of Invention: Brazilian Concrete Poetry and Intersemiotic Creation," *Harvard Library Bulletin,* New Series, 3, no. 2 (1992): 44–53.

46   This piece appeared in *achados e construidos* (São Paulo: Independent, 1980); reprinted in *nova leva: riocorrente construtiva* (1986), no pagination, keyed by semaphores.

47   The strip first appeared in *Código*, no. 8 (1983). Mattoso's homemade productions were distributed only by him, but widely known and reviewed in national news-magazines. His *samizdat*, an astounding anomaly, violated all copyright laws and senses of property.

48   For a general appreciation, see Luiz Fernando Valente, "Paulo Leminski: a poética do inútil," *Hispania* 76 (September 1993): 419–27.

49   Paulo Leminski, *Caprichos e relaxos* (São Paulo: Brasiliense, 1983). The title translates as "caprices and (re-) laxities." Examples that follow in the text are from this volume, except where noted. Translations in *Brasil Brazil* 7 (1992): 75–82.

50   Carlos Ávila, "Flashes de uma trajetória," *Revista USP* 3 (November 1989): 104.

51   Paulo Leminski, *Distraídos venceremos* (São Paulo: Brasiliense, 1987), p. 90.

6   Pagings and Postings: Historical
Imperatives of the Late Century

1   Two useful guides to multidisciplinary ideas and bibliography are Linda Hutcheon, *The Politics of Postmodernism* (London and New York: Routledge, 1989), especially the index to the bibliography, and Steven Connor, *Postmodernist Culture: An Introduction to Theories of the Contemporary* (New York and Oxford: Basil Blackwell, 1989). With specific regard to Brazil, see references passim, especially notes 17 and 23. Given the multiplicity of meanings associated with the postmodern, it is worthwhile to clarify that the present account does not propose a particular definition to be applied to the Brazilian cultural milieu in general, but rather an examination of the resonances of the postmodern in a realm of poetry.

2   José Guilherme Merquior, "Aranha e abelha: para uma crítica da ideologia pós-moderna," *Revista do Brasil* 2, no. 5 (1986): 22–27.

3   See John Beverley and José Oviedo, *The Postmodernism Debate in Latin America,* special issue of *Boundary 2,* vol. 20, no. 3 (Fall 1993), cited below by editors. For literature, see also the special issues of *Nuevo texto crítico,* vols. 6–7 (1990–91). An example of the exclusion of Latin America is Jochen Schulte-Sasse, "Modernity and Modernism, Postmodernity and Postmodernism: Framing the Issue," *Cultural Critique,* vol. 5 (Winter 1986–87). He assumes that the postmodern is solely a First World phenomenon and does not deal with any Third World case unless it criticizes "ethnographic categories"; cited by Guido Podestá, "An Ethnographic Reproach to the Theory of the Avant-Garde: Modernity and Modernism in Latin America and the Harlem Renaissance," *Modern Language Notes* 106 (1991): 395–422.

   In a review of contributions to a pertinent special issue, a leading critic notes how most approaches to the postmodern in the Third World / Latin America are "fraught with anxiety" and reservations about a postmodernism that cannot deliver on promises of de-centering; see George Yúdice, "Postmodernism in the Periphery," *South Atlantic Quarterly* 92, no. 3 (Summer 1993): 543–56. Yúdice's work is indispensable in the effort to formulate postmodernism judiciously in the Latin American context.

See especially his "Postmodernity and Transnational Capitalism in Latin America," in George Yúdice, Jean Franco, and Juan Flores, eds., *On Edge: The Crisis of Contemporary Latin American Culture* (Minneapolis: University of Minnesota Press, 1992), pp. 1–28; article cited below.

4   José Miguel Wisnik, "A interpretação do pós-modernismo na estética das produções culturais brasileiras (mass media, TV, filme, música popular)." Paper presented at "The Debate on Post-Modernism in Latin America: Brazil, Mexico and Peru," University of Texas, Austin, April 29, 1988, no pagination. Subsequent citations by author.

5   The collections of "text-cards" and poetic "objects," *Poemóbiles* (1974) and *Caixa preta* (Black box, 1975), were done in collaboration with designer Julio Plaza.

6   Jota de Moraes, "O pulsar quase mudo de Augusto de Campos," interview, *Código 5* (1981): no pagination. Originally in *Jornal da tarde* (São Paulo), April 26, 1980.

7   A 45 rpm record with Caetano's interpretation of "Pulsar" and "dias dias dias" (1953) accompanies the first edition of *VIVA VAIA Poesia 1949/1979* (São Paulo: Duas Cidades, 1979). The former song was rereleased on *Velô*, Polygram 824 024, 1984, with full reproduction of the text on the lyric sheet and, in an acoustic arrangement, on *Caetano Veloso*, US Nonesuch 79127, 1986.

8   "Memos," "Pulsar," and "Quasar" all appear in the excellent representation of Augusto's seventies work, including translations built on visual effects, in Emanuel Brasil and William Jay Smith, *Brazilian Poetry 1950–1980* (Middletown, Conn.: Wesleyan University Press, 1983). On "Memos" and other typical texts, see Claus Clüver, "Reflections on Verbivocovisual Ideograms," *Poetics Today* 3, no. 3 (1982): 137–48.

9   Augusto de Campos, *Expoemas 1980–1985* (São Paulo: Edições Serigráficas Entretempo, 1985). The thirteen poems in these colored serigraphic prints by Omar Guedes had appeared in the press or journals. These and other titles are collected in *Despoesia* (São Paulo: Perspectiva, 1994), often without the original color format.

10 Augusto de Campos, interview, *34 Letras* 4 (1989): 11; cited below by journal title.

11 On this intriguing link between advertising and the literary world, see Flora Sussekind, "Poesia & media," in *Papéis colados* (Rio de Janeiro: Editora UFRJ, 1993), pp. 227–35. Translations of "2ª via" and "Inestante" appear in *The Dirty Goat* 3 (1989): 21–23.

12 *34 letras,* 14–15, with reference also to "Quasar," "Pulsar," "Pó do cosmos," and "Anticéu."

13 Flora Sussekind, *Literatura e vida literária: polêmicas, diários & retratos* (Rio de Janeiro: Jorge Zahar, 1985), p. 82. Cited below by author and title.

14 Augusto de Campos, *poetamenos,* 2d ed. (1953; São Paulo: Edições Invenção, 1973), portfolio format.

15 Augusto de Campos, interview in *Póstudo* (Alfenas SP) 1 (1985–86): 4.

16 In a sociohistorical interpretation, the keen observer Sussekind (*Literatura e vida literária,* pp. 38–41) relates the polemic to a strategy of distraction on the part of the outgoing military regime.

17 Sérgio Paulo Rouanet, "Do pós-moderno ao neo-moderno," *Tempo brasileiro* 84 (January–March 1986): 86–87. Rouanet's literary intuition falls short of making explicit his sense of *how* the title translates the "post-" mood. This essay begins to develop a

philosophy of skepticism about postmodernism, further elaborated in "A verdade e a ilusão do pós-moderno," in *As razões do iluminismo* (São Paulo: Companhia das Letras, 1987), pp. 229–77, originally in *Revista do Brasil* 2, no. 5 (1986): 28–53. Rouanet's principal point of contention relevant to the idea of postmodern phenomena in Brazil, in Wisnik's assessment, is that a postmodern consciousness does not necessarily correspond to a postmodern reality.

18   "A Historic Landmark," in Roberto Schwarz, *Misplaced Ideas*, trans. and intro. John Gledson (London: Verso, 1992), pp. 187–96, from which citations in the text are taken; it originally appeared as "Marco histórico," in *Folhetim*, no. 428, cultural supplement of *Folha de São Paulo*, March 31, 1985, pp. 6–9, and later in *Que horas são?* (São Paulo: Companhia das Letras, 1987). Augusto de Campos's journalistic response, "A dialética da maledicência," in the form of a letter to the critic, first appeared in *Folhetim*, no. 429, April 7, 1985, pp. 6–8, and later appeared in *À margem da margem* (São Paulo: Companhia das Letras, 1989), pp. 174–79. The response objects to the targeting of concrete poetry under the pretext of poetic analysis of a single text, highlights textual features, and recapitulates the national and international recognition of concrete poetry. This final point has been subsequently fortified with four international uses of "Pós-tudo": on the cover of the special Brazilian issue of *Latin American Literary Review*, vol. 14 (1986); as the feature catalog text of the exhibition "Concrete Poetry: The Early Years" (July–September 1986) at the Metropolitan Museum of Art, New York; in the exhibition and catalog "Poesia concreta in Brasile," Archivio di Nuova Scrittura, Milan, 1991; and in the exhibition "Material Poetry of the Renaissance/The Renaissance of Material Poetry" at Widener Library, Harvard University, May 1992.

19   One analyst's observation about the minimalism of a younger Brazilian poet, Ronaldo Brito, is quite applicable to "Pós-tudo," which itself can be seen and heard to bring "echoes of the classical (Greek) ascertainment of the ephemeral, imperfect, and irrecoverable character of not only all things but also of the words that epigrammatic statement inscribed on the surface of such things"; see Italo Moriconi Jr., "Demarcando terreno, alinhavando notas (para uma história da poesia recente no Brasil)," *Travessia* 24 (1992): 10. See also the commentary of "Pós-tudo" by Moriconi in his *A provocação pós-moderna: razão histórica e política da teoria hoje* (Rio de Janeiro: Diadorim, 1994), pp. 22ff.

With respect to the codas to Spenser's *Faerie Queene*, Mexico's world-renowned poet-essayist affirms that they "are modern despite the oldness of their language, modern because of their subject — the dialogue between mutation and identity, between change and continuity — and because of the vitality of the phrasing, images, and expression." See Octavio Paz, *The Other Voice: Essays on Modern Poetry*, trans. Helen Lane (New York: HBJ, 1990), p. 17; cited below by author and title.

On a specific national level, "Pós-tudo" also alludes to an episode in the public life of Lamartine Babo, a leading figure of Brazilian popular music in the 1940s: the publication of "Humorismo," subtitled "Canção do ex-tudo"; cited by Suetônio Soares Valença, *Trá-la-lá* (Rio de Janeiro: MEC/FUNARTE, 1981), pp. 26–27.

20   Bell's position in *The Cultural Contradictions of Capitalism* are contextualized usefully by Matei Calinescu, *Five Faces of Modernity: Modernism, Avant-Garde, Decadence,*

Kitsch, Postmodernism, 2d ed. (Durham, N.C.: Duke University Press, 1987), pp. 6–7; further citations in text by author.

21 Mike Gonzalez and David Treece, *The Gathering of the Voices: The Twentieth-Century Poetry of Latin America* (London: Verso, 1992), pp. 308ff; cited in the text as Treece.

22 Fredric Jameson, *Postmodernism, or, The Cultural Logic of Late Capitalism* (Durham, N.C.: Duke University Press, 1991), p. xvi.

23 Wisnik notes the "diffuse" character of the discussion of the postmodern in Brazil up to 1988. The "generalist" approach of theoretical overviews — of Habermas, Lyotard, Jameson, and others — has dominated. One of Brazil's leading literary theorists writes that in Brazil postmodernism has been dealt with through "its aesthetic examination" or "as part of the debate between followers of Habermas and post-structuralists." See the engaging contribution of Luiz Costa Lima, "Pós-modernidade: contraponto tropical," in *Pensando nos trópicos* (Rio de Janeiro: Rocco, 1991), pp. 119–37. He reviews Habermas, Lyotard, and Jameson, vis-à-vis relations to modernism, adding a brief note of doubt about the validity of postmodernism as a concept for nonhegemonic nations. "In Latin America, for example, what does the euphoria of detemporalization mean beyond cynicism, the inconsequential, or mere robotization?" (p. 124). " . . . [T]he treatment of postmodernism becomes mystification when it is approached as a planetarily identical phenomenon" (p. 125). Numerous other studies in Brazil follow Hassan and a more specifically literary postmodernism, largely fiction, in the United States and Europe, with no real relation to Latin America or Brazil. For example, see F. F. dos Santos, "Barth, Pynchon e outras absurdetes: O pós-modernismo na ficção norteamericana," in Roberto Cardoso Oliveira et al., *A pós-modernidade* (Campinas: UNICAMP, 1987), pp. 57–72.

Studies that ponder the usefulness of postmodern angles in Brazilian fiction include: Silviano Santiago, "O narrador pós-moderno," in *Revista do Brasil* 2, no. 5 (1986): 4–13, which assumes postmodernism in a study of the stories of Edilberto Coutinho; Francisco Caetano Lopes, "A respeito da questão da pós-modernidade no Brasil," in Margo Milleret and Marshall Eakin, eds., *Homenagem a Alexandrino Severino: Essays on the Portuguese-Speaking World* (Austin: Host, 1993), pp. 229–48, which offers a general review of postmodern debates and raises the possibility of a Brazilian postmodern fiction, especially with regard to postcolonialism; and Eduardo Coutinho, "O pós-modernismo e a ficção latino-americana contemporânea: riscos e limites," *Terceira margem* (UFRJ) 1 (1993): 70–74, a concise examination of the barriers to acceptance of Latin American literature as postmodern in non-post-industrial societies where the critical concept may be viewed as an unwarranted foreign model and import. This professor of comparative literature recommends "extreme caution," even granting the heterogeneity of postmodern concepts and Latin America's idiosyncrasies.

24 On the reemergence of Left cultural criticism in the 1970s, see the case studies in Heloísa Buarque de Hollanda and Carlos Alberto Messeder Pereira, *Patrulhas ideológicas, marca reg. arte e engajamento em debate* (São Paulo: Brasiliense, 1980). On the 1960s, see the brief study by Heloísa Buarque de Hollanda and Marcos A. Gonçalves, *Cultura e participação nos anos 60* (São Paulo: Brasiliense, 1982).

In seeking to understand the 1980s, and the "Pós-tudo" affair in particular, Wisnik considers the residues of two modalities of modernizing utopia in Brazil in the sixties, competing projects with ideas of *emancipation* by culture: the nationalistic, Left, Centro Popular de Cultura camp (from which Schwarz emerged), and a camp more in tune with the experimental Oswald de Andrade, celebration of cultural difference, and integration into international spheres, influenced by concretism and reflected in Tropicalism. This last movement, to draw the relevant connection, was important in the local hippie counterculture via music. This development is broached in Charles A. Perrone, "Changing of the Guard: Questions and Contrasts of Brazilian Rock Phenomena," *Studies in Latin American Popular Culture* 9 (1990): 65–83.

25   Linda Hutcheon, *A Poetics of Postmodernism* (New York: Routledge, 1989), p. 22.

26   Interview with Augusto de Campos and Caetano Veloso, *Bric-a-Brac* 6 (1990): 87.

27   Augusto de Campos, "Pré pós tudo do concretismo" (interview), *Bric-a-Brac* 2 (1986), enclosure, no pagination.

28   Augusto de Campos, "Morte e vida da vanguarda: a questão do novo," *30 anos Semana Nacional de Poesia de Vanguarda 1963/93* (Belo Horizonte: Prefeitura Municipal/Secretaria Municipal de Cultura, 1993), p. 67.

29   Roland Greene, "From Dante to the Post-Concrete: An Interview with Augusto de Campos," *Harvard Library Bulletin*, New Series 3, no. 2 (Summer 1992): 34–35. Cf. Arnaldo Antunes and the final cadence of chapter 5.

30   Augusto's suspicious view of the "urge to relax" is clarified in the light of "Critiques of Postmodernism" presented by Calinescu, pp. 288ff.

31   Frederico Barbosa, "A tradição do rigor e depois . . . ," in Horácio Costa, ed., *A palavra poética na América Latina: avaliação de uma geração* (São Paulo: Memorial, 1992), p. 135, 137.

32   Benedito Nunes, "A recente poesia brasileira: expressão e forma," *Novos estudos CEBRAP* 31 (October 1991): 176; cited below by author.

33   Haroldo de Campos, *Deus e o diabo no Fausto de Goethe* (São Paulo: Perspectiva, 1981), p. 176.

34   Haroldo de Campos, "Poesia e modernidade: o poema pós-utópico," *Folhetim*, no. 404, supplement of *Folha de São Paulo*, October 14, 1984, pp. 3–5; citation in text.

35   The first part was "Poesia e modernidade: da morte da arte à constelação," *Folhetim*, no. 403, October 7, 1984, pp. 2–4. Written for the celebration of the seventieth birthday of Octavio Paz, the two parts appeared subsequently in *Vuelta*, no. 99 (February 1985).

36   Haroldo de Campos, in typescript (pp. 7–8) of in-press vol. 2 of Giovanni Ricciardi, *Auto-retratos* (Rio de Janeiro: Martins Fontes, 1991). See also "Concrete Poetry and Beyond: A Conversation Between Julio Ortega and Haroldo de Campos," trans. Alfred MacAdam, *Review: Latin American Literature and Arts* 36 (January–June 1986): 38–45.

37   The positions of "Poesia e modernidade: o poema pós-utópico" were maintained up to and beyond the commemorations of the Semana Nacional de Poesia de Vanguarda 1963/93.

38   For a more complete treatment of Haroldo's paper in light of Paz (through *The*

Children of the Mire) and Luiz Costa Lima's theory of mimesis and the imaginary, see Italo Moriconi Jr., "O pós-utópico: crítica do futuro e da razão imanente," *Tempo brasileiro* 84 (January–March 1986): 69–85.

39 Paz, *The Other Voice*, intro. and pp. 54ff. In an early assessment of the meaning of the thesis of postmodernism in literature, José Guilherme Merquior insisted that all efforts at corraling the postmodern revert to the concept of modernism and that what some were calling postmodern was an intensification of the romantic antibourgeois impulse within the "tradition of rupture" of Paz; see "O significado do pós-modernismo," in *O fantasma romântico e outros ensaios* (Petrópolis: Vozes, 1979), pp. 27–41. With respect to the final words of Paz quoted in the text, it should be kept in mind that while *modernismo* in Portuguese/Brazil refers to the decades of the avant-gardes, in Spanish/Spanish America the term refers to a late nineteenth-century aestheticism, the renovation of literature headed by poet Rubén Darío.

Paz concludes his essay "Breach and Convergence" with an update of a mid-seventies view: "The poetry that is beginning now, without beginning, is seeking the intersection of times, the point of convergence. It asserts that between the cluttered past and the uninhabited future, poetry is the present." To these words, written in 1974, he now adds: "the present is manifest in presence, and presence is the reconciliation of the three times. A poetry of reconciliation: the imagination made flesh in a *now* that has no dates" (p. 58). Paz, who spoke of the decentralization of cultural power as early as *The Labyrinth of Solitude* (1951), is critiqued in his postvanguard views as an essentialist by Yúdice in "Postmodernity and Transnational Capitalism in Latin America."

40 *A educação dos cinco sentidos* (São Paulo: Brasiliense, 1985), page citations for poems in the text. With respect to the other projects: *Livro de ensaios: galáxias* (São Paulo: Ex-Libris, 1984), in a large fine-press edition; *Qohélet/O-que-sabe/Eclesiastes* (São Paulo: Perspectiva, 1990). On this involvement with the Bible as literature, see Haroldo de Campos, "Inter-e-intratextualidade no Eclesiastes," *34 letras* 4 (June 1989): 188–212. *34 Letras* released a CD reading by the author of selected *Galáxias* in 1992.

41 A chronicler of recent poetry exemplifies containment in lyric with João Angelo Salvatori: "rigor do ofício / tudo que não seja haicai / é desperdício" (rigor of the craft / all that is not haikai / is waste), quoted by Domício Proença Filho, in "Tendências da poesia brasileira contemporânea," *Jornal de letras* (Lisbon), April 12, 1995, p. 20. Haroldo de Campos published the influential "Haicai: homenagem à síntese" in *A arte no horizonte do provável*, 4th ed. (1969; São Paulo: Perspectiva, 1977), pp. 55–62. See the study by Luiza Lobo, *O haikai e a crise da metafísica* (Rio de Janeiro: Numen, 1993).

42 Horácio Costa, "Dinámica de Haroldo de Campos en la cultura brasileña," *Cuadernos hispanoamericanos* 509 (November 1992): 67.

43 *Finismundo- a última viagem* (Ouro Preto: Tipografia do Fundo de Ouro Preto, 1990), no pagination; reprinted in Inês Oseki Dépré, ed., *Os melhores poemas de Haroldo de Campos* (São Paulo: Global, 1992), pp. 121–27.

44 W. B. Stanford, *The Ulysses Theme: A Study in the Adaptability of a Traditional Hero*, 2d ed. (Oxford: Basil Blackwell, 1963), p. 181. While Haroldo de Campos cites an Italian

reference for his access to Dante's passage, Anglo-American readers will find Stanford to be an indispensable study on this topic.

45   Haroldo de Campos, "De la poesía concreta a *Galaxias* y *Finismundo:* 40 años de actividad poética en Brasil," *Vuelta* 177 (August 1991): 25.

Postface: Coverage and Countenance

1   Alfredo Bosi, *História concisa da literatura brasileira,* rev. and exp. ed. (São Paulo: Cultrix, 1994), p. 488.

2   Eustáquio Gomes, "Para envenenar o banquete," *Estado de São Paulo,* February 20, 1988, pp. 2–4. The main three poets considered here maintain a dialogue with prominent names of (European) modernism in a contemplative vein: Rubens Rodrigues Torres Filho (b. 1942), Antonio di Francheschi (b. 1945), and Orides Fontela (b. 1940).

3   Benedito Nunes, "A recente poesia brasileira: expressão e forma," *Novos estudos CEBRAP* 31 (October 1991): 182, with reference to Ferreira Gullar, *Barulhos* (Rio de Janeiro: José Olympio, 1987). Other pertinent recent titles include a reedition of the poet's ground-breaking *A luta corporal* (1954; Rio de Janeiro: José Olympio, 1994) and a fine-press edition of the previously unpublished concretist exhibition piece *O formigueiro* (1955; Rio de Janeiro: Europa, 1991).

4   A prime epigrammatic practitioner is José Paulo Paes (b. 1926), a contemporary of the Noigandres poets. See limited samples of his work in translation in *Brasil Brazil* 2 (1989).

5   Nunes (p. 181) is referring to the work of Northeastern poet Marcus Accioly, *Narciso* (1984).

6   For elaborations on these points and the full text in translation, see Adriano Espínola, *Taxi or Poem of Love in Transit,* Library of World Literature in Translation, vol. 21 (New York: Garland Publishing, 1992); critical afterwords by Charles A. Perrone and Elizabeth Lowe. Original edition, *Táxi ou Poema de amor passageiro* (São Paulo: Global, 1986).

7   Horácio Costa, *O livro dos fracta* (São Paulo: Iluminuras, 1991); selections published as "From *The Book of Fracta,* " trans. Charles A. Perrone, *Sulfur: A Literary Bi-Annual of the Whole Art* 34 (1994): 150–57.

CHARLES A. PERRONE is Associate Professor of Por-
tuguese and Luso-Brazilian Culture and Literature at the
University of Florida. He is the author of *Masters of Contem-
porary Brazilian Song: MPB 1965–1985* and *Letras e Letras (da
Música Popular Brasileira)* and co-editor of *Crônicas
Brasileiras: Nova Fase.*

Library of Congress Cataloging-in-Publication Data
Perrone, Charles A.
Seven faces : Brazilian poetry since modernism / Charles A.
Perrone.
Includes index.
ISBN 0-8223-1807-5 (cloth : alk. paper). —
ISBN 0-8223-1814-8 (pbk. : alk. paper)
1. Brazilian poetry — 20th century — History and criticism.
I. Title.
PQ9571.P47   1996
869.1 — dc20   96-78 CIP